THE BOB DYLAN ALBUMS

A CRITICAL STUDY

ESSAY SERIES 44

ONTARIO ARTS COUNCIL
CONSEIL DES ARTS DE L'ONTARIO

Guernica Editions Inc. acknowledges support of
The Canada Council for the Arts.
Guernica Editions Inc. acknowledges support from the Ontario Arts Council.
Guernica Editions Inc. acknowledges the financial support of the
Government of Canada through the Book Publishing Industry Development
Program (BPIDP).

ANTHONY VARESI

THE BOB DYLAN ALBUMS

A CRITICAL STUDY

GUERNICA
TORONTO·BUFFALO·LANCASTER (U.K.)
2002

Copyright © 2002, by Anthony Varesi and Guernica Editions Inc.
All rights reserved. The use of any part of this publication, reproduced,
transmitted in any form or by any means, electronic, mechanical,
photocopying, recording or otherwise stored in a retrieval system, without
the prior consent of the publisher is an infringement of the copyright law.
Antonio D'Alfonso, editor
Guernica Editions Inc.
P.O. Box 117, Station P, Toronto (ON), Canada M5S 2S6
2250 Military Road, Tonawanda, N.Y. 14150-6000 U.S.A.
Gazelle, Falcon House, Queen Square, Lancaster LA1 1RN U.K.

Printed in Canada.
Typeset in Garamond by Selina.

Legal Deposit – Fourth Quarter
National Library of Canada
Library of Congress Catalog Card Number: 2001095259
National Library of Canada Catalog in Publication Data
Varesi, Anthony
The Bob Dylan albums
(Essays series ; 44)
Includes bibliographical references.
ISBN 1-55071-139-3
1. Dylan, Bob, 1941- . 2. Dylan, Bob, 1941–Discography.
I. Title. II. Series: Essays series (Toronto, Ont.); 44.
ML420.D98V296   2001   782.42164'092   C2001-902502-5

TABLE OF CONTENTS

PART VI: THE RENAISSANCE

PART VII: JOURNEY THROUGH DARK HEAT

PART VIII: SIGN ON THE CROSS

PART IX: SURVIVING IN A RUTHLESS WORLD

PART X: HAS ANYBODY SEEN MY STYLE?

PART XI: SERIES OF DREAMS

PART XII: BACK TO THE STARTING POINT

PART XIII: SKETCHES FROM MEMORY

ACKNOWLEDGMENTS

For their assistance, thanks to Libby Rohman, Robert Bower, and Jeff Rosen from Mr. Dylan's office. Thanks to my editor, Antonio D'Alfonso, for his enthusiasm and suggestions throughout this project. Stephen Scobie graciously and promptly answered my unsolicited correspondence, and provided me with a very valuable lead. Teresa Watson and Brad Haima helped with word processing. For their encouragement and support, thanks to Nora Varesi, Ann Walsh, the Hoogendoorn family, Lara Varesi, and Dr. James Rowse. My father, Joseph Varesi, gave innumerable hours of his time for the preparation of this manuscript, and never once complained or refused to help. How can I ever repay such patience and boundless generosity? Lastly, grudging thanks to the University of British Columbia libraries for unwittingly providing me with numerous clippings.

PERMISSIONS

Big Sky Music. "Foot of Pride" ©1983 Special Rider Music. "Fourth Time Around" ©1966; renewed 1994 Dwarf Music.

"Gates of Eden" ©1965; renewed 1993 Special Rider Music. "God Knows" ©1990 Special Rider Music. "Goin' to Acapulco" ©1975 Dwarf Music. "Gotta Serve Somebody" ©1979 Special Rider Music. "The Groom's Still Waiting at the Altar" ©1981 Special Rider Music.

"A Hard Rain's A-Gonna Fall" ©1963; renewed 1991 Special Rider Music. "Hard Times in New York Town" ©1962; renewed 1990 MCA. "Highlands" ©1996 Special Rider Music. "Highway 61 Revisited" ©1965; renewed 1993 Special Rider Music. *Highway 61 Revisited* liner notes ©1965 Special Rider Music. "Honey, Just Allow Me One More Chance" ©1963; renewed 1991 Special Rider Music. "Hurricane" ©1975 Ram's Horn Music.

"I Am A Lonesome Hobo" ©1968; renewed 1996 Dwarf Music. "I and I" ©1983 Special Rider Music. "I Dreamed I Saw St. Augustine" ©1968; renewed 1996 Dwarf Music. "I Pity the Poor Immigrant" ©1968; renewed 1996 Dwarf Music. "I Shall Be Free" ©1963; renewed 1991 Special Rider Music. "I Shall Be Free No. 10" ©1971 Special Rider Music. "I Threw It All Away" ©1969; renewed 1997 Big Sky Music. "Idiot Wind" ©1974 Ram's Horn Music. "If Dogs Run Free" ©1970 Big Sky Music. "If You See Her, Say Hello" ©1974 Ram's Horn Music. "I'll Remember You" ©1985 Special Rider Music. "I'm Not There" ©1997 Dwarf Music. "In the Summertime" ©1981 Special Rider Music. "Is Your Love in Vain?" ©1978 Special Rider Music. "Isis" ©1975 Ram's Horn Music. "It Ain't Me, Babe" ©1964; renewed 1992 Special Rider Music. "It Takes a Lot to Laugh, It Takes a Train to Cry" ©1965; renewed 1993 Special Rider Music. "It's All Over Now, Baby Blue" ©1965; renewed 1993 Special Rider Music.

"Jim Jones" ©1992 Special Rider Music. "John Wesley Harding" ©1968; renewed 1996 Dwarf Music. *John Wesley Harding* liner notes ©1968 Bob Dylan. "Joey" ©1975 Ram's Horn Music. "Jokerman" ©1983 Special Rider Music.

"Last Thoughts on Woody Guthrie" ©1993 Special Rider Music. "Lay, Lady, Lay" ©1969; renewed 1997 Dwarf Music. "Lenny Bruce" ©1981 Special Rider Music. "Let Me Die in My Footsteps" ©1963; renewed 1991 Special Rider Music. "License to Kill" ©1983 Special Rider Music. "Like a Rolling Stone" ©1965; renewed 1993 Special Rider Music. "Lo and Behold!" ©1967; renewed 1995 Dwarf Music. "Love Minus Zero / No Limit" ©1965; renewed 1993 Special Rider Music.

"Maggie's Farm" ©1965; renewed 1993 Special Rider Music. "Mama, You Been on My Mind" ©1964; renewed 1992 Special Rider Music. "The Man in the Long Black Coat" ©1989 Special Rider Music. "Man of Peace" ©1983 Special Rider Music. "Masters of War" ©1963; renewed 1991 Special Rider Music. "Million Dollar Bash" ©1967; renewed 1995 Dwarf Music. "Million Miles" ©1996 Special Rider Music. "Mr. Tambourine Man" ©1964; renewed 1992 Special Rider Music. "Most of the Time" ©1989 Special Rider Music. "Motorpsycho Nightmare" ©1964; renewed 1992 Special Rider Music. "My Back Pages" ©1964; renewed 1992 Special Rider Music.

"Neighborhood Bully" ©1983 Special Rider Music. "Never Gonna Be the Same Again" ©1985 Special Rider Music. "Never Say Goodbye" ©1973 Ram's Horn Music. "New Morning" ©1970 Big Sky Music. "New Pony" ©1978 Special Rider Music. "No Time to Think" ©1978 Special Rider Music. "North Country Blues" ©1963; renewed 1991 Special Rider Music. "Not Dark Yet" ©1996 Special Rider Music.

"Obviously Five Believers" ©1966; renewed 1994 Dwarf Music. "Oh, Sister" ©1975 Ram's Horn Music. "On a Night Like This" ©1973; renewed 1994 Dwarf Music. "One More Cup of Coffee (Valley Below)" ©1975 Ram's Horn Music. "One More Night" ©1969; renewed 1997 Dwarf Music. "One More Weekend" ©1970 Big Sky Music. "One Too Many Mornings" ©1964; renewed 1992 Special Rider Music. "Only a Pawn in Their Game" ©1963; renewed 1991 Special Rider Music. "Open the Door, Homer" ©1968; renewed 1994 Dwarf Music. "Oxford Town" ©1963; renewed 1991 Special Rider Music.

"Pledging My Time" ©1966; renewed 1994 Dwarf Music. "Political World" ©1989 Special Rider Music. "Positively 4th Street" ©1965; renewed 1993 Special Rider Music. "Precious Angel" ©1979 Special Rider Music. "Pressing On" ©1980 Special Rider Music.

"Rainy Day Women #12 & 35" ©1966; renewed 1994 Dwarf Music. "Restless Farewell" ©1964; renewed 1992 Special Rider Music. "Ring Them Bells" ©1989 Special Rider Music.

"Sad-Eyed Lady of the Lowlands" ©1966; renewed 1994 Dwarf Music. "Santa-Fe" ©1973 Dwarf Music. "Sara" ©1975 Ram's Horn Music. "Saving Grace" ©1980 Special Rider Music. "Seeing the Real You at Last" ©1985 Special Rider Music. "Senor (Tales of Yankee Power)" ©1978 Special Rider Music. "She's Your Lover Now" ©1971 Dwarf Music. "Shelter from the Storm" ©1974 Ram's Horn Music. "Shooting Star" ©1989 Special Rider Music. "Shot of Love" ©1981 Special Rider Music. "Sign on the Cross" ©1971 Dwarf Music. "Sign on the Window" ©1970 Big Sky Music. "Silvio" ©1988 Special Rider Music and Ice Nine Music. "Simple Twist of Fate" ©1974 Ram's Horn Music. "Slow Train" ©1979 Special Rider Music. "Something There Is About You" ©1973 Ram's Horn Music. "Something's Burning, Baby" ©1985 Special Rider Music. "Song to Woody" ©1962; renewed 1990 MCA. "Spanish Harlem Incident" ©1964; renewed 1992 Special Rider Music. "Standing In The Doorway" ©1996 Special Rider Music. "Subterranean Homesick Blues" ©1965; renewed 1993 Special Rider Music. "Sweetheart Like You" ©1983 Special Rider Music.

"Talkin' New York" ©1962; renewed 1990 MCA. "Talkin' World War III Blues" ©1963; renewed 1991 Special Rider Music. "Tangled Up in Blue" ©1974 Ram's Horn Music. *Tarantula* ©1966 Bob Dylan. "Tears of Rage" ©1968; renewed 1996 Dwarf Music. "Tell Me, Momma" ©1971; renewed 1995 Dwarf Music. "Tell Me That It Isn't True" ©1969; renewed 1997 Dwarf Music. "Temporary Like Achilles" copyright 1966; renewed 1994 Dwarf Music. "10,000 Men" ©1990 Special Rider Music. "This Wheel's on Fire" ©1967; renewed 1995 Dwarf Music. "'Til I Fell In Love With You" ©1996

Special Rider Music. "Time Passes Slowly" ©1970 Big Sky Music. "The Times They Are A-Changin'" ©1963; renewed 1996 Special Rider Music. "Tiny Montgomery" ©1967; renewed 1995 Dwarf Music. "To Ramona" ©1964; renewed 1992 Special Rider Music. "Tombstone Blues" ©1965; renewed 1993 Special Rider Music. "Tonight I'll Be Staying Here With You" ©1969; renewed 1997 Dwarf Music. "Too Much of Nothing" ©1967; renewed 1995 Dwarf Music. "Train A-Travelin'" ©1968; renewed 1996 Special Rider Music. "Trouble in Mind" ©1979 Special Rider Music. "True Love Tends to Forget" ©1978 Special Rider Music. "Tryin' to Get to Heaven" ©1996 Special Rider Music. "2 * 2" ©1990 Special Rider Music.

"Ugliest Girl in the World" ©1987 Special Rider Music and Ice Nine Music. "Unbelievable" ©1990 Special Rider Music. "Under the Red Sky" ©1990 Special Rider Music. "Union Sundown" ©1983 Special Rider Music. "Up to Me" ©1974 Ram's Head Music.

"Visions of Johanna" ©1966; renewed 1994 Dwarf Music.

"Watching the River Flow" ©1971 Big Sky Music. "Watered-Down Love" ©1981 Special Rider Music. "We Better Talk This Over" ©1978 Special Rider Music. "Wedding Song" ©1973 Ram's Horn Music. "Went to See the Gypsy" ©1970 Big Sky Music. "What Can I Do for You?" ©1980 Special Rider Music. "What Good Am I?" ©1989 Special Rider Music. "What Was It You Wanted?" ©1989 Special Rider Music. "When He Returns" ©1979 Special Rider Music. "When the Night Comes Falling from the Sky" ©1985 Special Rider Music. "When the Ship Comes In" copyright 1963; renewed 1991 Special Rider Music. "Where Are You Tonight? (Journey Through Dark Heat)" ©1978 Special Rider Music. "Where Teardrops Fall" ©1989 Special Rider Music. "Wiggle Wiggle" ©1990 Special Rider Music. "Winterlude" ©1970 Big Sky Music. "With God on Our Side" ©1963; renewed 1991 Special Rider Music. "World Gone Wrong" ©1993 Special Rider Music. *World Gone Wrong* liner notes ©1993 Bob Dylan.

"Yea! Heavy and a Bottle of Bread" ©1967; renewed 1995 Dwarf Music. "You're a Big Girl Now" ©1974 Ram's Horn Music. "You're Gonna Make Me Lonesome When You Go" ©1974 Ram's Horn Music.

INTRODUCTION

It is now almost a casual observation in the works of pop and rock historians that "Bob Dylan changed the face of popular music."

Cameron Crowe, *Biograph* notes[1]

Bob Dylan's career started out modestly enough. He lived an ordinary childhood in Hibbing, headed to Minneapolis, spent a semester at university, then began playing to folk crowds in Dinkytown and, later, after journeying to New York, in Greenwich Village. Over forty years after that trek, Dylan is "still on the road / Heading for another joint."

During that time, Dylan has almost single-handedly "changed the face of popular music." As a songwriter, Dylan rescued music from the largely content-free lyrics that had pervaded the airwaves up until the 1960s. Early in his career, Dylan demonstrated an extensive knowledge of folk, blues, country and rock songs, and he began building upon traditional material to create songs that were new and invigorating. Bob Dylan's first songs are very much styled after Woody Guthrie's works, but they bear the unmistakable stamp of originality ("Song to Woody," for instance).

By 1962, Dylan had assimilated these styles and forged his own songwriting technique, a technique that first appears on the monumental record *The Freewheelin' Bob Dylan*. The album combined love songs, topical songs and humorous pieces, and people had a difficult time believing that the kid was only twenty-two years old.

The above quotation by Crowe is framed in the context of a discussion about "Blowin' in the Wind," possibly the most famous song to have been written in the twentieth century.[2] Now sung universally, the song also served to increase social awareness of one of the major issues in the United States: segregation. Blacks adopted the song as part of the civil rights movement: a form of non-violent civil disobedience. Dylan's topical songs became legendary, in part because, as Crowe writes, they never approached the heavy-handed.[3]

With 1964's *Another Side of Bob Dylan*, Dylan's language began to become increasingly complex, and his next three albums, *Bringing It All Back Home*, *Highway 61 Revisited* and *Blonde on Blonde*, integrated literary allusions with poetic language in a stream-of-consciousness style that expanded the boundaries for songwriting.

By employing backing musicians, Dylan took these songs and charged them to a rock beat, leaving the rest of the music world scrambling to catch up to him. Dylan's break with the folkie crowd at the 1965 Newport Festival (Dylan appeared with a rhythm and blues band at what was, after all, a folk festival) is understandable, a desire to bring his new songs to the country in a manner that was bound to bring acclaim as well as controversy. Dylan's dissatisfaction with the folk audience was due partly to the fact that, as Jerome Rodnitzky observed in a study of folk music, they liked the songs he was writing but not his voice.

Dylan's voice is his other lasting gift to music. It is a testament to his range as a singer that no two Bob Dylan albums sound completely alike. When he broke into the music scene, some of the older folk crowd regarded his singing as rude and uncultured. The irony is that the clean-voiced singers of this period quickly faded into obscurity, while those performers willing to take risks with their voice (such as Dylan, Elvis Presley, The Beatles and Mick Jagger) became models for other singers.

From the start, Dylan began combining different musical dialects into one voice. Talent scout John Hammond was so impressed by Dylan (as was *New York Times* music critic Robert Shelton, who enthusiastically reviewed Dylan's stage show) that he gave him a recording contract almost immediately. What Hammond and Shelton saw that many others did not was Dylan's uniqueness as a singer, his ability to convey a tremendous amount of feeling with his voice. When "Like a Rolling Stone" hit the airwaves in 1965, the rock world suddenly realized that brilliant lyrics fused with an incredible voice was a potent combination. Dylan's influence as a singer ranges throughout popular music, from artists such as Neil Young, Bruce Springsteen, Lou Reed and Patti Smith, and into such musical genres as New Wave, punk and grunge.

Some people claim that Dylan used his 1966 motorcycle accident as a pretext for distancing himself from the rock scene that he had fostered, but that explanation seems rather petty. Certainly, Dylan has never been content to make the same type of music continuously, and *The Basement Tapes*, *John Wesley Harding* and *Nashville Skyline* are explorations into a rootsy, country and western style of music. Consequently, his language gets pared down to make it more accessible to the musical idiom.

After the 1960s, Dylan's musical and lyrical shifts become somewhat less abrupt. Discarding *Self Portrait*, *New Morning* is a marginally successful return to rock, but it's not until his work with The Band in 1973 and 1974 (with *Planet Waves* and an American tour) that Dylan finds a relative degree of musical stability. Meanwhile, his lyrics are rooted in a domestic setting. On *Blood on the Tracks*, Dylan slims the music down to suit the lyrics, the result being something similar to a folk album. The songs he writes during this period quickly become classic expressions of lost love. With *Desire*, he employs a violin sound and vocal harmonies, and writes exceptional story-songs. The 1978 tour and the album *Street Legal* use a much larger band than in the past, and the songs become dense, dark and mysterious. His evangelical trilogy, *Slow Train Coming*, *Saved* and *Shot of Love*, is gospel-tinged. 1983's *Infidels* is a welcome return to skilled songwriting and gritty music. After experimenting with various styles during the 1980s, Dylan returns to acoustic music in 1992 with *Good As I Been to You*.

Dylan is the type of musician whose wide-ranging knowledge of music enables strains from various styles to appear throughout his career. Elements of folk, blues, rock, country and gospel seep into all his music, and his voice, at its best, has the ability to blend these modes. On some albums, certain styles find fuller expression than others. In the *London Review of Books*, writer Danny Karlin contended that "the notion that the 'folk Dylan' or the 'electric Dylan' or the 'country Dylan' or the 'gospel Dylan' is *the* Dylan, and hence the hero of his own apotheosis or the demon of his own decline" is a fallacy, and Karlin's comments are important to consider in looking at Dylan's career.[4] As Karlin implies, the trap that Dylan's critics often fall into is believing that Dylan is true to only one musical style and that the others are simply digressions as he searches for a way to perfect that one particular style. The critics that praise the "electric Dylan (circa 1965-66)" and the "*Blood on the Tracks* Dylan" the most are always the first ones to condemn Dylan when his music or language is different. This is how the rather irksome distinction arose of dividing Dylan's music into two periods: everything up to and including *Blonde on Blonde* is one period, *Blood on the Tracks* is the other, with everything between the two and after *Blood on the Tracks* deemed unimportant, with rare exceptions. *The Basement Tapes* and *John Wesley Harding* are the only albums that fall outside these categories to be granted significant standing.

This isn't to suggest that all of Dylan's other studio albums are of the same high quality. But at least two of them (*Desire* and *Infidels*) are worthy of such accolades, several others are excellent (*Nashville Skyline, Street Legal, Good As I Been to You, World Gone Wrong* and *Time Out of Mind*), and a few are commendable (*Pat Garrett & Billy the Kid, Oh Mercy* and the first side of *Slow Train Coming*). The mistake many critics make is to approach a Dylan album expecting it to sound like *Blonde on Blonde* or *Blood on the Tracks*; obviously, they will be disappointed. It's best to look at each album individually rather than rigidly compare them to other albums: Does the album achieve what Dylan was aiming at? Is it cohesive? Are the individual songs musically and lyrically strong? These are the questions I found myself asking when studying these albums.

Dylan's recorded output is not perfect. 1970s *Self Portrait* is an utter disaster, and his 1980s work is spotty. But considering the high standards he set with his 1960s work, much of Dylan's other albums can easily stand on their own merits.

Of course, Dylan's body of work also includes unreleased material and concert performances. Throughout his career, Dylan has continually reworked songs on stage. For the purposes of this volume, however, I have limited myself primarily to a comprehensive study of Dylan's individual albums, with a brief concluding chapter at the end of each section that deals with the significance of the period and sometimes addresses larger issues surrounding these records. Bootlegged material is undoubtedly interesting, but the limited availability of unofficial recordings to the general public, poor sound quality of many such recordings, and often sketchy information surrounding such material precludes any lengthy discussion on my part of these works. By examining Dylan's records and the songs on them, one can conveniently chart the movements in his art, look closely at how Dylan uses language, and discuss his vocal techniques. Since Dylan's official releases, good or bad, are the signposts in his career, a thorough understanding of his records enables one to more fully appreciate Dylan's contribution to popular music.

PART I

MY BACK PAGES

BOB DYLAN

RELEASED: MARCH 1962

The folk music revival of the mid-to-late 1950s and the early 1960s brought traditional music back to the forefront of American popular culture. The movement is explicable on a number of grounds. On one level, it reflected the bohemian movement that flourished in the coffeehouses of Greenwich village and the Dinkytown district of the University of Minnesota (among other places). To angst-filled youths, folk music did more for them than contemporary rock 'n' roll was doing. Although this period produced some fine singles, notably Wilbert Harrison's "Kansas City," "Tutti Frutti" by Little Richard, "Whole Lotta Shakin' Goin' On" by Jerry Lee Lewis, and almost everything Chuck Berry put out, the pop charts consisted mainly of songs such as Jan and Dean's "Baby Talk," The Coasters' "Yakety Yak," Bobby Day's "Rockin' Robin" and Frankie Lymon's "Why Do Fools Fall In Love?," to name a few. And with Elvis in the army, it is no surprise that more people turned to folk songs for inspiration. Another reason for folk music's resurgence was that folk songs were historically, from union ballads to anti-slavery songs, a tool that could be used by the populace to make a point about social conditions. To many, the 1950s were rife with problems.

The Kingston Trio's pleasant version of "Tom Dooley" gave the folkie crowd the hit single it needed to gather momentum, and from there the genre boomed, with groups like The Brothers Four, The Seekers and The Clancy Brothers, and individuals like Pete Seeger and Joan Baez gaining popularity with their own interpretations of older folk songs and a smattering of originals.

Dylan's role in this emerging folk scene has been well documented; suffice to say that by late 1959-early 1960 he had a regular gig at coffeehouses in Minneapolis. Dylan landed in New York in January 1961 and performed well enough to earn a recording contract with Columbia. The result of two recording sessions in 1961 was *Bob Dylan*, consisting mostly of folk and blues standards, with a couple of strong original compositions included. The album sold poorly on its release and did not garner much attention; artistically, nonetheless, it holds up well alongside the other albums in Dylan's canon. Dylan's singing must have struck listeners as unorthodox, to say the least, but his voice often has an assurance that foreshadows his later vocal techniques. On "You're No Good," he sings with true verve, pulling off a wild performance (similar to "Honey, Just Allow Me One More Chance"). The standard "Pretty Peggy-O" is reinvented with a whooping harmonica and Dylan's jovial "whoo-hoo"'s. "Fixin' to Die" gains a ferocity that fits the lyrics. Occasionally, Dylan's singing gets away from him: when he tries to stretch the word "blues" on "Freight Train Blue" and his voice goes to shreds, it's an embarrassment.

Vocally, the four strongest performances are "Baby, Let Me Follow You Down," "Man of Constant Sorrow," "House of the Risin' Sun" and "Song to Woody." "Song to Woody" is heartfelt and "Man of Constant Sorrow" is sung with a weariness that gives the song a beautiful quality. "Baby, Let Me Follow You Down" benefits from a warm, endearing, spoken introduction, some good harmonica work, and a wonderful conclusion, as Dylan's voice bursts free before the final guitar strum. The song became a regular on Dylan's famous 1965-66 concerts, performed amidst much hostility.

Although the arrangement of "House of the Risin' Sun" was purportedly stolen from Dave van Ronk, Dylan's singing is ambitious, and his version is often credited as a forerunner of The Animals' folk-rock version.[5] Dylan adopts the persona of a young girl dragged into prostitution and recounts the tragedy with a mixture of fear and abhorrence. In verses one to four, the singer sounds troubled; in the final verses Dylan gives the song a real urgency, as if the heroine realizes how deplorable her condition really is.

At the time of Bob Dylan's recording, Dylan had written few original songs. Aside from "Talkin' New York" and "Song to Woody," the only significant compositions were two out-takes from those first Columbia recording sessions, the tender "He Was a Friend of Mine" and "Man on the Street" (both on *The Bootleg Series*), "Hard Times in New York Town," and the disaster parody "Talking Bear Mountain Picnic Massacre Blues," a country bumpkin's version of the Titanic, which was recorded for *The Freewheelin' Bob Dylan* but would not appear until *The Bootleg Series*.

These songs hint at where Dylan is headed as a lyricist. In particular, "Talkin' New York" and "Song to Woody" suggest a talent for songwriting. "Talkin' New York" is similar to the folk song "The State of Arkansas" and Guthrie's "Talkin' Subway," and Dylan drops a reference to Guthrie's "Pretty Boy Floyd" (performed brilliantly by Dylan on the 1988 lp *Folkways: A Vision Shared*) when he writes that "a very great man once said / That some people rob you with a fountain pen"; meaning corrupt bankers who steal from the poor, but also writers who criticize with their pens.

Despite these references, there are some good original lines in "Talkin' New York": the opening verse about leaving "the wild West . . . the towns I love the best" in search of glory, contrasting the charm of the mid-West with the opulence and turmoil of the East; Dylan's joke about the club owner who rejects him on the grounds that he sounds "like a hillbilly; we want folk singers here" pokes fun at the prevailing misconception that a folk singer had to have a bland, modest voice; and Dylan's version of the have-nots vs. the haves, anticipating problems with increasing disparities in the levels of wealth in American society:

> A lot of people don't have much food on their table,
> But they got a lot of forks 'n' knives,
> And they gotta cut somethin'.

"Song to Woody," written at the time that Dylan was visiting Guthrie in the hospital, is the record's standout.[6] Sung in Guthriesque fashion, Dylan pays homage to the man he once called his first, and last, idol.[7] Dylan recognizes all that Guthrie has done and, in the process, foreshadows the turbulence of the 1960s:

> Hey, hey, Woody Guthrie, I wrote you a song
> 'Bout a funny ol' world that's a-comin' along.
> Seems sick an' it's hungry, it's tired an' it's torn,
> It looks like it's a-dyin' an' it's hardly been born.

In the conclusion ("The very last thing that I'd want to do is to say I've been hittin' some hard travelin too"), Dylan voices his hopes that he won't face the same hard times that Guthrie endured, that his road will be an easier one.

When Dylan returned to the song thirty years later at his anniversary celebration, he sang it poorly but acknowledged that he had not forgotten Guthrie, and that his debt to him can never fully be repaid ("I can't sing enough"). There is no doubt that Dylan had learned Guthrie's massive catalogue inside-out; Dylan's topical songs on *The Freewheelin' Bob Dylan* and *The Times They Are A-Changin'* are in the tradition of Guthrie's songs of social injustice, while Dylan's later anti-hero outlaw sagas like "John Wesley Harding," "Billy" and "Joey" mine the same vein as Guthrie's dust-bowl ballads (like "Pretty Boy Floyd"). When Dylan lied about his antecedents during his formative years (as in his poem "My Life in a Stolen Moment," which begins with a truthful retelling of his early life but soon lapses into falsehood – "I ran away from [Hibbing] when I was 10, 12, 13, 15, 15 1/2, 17 an' 18") he wasn't rejecting his heritage but fashioning himself along the lines of the Guthrie legend as a hobo figure who traversed America. In that light, "Song to Woody" may be read as a statement of faith, a pledge to carry the Guthrie legacy.

Part of Guthrie's populist appeal was his ability to put himself in the shoes of those people he wrote about. By working alongside migrants or riding the rails, Guthrie's humility endeared him to "the common folk." Dylan was fascinated by such selflessness, and several of his early writings concern this facet of Guthrie's career. In "11 Outlined Epitaphs," Dylan writes that Guthrie "taught me / face t' face / that men are men / shatterin' even himself / as an idol." In "My Life in a Stolen Moment," he speaks of being influenced by "the faces you can't find again." Dylan mentions Guthrie's hobo mystique in his poem "Last Thoughts on Woody Guthrie":

You need something special all right
You need a fast flyin' train on a tornado track
To shoot you someplace and shoot you back.

Dylan followed Guthrie's example by playing at hootenanies and at events like the March on Washington. Part of what rankles about *Renaldo and Clara* is that the film largely ignores such precedent and tries to make Dylan appear as a larger than life figure.

Bob Dylan has much of the communal spirit to it, a theme that gets developed more fully in his next two albums. The traditional songs on *Bob Dylan* show at least a bit of Dylan's musical roots and the originals reveal a gift for songwriting. But not until his second album do Dylan's songwriting talents come to fruition.

THE FREEWHEELIN' BOB DYLAN

RELEASED: MAY 1963

At the time, Dylan's debut album went almost unnoticed, selling a measly five thousand copies.[8] After the recording of *Bob Dylan*, Dylan began writing more of his own material, and he had plenty of original songs for *The Freewheelin' Bob Dylan*. Few sophomore albums have had the type of impact that *The Freewheelin'* had.

"Blowin' in the Wind" is the song that first brought Dylan recognition. Popularized by Peter, Paul and Mary, who reduced the song to a catchy jingle, "Blowin' in the Wind" became a civil rights anthem and spawned a plethora of cover versions, most of them awful.

Dylan's simple, moving original recording is still the best, and it marks an introduction to the topical music of the

1960s. "Blowin' in the Wind" has the same broad appeal of Guthrie's "This Land is Your Land"; its unforgettable chorus is uplifting. The song remains Dylan's best known composition, in the sense that its lyrics are recognized worldwide. In one of the few good scenes in *Renaldo and Clara,* David Blue talks about "Blowin' in the Wind"'s composition:

> It was a Monday at "The Fat Black Pussycat." Bob came in and he had the guitar. And he sat there writing. . . . And that was "Blowin' in the Wind." When it was finished . . . we went over to Gerde's Folk City – and he went to Gil Turner [a folk singer] and he took out his guitar and sang "Blowin' in the Wind." And this guy said, ' . . . I've never heard anything like that in my entire life! That's the most incredible song I've ever heard!' And that's the first time anybody, to my knowledge, had ever heard "Blowin' in the Wind."

The first verse deals with warfare, as the white dove, a symbol of peace, contrasts with the flying cannon balls. Verse two, which is out of sequence in *Lyrics, 1962-1985,* continues on the issue of freedom that opens the song ("How many roads must a man walk down / Before you call him a man?"). The final verse flows naturally from the second, condemning those who are blind to human suffering. The chorus is somewhat ambiguous: does the wind bring the answers or scatter them? Dylan perhaps intended to provoke neither question; the key may lie in the opening lines of verse two, which asks, "How many years can a mountain exist / Before it is washed to the sea?" Dylan suggests that, like the wind, these questions are eternal.

"Masters of War" is an extension of "Blowin' in the Wind"'s first verse. The song is a biting attack on merchants of death. Dylan pulls no punches, likening them to Judas and then wishing for their death. He presents images of warfare ("young people's blood / Flows out of their bodies / And is buried in the mud") to stress the waste of human life.

The song may be read as a forerunner to the protests against the Vietnam War. Written at a time when the conflict in Vietnam stood on the periphery of American awareness (January 1963), the song's release coincided with Buddhist-led demonstrations in South Vietnam, which awakened anti-war sentiments in the American public, attitudes that would become more pronounced with increased United States in-volvement in the war in 1964 and 1965. The warmongers in question, however, are not specified, and so the song can easily refer to any battle in which men profit at the expense of the lives of others, a point Dylan made clear when he performed a snarling, full-throttle rendition of "Masters of War" at the 1991 Grammy Awards while the U.S. was at war in the Persian Gulf.

"A Hard Rain's A-Gonna Fall" is a post-apocalyptic nightmare, as Dylan assumes the role of seer foretelling horrible events. The scenes he presents are vivid: "a black branch with blood that kept drippin'"; "a newborn baby with wild wolves all around it"; "a young woman whose body was burning." As Tim Riley notes in his sound Dylan study *Hard Rain* "much of the imagery is darkly visionary: he pictures weapons held by children, which summons the spectre of adolescent warriors in Ireland, Central America, and the Middle East three decades on," while the lines "Where the people are many and their hands are all empty," and "Where hunger is ugly, where souls are forgotten" may be applied to the famines that swept Bangladesh in the early 1970s and Ethiopia in the mid-1980s.[9] In verse three, Dylan contrasts one person starving with "many people laughin'."

Dylan's straightforward performance invests the lyrics with more despair. But the breathtaking final lines offer a glimmer of hope:

And I'll tell it and speak it and think it and breathe it,
And reflect from the mountains so all souls can see it.
Then I'll stand on the ocean until I start sinkin',
But I'll know my song well before I start singin'.

Although the song is looking at the past ("where have you been?", "what did you see?", etc.), the above lines seem to make the song's terrors into prophecies. This is the type of complex tense shifting that Dylan perfects on *Blood on the Tracks*.

"Hard Rain," "Blowin' in the Wind," "Masters of War" and "Oxford Town" (concerning James Meredith's attempts to become the first black to enrol at the University of Mississippi) are often described as "political statements," but pigeonholing these songs upsets their timelessness. Danny Karlin points to a misconception that "focuses on Dylan's 'relevance' or 'significance' as the time-bound representative of some cultural moment or other, whether anti-war or pro-flag, the student Left or the religious Right."[10]

Dylan has always been unhappy with labels of any kind, and to call his topical songs "Leftist statements," as many did during the early part of Dylan's career, is a curious misnomer. Dylan has never fallen into any one "political camp," and his songs outlast those of his more adamantly politically affiliated contemporaries (such as Pete Seeger).

Dylan leavens the serious nature of *The Freewheelin'* with songs of gentle yearning, and with songs of a playful yet cutting humour. "Girl from the North Country" and "Down the Highway" establish a mood of loneliness, but the narrator never sounds self-pitying. "Bob Dylan's Dream" finds the narrator reminiscing about his adolescence. There is a maturity to this sad tale that comes through in the fifth verse:

And our choices they was few so the thought never hit
That the one road we travelled would ever shatter or split.

"Don't Think Twice, It's All Right" seems like a much more
jaded farewell, but the speaker still harbours deep feelings
for the girl ("But I wish there was somethin' you could do or
say / To try and make me change my mind and stay").

"Talkin' World War III Blues" is the best of the humorous songs on the album. The song skewers the Cold War
paranoia about the world coming to an end, and sends up
the individual's misconception that he will somehow survive. "Talkin' World War III Blues" reads like a hilarious
Twilight Zone episode. When Dylan encounters other people in his dream, he mixes reality with illusion, the result
being a quick trip to the shrink, who informs Dylan that he,
too, has been having the same dreams. The song also parodies hackneyed pop music:

> Turned on my record player –
> It was Rock-A-Day Johnny singin'
> "Tell Your Ma, Tell Your Pa;
> Our Love's A-Gonna Grow Ooh-wah, Ooh-wah."

These lines lead back to the introduction to "Bob Dylan's
Blues," in which Dylan makes fun of the Tin Pan Alley
method of songwriting to order. Dylan told Cameron Crowe
for *Biograph* that "Tin Pan Alley is gone. I put an end to it."[11]

The *Freewheelin'* represents a significant step for Dylan
not only as a songwriter, but as a singer. His voice is more
controlled than on his first album. It has more depth, and
more sway from song to song. "Blowin' in the Wind" and
"Hard Rain" are pitched in the voice of a troubadour; "Girl
from the North Country" is gently performed; "Masters of
War" is sung angrily; "Bob Dylan's Blues," "I Shall Be Free"

and "Honey, Just Allow Me One More Chance" are done in a carefree manner. In "Oxford Town," Dylan does not sing the song sarcastically (the lyrics have just a touch of sarcasm to them); if he had, the emotional effect would be lessened. Dylan sings about the lackadaisical attitude the South took towards probing civil rights problems ("Two men died 'neath the Mississippi moon / Somebody better investigate soon") in a wry manner.

Dylan's singing on many of the album's topical songs is that of a voice urging to be recognized. In an outtake from these sessions, "Let Me Die in My Footsteps" Dylan sings, "But now, Lawd God, let my poor voice be heard." By "poor voice," Dylan does not mean bad voice, he means the voice of the "little people' in society. In much of his writing from this period, Dylan tells the story from the perspective of these "little people."

This concern for the downtrodden in society has always been a part of the folk tradition. *The Freewheelin'* honours this tradition while at the same time advancing past it. Some of the songs written by Dylan during this time have their antecedents in folk material. Dylan recorded "Dink's Song" in late 1961; he wrote "Farewell" in January 1963. "Dink's Song," a Negro ballad, has the refrain "Fare thee well, O honey, fare thee well." In "Farewell," the chorus includes:

> So it's fare thee well my own true love,
> We'll meet another day, another time.

Dylan adopted the melody for "Blowin' in the Wind" from "No More Auction Block," another Negro song. "Scarborough Fair" provides the working melody to "Girl from the North Country" and the lines "Remember me to one who lives there, / For she once was a true love of mine." Dylan's "talking blues" songs on the album are very much modelled after "The Original Talking Blues." One verse in the latter song opens this way: "I was down in the holler just a-settin' on a log." In "Talkin' World War III Blues," Dylan sings, "I was down in the sewer with some little lover." Verse five of "The Original Talking Blues" runs:

> Ain't no use me workin' so hard,
> I got a gal in the rich folks' yard,
> They kill a chicken, she sends me the head;
> She thinks I'm workin', I'm a layin' up in bed.
> Just dreamin' about her. Havin' a good time . . . two
>   other women . . .

In "I Shall Be Free," Dylan reworks this verse into:

> Oh, there ain't no use in me workin' all the time,
> I got a woman who works herself blind.
> Works up to her britches, up to her neck,
> Writes me letters and sends me checks.
> She's a humdinger . . . folk singer.

In fact, "I Shall Be Free" is almost entirely based on the earlier song. (Incidentally, "The Original Talking Blues" appears in two other Dylan songs: "Subterranean Homesick Blues," which turns "Mama's in the kitchen fixin' the yeast, / Poppa's in the bedroom greasin' his feet, / Sister's in the cellar squeezin' up the hops, / Brother's at the window just-a-watchin' for the cops" into "Johnny's in the basement / Mixing up the medicine / I'm on the pavement / Thinking about the government"; and "Don't Ya Tell Henry," which adapts "Down in the hen house on my knees, / I thought I heard a chicken sneeze" into "I found a little chicken down on his knees, / I went up and yelled to him, / 'Please, please, please!'")

Folk, blues, gospel, and even rockabilly (with "Mixed-Up Confusion") influenced *The Freewheelin' Bob Dylan*. On the album, Dylan combines these various styles. But the lyrics he writes are unconventional, different from folk ballads. In "Hard Rain," the opening couplet of each stanza may be a variant on the traditional ballad "Lord Randall," but the images Dylan creates could not be described as folk lyrics. "Don't Think Twice" is a song freed from the sentimentality of many folk "love songs." "Blowin' in the Wind," for all its gospel and folk strains, is a very unique song.

The Freewheelin' heavily impacted popular music. It introduced more complex imagery to songwriting; it led to an increase in the number of "singer-songwriters"; the topical song movement of the 1960s began; "Blowin' in the Wind" had an influence on society; Dylan's voice allowed other singers greater room for expression. The album's lustre has not faded over the years, and its songs still have meaning in today's society.

THE TIMES THEY ARE A-CHANGIN'

RELEASED: JANUARY 1964

The trouble with folk music in the years preceding Dylan's ascension is that there were simply not enough original songs being written. Joan Baez was doing traditional ballads like "East Virginia" and "John Hardy"; Peter, Paul and Mary reworked staples like "This Train" and "500 Miles"; The Brothers Four and The Kingston Trio wrote very few of their own songs. Even Pete Seeger did mostly older material. While these artists produced many fine cover versions, the songs could not truly reflect topical issues. With the release of *The Times They Are A-Changin'*, Dylan solidified his status as a unique folksinger – one who wrote almost entirely his own material – and as a social commentator. No wonder the folk crowd so readily covered Dylan's songs. Dylan involuntarily became the centrepiece for folk's resurgence (hence the outrage when he turned to rock and roll).

Although not as diverse as *The Freewheelin'*, *The Times They Are A-Changin'* successfully captures a phase in Dylan's career when he was heavily concerned with topical issues. The album speaks to the downtrodden, the poor, the "little people" in society; manifesting a broad concern for morality and a need for change. Social protest is long a part of folk music: the negro spirituals "John Brown's Body" and "O Freedom," anti-war songs like "Arthur McBride" and "Johnny Has Gone for a Soldier," and the union ballad "Joe Hill" are merely a few examples.

Before Dylan, Woody Guthrie was the pre-eminent topical songwriter. In songs such as "Pastures of Plenty" and "Do-Re-Mi" he expressed the hardships endured by Dust Bowl migrants, in "Lindbergh" and "Sinking of the Reuben James" he dealt with World War II; in "Grand Coulee Dam" he attacked the rich and famous. Guthrie's songs resonate with heartache, hope, spirituality, and an inherent kindness that makes his life a triumph and his death by Huntington's chorea even sadder. His autobiography, *Bound For Glory*, is a marvellous collection of anecdotes; the movie is worth seeing for the final thirty minutes, which finally capture the book's positive energy.

Dylan's protest songs are by no means copycats of Guthrie's, but Guthrie's spirit tints them. In the liner notes to *The Times*, Dylan writes:

Woody never made me fear
and he didn't trample any hopes

for he just carried a book of Man
an' gave it t'me t'read awhile
an' from it I learned my greatest lesson.

Like Guthrie, Dylan often structured songs around current events. Dylan based "The Lonesome Death of Hattie Carroll" on a newspaper account he had read of the murder of a barmaid by the son of a wealthy Maryland family. Dylan's performance instills in the listener great empathy for Hattie Carroll and disgust for William Zanzinger. Zanzinger represents the establishment; Hattie Carroll is the poor black with low status. Dylan hints that maybe the Maryland elite would have felt sorrier for Zanzinger going to jail than for Hattie Carroll's fate, and perhaps that's the true tragedy of the incident.

In "Only a Pawn in Their Game," Dylan takes a different perspective on the murder of Mississippi NAACP leader Medgar Evers. He presents the event as a crime nurtured by southern attitudes. The killer (who was finally sentenced in early 1994) is white trash conditioned to hate the negro:

He's taught in his school
From the start by the rule
That the laws are with him
To protect his white skin
To keep up his hate.

"But it ain't him to blame / He's only a pawn in their game," Dylan sings, fingering a society that did little to discourage racism. *Don't Look Back* features a clip of Dylan singing "Only a Pawn in Their Game" in a cotton field outside Greenwood, Mississippi in July 1963 to a crowd of negroes; it is a touching moment, showing Dylan's genuine concern for the black plight. In his final poem in the "11 Outlined Epitaphs," Dylan's comment on segregation achieves a universal significance: "all people / no matter what creed / no matter what colour skin / no matter what language an no matter what land / . . . laugh / in the same tongue / an' cry / in the same tongue."

Other songs chronicle the experiences of struggling individuals, recalling Guthrie's treatment of migrant workers. "Ballad of Hollis Brown" is a disturbing song about an impoverished farmer who goes insane and commits suicide, taking his family with him. Dylan summons up images of depression to convey the extent of the man's despair: "cabin broken down," starving children, a dying mare, a well devoid of water. The final lines may be pessimistic or optimistic: either the seven new people will have a better life than Hollis Brown or a similar one.

"North Country Blues" describes the effect of a mine closure (the locale is clearly Hibbing, Dylan's hometown) on a worker's wife. The performance is morose, generating a sense of this woman's suffering as domestic tragedy coincides with economic downturn. Dylan brings out the innate dignity of the woman and her endurance in the face of continual hardships.

Dylan's social criticisms are wide-ranging on the album. "With God on Our Side" attacks the patriotic propaganda of countries that use God's name to rationalize their actions. The second and third verses send up conventional history texts in which leaders are presented as heroic figures who almost invariably had God on their side. Verse four questions World War I: "The reason for fighting / I never did get." In the following verses, Dylan wonders why the Russians became the enemy after the second World War, while noting the irony of the Germans being readily forgiven despite their atrocious crimes against humanity. Dylan's point is that it is easy to build up hatred against certain groups of people and then shift that hatred to others.

If "With God on Our Side" looks to the past, the title track finds Dylan ahead of his time. "The Times They Are A-Changin" stands as a prelude to the radical decade which the 1960s was to become, an era of "flower power," the drug culture, the New Left, free speech, Black Power and an order "rapidly fadin'." The fourth verse anticipates teenage rebellion, and the lines "Don't block up the hall / For he that gets hurt / Will be he who has stalled" are Dylan's warning that people have to adapt with the times.

It is difficult to say whether Dylan is welcoming change or not, but he certainly understood that the coming years would bring change. The song did prove beneficial to Dylan, becoming an instant success, thanks not only to its message, but to Dylan's vibrant performance. Unfortunately, the recent use of the song in advertisements has tainted "The Times"'s appeal, and the title has become the last refuge of a hack, a cliché now used to bemoan the current generation (as in, "The times, they sure have a-changed").

Knowing an entire album of protest songs would appear self-righteous, Dylan included four compositions with more general themes. "When the Ship Comes In" is as anthemic as "The Times," with Biblical imagery replacing social commentary. Dylan's singing approaches exaltation, punctuated by the piercing harmonica refrain that precedes the final verse. The imagery is precise and evocative, and the lines "Then the sands will roll / Out a carpet of gold" are a precursor for the language of "Mr. Tambourine Man" ("silhouetted by the sea, circled by the circus sands"). The song celebrates the beauty and the majesty of God's Nature (similar to "Lay Down Your Weary Tune"). The ship becomes a symbol of salvation, and the prophetic conclusion, as Shelton points out, heralds the day when evil will be purged:

And like Pharaoh's tribe,
They'll be drownded in the tide,
And like Goliath, they'll be conquered.[12]

"One Too Many Mornings" and "Boots of Spanish Leather" are love songs similar to "Girl from the North Country." The melancholy "One Too Many Mornings" is atmospheric, evoking the uneasy calm of the early morning. The song actually begins in the evening, while the second verse has the narrator leaving his love at dawn. "The crossroads of my doorstep" suggests the line in "Bob Dylan's Dream," "And many a road taken by many a first friend," and Robert Frost's "The Road Not Taken," anticipating the choices of youth. In verse three, Dylan's restlessness gives way to a feeling of compromise and understanding:

You're right from your side,
And I'm right from mine.
We're both just one too many mornings
And a thousand miles behind.

These lines would assume a different meaning when Dylan sang them during his 1966 concerts to an audience decrying his going electric.

"Boots of Spanish Leather" is a similar lament, with the pathos inherent in Dylan's voice complementing the gentle guitar picking. The first six verses take the form of an alternating dialogue between lovers; the final three are the narrator's alone. The prevailing mood is one of longing, a wish for a safe return for his love, as embodied in verse four:

If I had the stars of the darkest night
And the diamonds from the deepest ocean,
I'd forsake them all for your sweet kiss,
For that's all I'm wishin' to be ownin'.

The theme of uneasiness gets developed further in the album's postlude, "Restless Farewell." The performance and lyrics have an after-hours feel to them; Dylan sitting in a bar reflecting on his past experiences. Dylan refers to his writing of topical songs ("And ev'ry cause that ever I fought, / I fought it full without regret or shame") and his subsequent need to move on.

He continues to develop these ideas in verse five. The verse begins with an overt reference to a mean-spirited *Newsweek* article which claimed that Dylan had bought "Blowin' in the Wind" from a New Jersey high school student.[13] "But if the arrow is straight / and the point is slick, / It can pierce through dust no matter how thick" celebrates one's capacity for creativity and change in the face of hostility. Dylan pledges to stay true to himself. "Restless Farewell" implies a farewell to this particular period of Dylan's life and a move "down the road."

The album also includes a collection of decent, if unremarkable, prose poems on the back of the cover and inner sleeve. Number two deals with Hibbing; number six idolizes Guthrie. Number nine refers again to the *Newsweek* piece. Some of the prose is shocking in its bluntness, as in the reference to Christ in number four:

an' I am on the side a them hurt feelings
plunged on by unsensitive hammers
an' made t' bleed by rusty nails

In the final poem, Dylan drops names with a rapidity that foreshadows his language of the 1964-66 period.

Despite the common criticism that the album seems dated, *The Times* is an important record, capturing Dylan at the height of his association with topical songs.[14] In all the

songs, there is a premonition of change, be it racial, romantic, or personal.

CONCLUSION

Bob Dylan's first three albums immediately established him
as a songwriter of great distinction. Writing original material
was new to folk music at the time, for the Greenwich Village
scene and Dinkytown coffee houses where Dylan got his
start consisted largely of singers performing the same standards night after night. *Bob Dylan* does contain some of these
traditional songs, yet the performances on the record reflect
Dylan's style. At the same time, Dylan began writing his own
compositions, works of high quality. Many of the songs on
his next album (like "Blowin' in the Wind" and "Don't
Think Twice, It's All Right") would become staples of the
folk scene. In 1962 and 1963, Dylan wrote around forty
songs each year, and he would continue to write songs at an
incredible pace up until the late 1960s. *Freewheelin'* and *The
Times They Are A-Changin'* set a new standard for folk
music, one that none of his contemporaries could measure
up to (although many were to try). For *Biograph*, Dylan
discussed the factors that made him a unique interpreter of
traditional folk songs and, moreover, allowed him to write
such profound social criticisms:

> . . . I was singing stuff like "Ruby Lee" by the Sunny
> Mountain Boys, and "Jack O' Diamonds" by Odetta and
> somehow because of my earlier rock 'n' roll background
> was unconsciously crossing the two styles. This made me
> different from your regular folk singers, who were either
> folk song purists or concert-hall singers, who just hap-
> pened to be singing folk songs. When I started writing
> those kinds of songs, there wasn't anybody doing things

like that . . . Woody Guthrie had done similar things but he hadn't really done that type of song. Besides, I had learned from Woody Guthrie and knew and could sing anything he had done. But now the times had changed and things would be different. He contributed a lot to my style lyrically and dynamically but my musical background had been different, with rock 'n' roll and rhythm and blues playing a big part earlier on. Actually attitude had more to do with it than technical ability and that's what the folk movement lacked. In other words, I played all the folk songs with a rock 'n' roll attitude. This is what made me different and allowed me to cut through all the mess and be heard.[15]

These comments are meaningful in light of the folkies' claims that Dylan would "sell out" when he went electric. People forget that Dylan grew up listening to a wide range of music, from Leadbelly to Guthrie to Hank Williams to Chuck Berry to Elvis Presley. Dylan certainly harboured ambitions to be a rock star, but there was little interest in rock and roll at the time he entered the music scene. As biographer Bob Spitz wrote, "The doo-wop and rhythm and blues groups had given way to a group of white-bucked, white-skinned choirboys who projected decidedly whole-some, clean-cut images on the order of Frankie Avalon, Bobby Darin, Ricky Nelson, Dion and Paul Anka."[16]

In 1959, rock was in decline; folk music offered oppor-tunity for advancement and had considerably more sub-stance. Dylan acknowledged this in the notes to *Biograph*:

The thing about rock 'n' roll is that for me anyway it wasn't enough, "Tutti Frutti" and "Blue Suede Shoes" were great catch phrases and driving pulse rhythms and you could get high on the energy but they weren't serious or didn't reflect life in a realistic way. I knew that when I got into folk music, it was more of a serious type of thing. There

is more real life in one line than there was in all the rock
'n' roll themes. Life is full of complexities and rock 'n' roll
didn't reflect that. If I did anything, I brought one to the
other.[17]

Furthermore, Dylan realized that he couldn't go on making
records such as *The Times They Are A-Changin'* for his whole
career. Every artist fears becoming a caricature of himself,
and the last thing Bob Dylan must have wanted was to make
sound-alike records for years.

Years later, some writers would charge that Dylan had
used the Civil Rights Movement to advance himself. As
Patrick Humphries wrote, "Dylan's appearance in Mississippi gave the lie to those who saw him as an opportunist,
riding to his early success on the suffering of the blacks and
the coat-tails of the folk-protest movement."[18] Dylan has
always written social commentary, from "It's Alright, Ma
(I'm Only Bleeding)" to "George Jackson" to "Idiot Wind"
to "Hurricane" to "Union Sundown" to "Political World."
In the notes to "Masters of War" on *Biograph*, Dylan states
that he is "always in the struggle for peoples' freedom,
individual or otherwise. I hate oppression, especially on
children."[19]

Lastly, it is important to remember that Dylan was in his
early twenties at the time of his first three albums, and that
he had a young person's intensity about issues, yet he voiced
these concerns with the eloquence of someone much older.
Dylan's later songs on albums such as *Blood on the Tracks*
and *Street Legal* become more introspective, dealing with the
trials that age brings. For the same reason, Dylan's sense of
humour is more pronounced in his 1960s songs; he could
still be freewheelin' back then.

Hence, it is clear that Dylan was fully committed to the
causes he sang for, and, if anybody doubted his love for and

knowledge of folk music, in 1992 he recorded *Good As I Been to* You, a collection of obscure folk songs, and followed it up with *World Gone Wrong*, an album of folk and blues music. When *The Times They Are A-Changin'* was released, however, it was time for Bob Dylan to move on.

PART II

SOME OTHER KINDS OF SONGS

ANOTHER SIDE OF BOB DYLAN

RELEASED: AUGUST 1964

Another Side of Bob Dylan represents a point in Dylan's career where he began to experiment more with language. His biographers report that Dylan had done extensive reading of the French symbolist poets such as Arthur Rimbaud; consequently, some of the songs on *Another Side* tend towards the impressionistic.[20]

The album's title seems to reflect the shift in Dylan's writing. The compositions "Spanish Harlem Incident," "Chimes of Freedom," "My Back Pages" and "Mama, You Been on My Mind" show "another side" of Dylan, exploring the possibilities suggested by some of his earlier songs ("A Hard Rain's A-Gonna Fall").

The eroticism of "Spanish Harlem Incident" is generated through the sharpness of images such as "Your pearly eyes, so fast an' slashing, / An' your flashing diamond teeth." "On the cliffs of your wildcat charms I'm riding" suggests the mysteriousness of the woman.

"Chimes of Freedom" and "My Back Pages" are the two major songs on the album. In "Chimes of Freedom," when

Dylan witnesses the lightning, it seems to unlock his descriptive powers, so he can depict a commonplace event as "a cloud's white curtain in a far off corner flared" and "Electric light struck like arrows." Dylan evokes the grandeur of nature throughout, from the Poe-like opening line of verse three to "The sky cracked its poems in naked wonder" to "the rain unravelled tales."

Thematically, each flash of lightning implies the promise of freedom for an individual or group of people. "Chimes of Freedom" encompasses civil rights but goes beyond that to include political prisoners, those who would practice civil disobedience, rebels, outcasts and "every hung-up person in the whole wide universe." The totality of Dylan's vision of emancipation elevates "Chimes of Freedom" to the status of anthem.

"My Back Pages" is a statement of growth, a move beyond "lies that life is black and white" to deal with the complexities of life. In the fourth verse, Dylan asserts that there is more to liberty then just "equality in school," that entrenched racial attitudes have to be done away with before the struggle for civil rights ends. Dylan isn't disavowing his earlier songs, he's just viewing the situation from a different angle. The paradoxical refrain refers to Dylan's penchant in his first three albums for portraying himself as someone who has had a lot of experience in the world. Songs such as "Bob Dylan's Dream" and "Restless Farewell," and the songs on his debut album that deal with death, all give the impression of a man who is in middle age, not his early twenties.

But most of the song is a riddle, compounded by Dylan's eerie, almost trance-inducing performance. One has to wonder what the opening lines "Crimson flames tied through my ears / Brewing high and mighty traps / Pounced with fire on flaming roads" might mean, but they certainly sound beatific when Dylan sings them. "My Back Pages" occupies a unique position on the album: although not out of place, it stands out because of its enigmatic qualities. It achieves similar status on *Greatest Hits, Volume II*. The Byrds' cover version, a lighter, jingly take, is appealing in its own right.

"Mama, You Been on My Mind," recorded for the album but not released until *The Bootleg Series*, slots in somewhere between *Another Side*'s fantasies and the album's relationship songs. Most of the song fits the latter description, but "The colour of the sun cut flat / An' cov'rin' the cross-roads I'm standing at" is as impressionistic as anything on the album. Dylan's intentionally lazy delivery makes the song's detached obsession seem more like a backhanded compliment ("I don't even mind who you'll be wakin' with tomorrow, / But mama, you're just on my mind").

If "Mama, You Been on My Mind" is a backhanded compliment, "Ballad in Plain D" is closer to a slap in the face. Detailing the break-up between Dylan and his girlfriend Suze Rotolo, Dylan resorts to name-calling (Suze's sister is the "parasite sister") and nasty put-downs (Suze's mother and sister suffer "from the failures of their day").[21] Worse, the song plods, showcasing bad writing, as in "Beneath a bare light bulb the plaster did pound," "I gagged in contradiction" and "A magnificent mantelpiece, though its heart being chipped." Meanwhile, promising phrases like "manufactured peace" and "Are birds free from the chains of the skyway?" get lost amidst this diatribe's uneloquent vitriol. Dylan would later admit: "I look back at that particular [song] and say . . . maybe I could have left that alone."[22]

"To Ramona" handles third party intervention in a relationship with slightly more tact. Although the narrator is highly resentful of the intrusion of the woman's friends into their affairs, the song ends with an acceptance of change that also works in the context of Dylan's artistic growth:

Everything passes,
Everything changes,
Just do what you think you should do.

The other "love songs" on the album are similarly unconventional. In "I Don't Believe You (She Acts Like We Never Have Met)," about a woman who ignores the narrator after a night of passion with him, the mood is more bewilderment than bitterness, and Dylan even giggles about the situation in verse three.

"It Ain't Me, Babe" seems as much addressed to Dylan's folk audience as it does to his lover, spurning the misperception of him as "someone / Who will promise never to part." It ranks among Dylan's greatest songs, undoubtedly due to the manner in which Dylan holds the last word before the chorus, and the unforgettable chant "No, no, no."

"It Ain't Me, Babe"'s chorus hints at how Dylan's vocal technique was becoming more wonderfully untamed even before his electric period. Such hints pop up throughout the album. In "All I Really Want to Do," Dylan's voice breaks into a yodel on the word "do." On "Black Crow Blues," Dylan jauntily bangs out the tune on the piano, letting his voice go on the lines "But my nerves were kickin' / Tickin' like a clock."

Dylan's pronunciations are more daring and innovative. "Now they asked me to read a *po-em*," Dylan deadpans on "I Shall Be Free No. 10," caricaturing the tiring debate over whether song lyrics are or are not poetry, and he ends up stating his own view in gleefully ambiguous fashion: "Yippee! I'm a poet / and I know it / Hope I don't blow it."[23] The internal rhyme of "All I Really Want to Do" is clever. And only Dylan could rhyme "something jerkin'" with "Tony Perkins" (in "Motorpsycho Nightmare").

Moreover, *Another Side* made Dylan's influence as a songwriter more pervasive: both Sonny and Cher and The Byrds covered "All I Really Want to Do" (the *At Budokan* version sounds like the bastard offspring of these arrangements); The Byrds also did "My Back Pages" and "Chimes of Freedom," The Turtles scored a hit with "It Ain't Me, Babe," and Joan Baez made "Mama, You Been on My Mind" her own. Baez is a good interpreter of Dylan's material, not because she does so much of it, but because her voice allows her to shade the songs differently (compare her version of "Sad-Eyed Lady of the Lowlands" with Dylan's, to cite one example). When Baez loses her focus, as when she parodies Dylan on "Simple Twist of Fate" (how many third-rate comedians have used that same gag?), she only succeeds in making herself, not Dylan, look foolish.

Another Side gains additional importance because it bridges the gap between Dylan's early records and his electric triumphs of the mid-1960s. Dylan's language doesn't reach the staggering dimensions it achieves on *Bringing It All Back Home*, but that only makes the transition smoother. Although a solo album, *Another Side* is often described as a rock album without a band; indeed, songs such as "Black Crow Blues" and "I Don't Believe You" invite backing. With The Hawks on his 1966 tour, Dylan transformed "I Don't Believe You" into a riotous electric performance, captured for posterity on *Biograph*. In retrospect, it is easy to see how *Another Side* evolved into *Bringing It All Back Home*.

PART III

BRINGING IT ALL BACK HOME

RELEASED: MARCH 1965

Bob Dylan's career has had numerous turning points; most successful, some less so (*Self Portrait*; *Renaldo and Clara*). The making of *Bringing It All Back Home* is one of the most significant of these turning points. The sessions for the album marked the first time that Dylan had made a serious attempt at recording songs with a band. His earlier tries (a couple of songs at *The Freewheelin' Bob Dylan* sessions) seemed uncommitted. With *Bringing It All Back Home*, Dylan developed a rapport with his musicians that, presumably, was missing on the past attempt. The tactful accompaniment allowed Dylan to fuse the energy of rock and roll with the intelligent lyrics of folk music, which is what people are talking about when they say that Bob Dylan invented "folk-rock." But to label *Bringing It All Back Home* "folk-rock" is somewhat inappropriate because the lyrics are much different from standard folk fare, and the music aims less at imitating existing forms of rock and roll (although, to some extent, it does) and more at giving Dylan some room for experimentation. In this sense, Dylan's decision to play acoustic on side two seems not a concession to the folk crowd but a slight unease about whether a rock sound would suit the lyrical complexities of "Mr. Tambourine Man," "Gates of Eden" and "It's Alright, Ma (I'm Only Bleeding)."

The sound of *Bringing It All Back Home* is a prototype for the revolutionary music of *Highway 61 Revisited*, *Blonde on Blonde*, the 1965 and 1966 electric tours, and even the 1965 Newport Folk Festival (the sound of Dylan's set may be distorted, but it is certainly revolutionary, especially considering the locale). The clang of songs such as "Subterranean Homesick Blues," "Maggie's Farm" and "Outlaw Blues" evolves into the rock on *Highway 61 Revisited*. The listener can sense that there is a difference to the music of *Bringing It All Back Home*, that Dylan is creating his own unique style. In a 1977 interview for *Playboy*, Dylan explained that there was something special about this music:

> The closest I ever got to the sound I hear in my mind was on individual bands in the *Blonde on Blonde* album. It's that thin, that wild mercury sound. It's metallic and bright gold, with whatever that conjures up. That's my particular sound . . . It was in the album before that too [*Highway 61 Revisited*]. Also in *Bringing It All Back Home*. That's the sound I've always heard.[24]

The missing link to this sound turns out to be the organ, which is introduced on *Highway 61 Revisited*. The organ serves a dual purpose: it can waft through the song ("Queen Jane Approximately"; "Visions of Johanna") or acquire a force all its own ("Like a Rolling Stone," "Positively 4th Street," "I Want You," Garth Hudson's playing on tour). It should be noted that a defining characteristic of this music is that the instruments are never tangential. Throughout his career, Dylan has frowned upon self-indulgent playing by his band mates.

If the sound on *Bringing It All Back Home* doesn't quite achieve the proportions of *Highway 61 Revisited* and *Blonde on Blonde,* the music is nonetheless engrossing. When the first guitar chords of "Subterranean Homesick Blues" chime in, the sound immediately captures the listener's attention. It doesn't matter that Dylan has lifted the structure from

Chuck Berry's "Too Much Monkey Business"; the point is that Dylan is turning to his rock roots and then building upon his extensive musical knowledge. "On the Road Again" may be sloppy, but the song does have a rhythm and blues mood about it. The scratchy riffing on "Outlaw Blues" recalls early rock and roll. Its affinities with older rock and rhythm and blues notwithstanding, the sound of *Bringing It All Back Home* is largely unique from both its predecessors and its contemporaries.

Much of this uniqueness is a product of Dylan's singing. Due to the sweep of Dylan's vocals, the music becomes more expressive. The band hones in on Dylan's vocal inflections, as in the blitzkrieg pace of "Subterranean Homesick Blues," the raw surge that drives "Outlaw Blues," or the lissomeness of "Love Minus Zero / No Limit" and "She Belongs to Me." The bass lines to "She Belongs to Me" and "Love Minus Zero" complement Dylan's delivery. In "Subterranean Homesick Blues," Dylan delivers the lyrics with impeccable timing, and the band never misses a beat. Not even Chuck Berry could string together as many lines as Dylan does. This same expressiveness is true of the second side. Only two songs – "Mr. Tambourine Man" and "It's All Over Now, Baby Blue"– feature musicians other than Dylan, but Bruce Langhorne's guitar in the former and Bill Lee's bass in the latter are strong components of these songs.

Dylan going electric with the album is only part of *Bringing It All Back Home*'s importance. Finally, the lyrics to a rock song could explore a whole range of subjects. Granted, there were fine rock lyricists before Dylan (like Chuck Berry, Buddy Holly and Jerry Lee Lewis), but none with nearly the same skill with words as Dylan. The first four songs of *Bringing It All Back Home* became landmarks for other songwriters. It is no surprise that both The Beatles and

The Rolling Stones wrote more varied material after the album's release.

"Subterranean Homesick Blues" is a burst of creative spirit. The lines fly by so fast that repeated listenings of the song are necessary to take everything in. The narrative, about a kid looking for drugs while trying to avoid the law, is structured so that Dylan can poke fun at everything from the army to education ("Twenty years of schoolin' / And they put you on the day shift") to the police (". . . the heat put / Plants in the bed but / The phone's tapped anyway / . . . Watch the plain clothes"). Dylan mocks the song's disenchanted youth as much as he does "the system"; the kid's paranoia becomes a target for Dylan's satire and, as such, "Subterranean Homesick Blues" shares an unconscious link with "Stuck Inside of Mobile with the Memphis Blues Again."

"Subterranean Homesick Blues" is an expression of individuality, as is "Maggie's Farm." The closing lines of "Maggie's Farm" sum up Dylan's attitude towards the press and the narrow expectations of his audience:

> Well, I try my best
> To be just like I am,
> But everybody wants you
> To be just like them.
> They say sing while you slave and I just get bored.

"She Belongs to Me" and "Love Minus Zero/No Limit" are similar in nature; both deal with an enigmatic female who is attractive precisely because of her inscrutability. In "She Belongs to Me," Dylan invests the woman with the unreality of an Egyptian goddess who reduces men to their knees. The title is deliberately ironic; this woman doesn't really belong to the narrator, as much as he would like her to. In "Love

Minus Zero," the adoration is tempered by the closing simile of his love tapping at his window (bypassing the chamber door) like a raven, indicative of either a flaw or the need for shelter. The appearance of a raven is not the only nod to Edgar Allan Poe in the song: "The cloak and dagger dangles," "The bridge at midnight trembles," and "The wind howls like a hammer / The night blows rainy" are spooky lines that Poe would have been proud of.

Dylan admires the woman not only for her faithfulness, which is emphasized through her silence, but also because she is above the phony symbols of romantic love:

> People carry roses,
> Make promises by the hours,
> My love she laughs like the flowers,
> Valentines can't buy her.

Verse two punctures the pretensions of pseudo-intellectuals, who "Read books" and "Repeat quotations," while their "conclusions on the wall" are little more than literary graffiti. The paradox "She knows there's no success like failure / And that failure's no success at all" is one of Dylan's most famous statements. The following verse introduces the element of the occult, while prophesying the fate of false idols ("Statues made of matchsticks, / Crumble into one another"). Imagery-wise, "Love Minus Zero" would not be out of place on side two of the album.

Dylan's genius as a songwriter is nowhere more evident than on the second side of *Bringing It All Back Home*. "Mr. Tambourine Man," "It's Alright, Ma (I'm Only Bleeding)," "Gates of Eden" and "It's All Over Now, Baby Blue" are among the top compositions in Dylan's catalogue. The released versions of "Mr. Tambourine Man," "Gates of Eden" and "It's Alright, Ma" were reported by photographer

Daniel Kramer to have been recorded one after the other, without stopping.[25] As with the rumour that "Like a Rolling Stone" was done in one take, this feat has gone down as one of the most fabled moments in Dylan lore.[26] Alas, all myths are eventually debunked, and in his book *Bob Dylan: The Recording Sessions (1960-1994)*, Clinton Heylin writes that Dylan performed the first two songs but had trouble with "Mr. Tambourine Man" and ended up doing six takes of the song (the sixth being the released version).[27]

Whatever the real story is, these three performances are nothing less than remarkable. From the opening guitar chords through to the harmonica fade-out, "Mr. Tambourine Man" could not be done better. Dylan's voice is rich and powerful, and Bruce Langhorne's guitar accompaniment sounds almost like an extension of Dylan's singing.

Too often, "Mr. Tambourine Man" gets tagged with the simplistic label of "drug song." While there is little doubt that Dylan was experimenting with drugs during this period, the song touches on something more universal than drugs. "Mr. Tambourine Man" is the music's source, Dylan's inspiration for the "skippin' reels of rhyme" that are his songs. The Tambourine Man is Dylan's pied piper, and he casts a euphoric spell over the narrator.

In the liner notes to *Biograph*, Dylan cites Fellini's *La Strada* as a probable source for the song, and much of the imagery is Felliniesque, particularly in the final verse, wherein the dark trees contrast with the lighted sky.[28] The fourth verse contains what may be the finest lines Dylan has ever written:

> Then take me disappearin' through the smoke rings of
>   my mind,
> Down the foggy ruins of time, far past the frozen leaves,
> The haunted, frightened trees, out to the windy beach,

Far from the twisted reach of crazy sorrow.

The "foggy ruins of time" seem part of "Gates of Eden," Dylan's vision of paradise, where there are no rulers, sins or trials.

The contrast between the earth and paradise is continually reinforced throughout "Gates of Eden." The opening line ("Of war and peace the truth just twists") recalls "With God on Our Side," calling into question the issue of right and wrong in secular relations. Verse four branches into the mythical, as "Aladdin and his lamp / Sits with Utopian hermit monks"; here, Dylan exposes man's tendency to invent both creatures with magical powers (Aladdin) and places of perfection (Utopia) to reassure himself of salvation.

Other lines range from the personal – "And I try to harmonize with songs / The lonesome sparrow sings" suggests both an association with nature and an invocation to Dylan's muse – to the sweeping ("As friends and other strangers / From their fates try to resign" has Faustian overtones). The key to the song's meaning may lie in the conclusion (notice how Dylan shifts from inside the Gates to outside):

> At times I think there are no words
> But these to tell what's true
> And there are no truths outside the Gates of Eden.

Again, the song contrasts the earth with paradise. As Tim Riley described these lines: "Truth . . . is a gliding 'curfew gull' that twists itself to suit what each individual sees, feels and hears."[29]

"It's Alright, Ma" is even longer than "Gates of Eden," encompassing fifteen verses, each one memorable in some way. Dylan's concern in "It's Alright, Ma" is with detailing the ills of society as he sees them. In verse five, Dylan attacks those who manufacture religious faith, concluding that "It's easy to see without looking too far / That not much / Is really sacred." In the following refrain, "the rules of the road have been lodged" refers to the entrenched tenets of society. This idea reappears in the next chorus; as "the masters make the rules / For the wise men and the fools." Dylan counters by intoning that "I got nothing, Ma, to live up to," a phrase which assumes ironic overtones in the context of the often negative critical reaction to his post-1960s albums.

Elsewhere in the song, Dylan rails against the fraudulence of advertising, propaganda, riches, and those people trapped in society's "vault" who attempt to pull down the ambitious:

> While one who sings with his tongue on fire
> Gargles in the rat race choir
> Bent out of shape from society's pliers
> Cares not to come up any higher
> But rather get you down in the hole
> That he's in.

In another of the song's renowned lines, Dylan urges individuals to get the most out of life, while maintaining that a man has to constantly adapt or else succumb to lifelessness (something Dylan understands better than most musicians): "he not busy being born / Is busy dying." The final lines play on the concept of Orwellian thought crime:

> And if my thought-dreams could be seen
> They'd probably put my head in a guillotine

"It's All Over Now, Baby Blue" may not have the grandeur of the other three songs on side two, but it is an undeniable classic. Historically, the song indicates a break with the past and a move onwards. Dylan may be addressing his folk audience; when he appeared at the 1965 Newport Folk Festival, Dylan closed his set with a solo rendition of this song, after blasting his way through "Maggie's Farm," "Like a Rolling Stone" and "It Takes a Lot to Laugh, It Takes a Train to Cry" with The Paul Butterfield Blues Band, and doing an acoustic "Mr. Tambourine Man." This is the moment when the folk crowd became convinced that Dylan had "sold out."

As Bob Spitz wrote, *"Bringing It All Back Home* had a tremendous influence on the shaping of popular music. It inspired every rock 'n' roller for the next twenty years, from The Beatles to Bruce Springsteen."[30] A Springsteen song such as "Blinded by the Light" (on his Dylanesque first album) is modeled after "Subterranean Homesick Blues," while "Mr. Tambourine Man"'s "diamond sky" may be the source for The Beatles' "Lucy in the Sky with Diamonds." After *Bringing It All Back Home*, the "folk-rock" genre proliferated, as The Byrds continued with the sound and groups such as Buffalo Springfield emerged.

Further, *Bringing It All Back Home* gave a certain credibility to rock and roll that had been lacking in the past. Many writers (Paul Williams and Clinton Heylin) have commented on the album's aphoristic value ("She's an artist, she don't look back," "a poem is a naked person," "the Great books've been written. The Great sayings have all been said," and numerous other examples), and as these lyrics filtered into the mass media, rock gained more recognition as a serious medium and as a form of artistic expression.[31] *Bringing It All Back Home* opened up new routes for songwriters; and it gave Bob Dylan a new sound.

HIGHWAY 61 REVISITED

RELEASED: AUGUST 1965

Only five months after recording *Bringing It All Back Home* in January 1965, Dylan was back in Columbia Studios to make *Highway 61 Revisited*, and he had finished the album by early August. As Dylan's first complete rock record, the sound is crisper than on his previous album. Central to this sound are Al Kooper on organ and Michael Bloomfield on guitar. Bloomfield, a crack guitarist and a member of The Paul Butterfield Blues Band, blazes a path throughout *Highway 61*. His playing on, in particular, "Tombstone Blues" (especially between verses), "From a Buick 6" and "Highway 61 Revisited" is inspired musicianship, and a splendid counterpart to Dylan's lyrical jaunts into the worlds of John the Baptist, junkyard angels, Mack the Finger et al.

Kooper, however, had enjoyed no such renown as an organist. In fact, according to legend, Kooper had never played organ in his life prior to these sessions; he just happened to fill the seat during the making of "Like a Rolling Stone" and improvise his way into music history.[32] Kooper is now best remembered, above all else, for his playing on this song. His swirling organ helps make "Like a Rolling Stone" one of the most memorable singles in rock.

As with, for instance, the beginning of The Rolling Stones' "Satisfaction" or The Who's "Substitute," the opening to "Like a Rolling Stone" is one of those moments in music that draw the listener to the song immediately. Bruce Springsteen later said that, upon first hearing it, the snare-drum sounds "like somebody'd kicked open the door to your mind."[33] Then Kooper's organ notes are heard and, consequently, "Like a Rolling Stone" sounds like a classic even before Dylan starts singing.

Biting into the words (as when he sings "didn't you?"), Dylan's voice builds until there is an incredible release of energy when he asks, "How does it feel [?]" Kooper's organ playing between the lines of the chorus accentuates the words, and the instruments reach an ensemble before Dylan cries "aah."

The tale itself chronicles the decline of a haughty ex-lover, as Dylan charges the little rich girl with complacency. Nevertheless, there is an element of tragedy to the song which moderates the put-down; it is as if Dylan innately sympathizes with what has happened to this woman, fearing the same thing could happen to him.

The opening verse shows how Dylan can take a cliché and reinvent it completely. The story-book phrase "Once upon a time . . . " is a brilliantly ironic beginning; in this context, it parodies the phrase at the same time it gives it an entirely new meaning. (Another great example of this skill of Dylan's occurs in 1974's "Tangled Up in Blue," which begins with "Early one mornin' the sun was shinin'." In *Hard Rain*, Tim Riley criticizes Dylan for using the cliché, but Riley misses the point: when Dylan fleshes out the cliché in the following lines, he makes it seem like one of the most telling phrases of all time).[34]

The finished arrangement of "Like a Rolling Stone" was done in one try, after Dylan had fiddled around with the structure. *The Bootleg Series* contains an interesting minute of Dylan playing the song (in waltz time) at the piano. His voice keeps breaking throughout, and he stops the song short after the first chorus, saying, "My voice is gone, man. You wanna try it again?" There are nine versions of the song available on the Dylan CD-rom (*Bob Dylan: Highway 61 Interactive*), and they show how the song progressed into the album cut, with Kooper making his first appearance on the organ. The session that produced "Like a Rolling Stone" provides an example of how Dylan works in the studio; radically altering songs and bringing out the best in his musicians in the process. In the *Biograph* notes to "Abandoned Love," Eric Clapton is quoted as saying, "When you rehearse with Dylan . . . you listen hard and watch his hands for the changes. It may be your only take."[35]

Highway 61 Revisited is full of references to the corroding effects of fame and this subtopic reveals that Dylan was somewhat leery about his success. "Like a Rolling Stone" rebuts the air of superiority that often accompanies celebrity status. "Just Like Tom Thumb's Blues" looks at the paradox of success:

> Up on Housing Project Hill
> It's either fortune or fame
> You must pick one or the other
> Though neither of them are to be what they claim

"Ballad of a Thin Man" takes a lighter approach to the subject, portraying dealing with reporters as one of the pratfalls of fame. The "thin man" is a bit mentally thin, an older generation writer who is trying to keep up with the Joneses, who tries so hard but just doesn't understand.

Many of the lines, such as the absurd dialogue Mr. Jones gets trapped in in verse seven, read like comical take-offs on Dylan's own interviews at the time, which always seemed to make reporters look foolish. The line "What does this mean?" refers to interviews where reporters persistently asked Dylan what his songs were about. At the end of the song, all the reporter can do is put his glasses away and sniff the ground for clues. The chorus includes the music scene, as people knew Dylan was up to something but couldn't quite pinpoint what.

The song has the same fanciful nature as much of the other material on the album. Beginning with "Farewell Angelina" (a *Bringing It All Back Home* outtake), Dylan started mixing historical and fictional characters into his songs. This approach works quite well, as the situations depicted, albeit ludicrous, build upon and interact with each other to create a likeable mood (as in "Tombstone Blues" and "Highway 61 Revisited").

"Tombstone Blues," with its outrageous cast, invites comparisons to *Highway 61 Revisited*'s zany liner notes ("Lifelessness said when introducing everybody, 'go save the world' & 'involvement! That's the issue' & things like that & Savage Rose winked at Fixable & the Cream went off with his arm in a sling singing 'summertime & the living is easy'"). Additionally, "Tombstone Blues" has obvious connections with Dylan's book *Tarantula*, as the line "'The sun's not yellow it's chicken'" appears in both, and verse five of "Tombstone Blues" would not be out of place in *Tarantula*:

> Well, John the Baptist after torturing a thief
> Looks up at his hero the Commander-in-Chief
> Saying, "Tell me great hero, but please make it brief
> Is there a hole for me to get sick in?"

Dylan balances some of the song's ridiculousness with seriousness, and part of "Tombstone Blues" is a critique of the Vietnam War. Verse seven contains the most overt reference; many writers have seen Lyndon Johnson as "The king of the Philistines" who sends American troops to the jungles of Vietnam.[36] The next verse seems to be a parody of fictional war heroes who hope to win friends in the American government and influence Uncle Sam. The title itself suggests that Dylan remains bothered by the killing in Vietnam – the "tombstone blues."

One doesn't have to read such references into the song to find "Tombstone Blues" enjoyable nonetheless. The band plays with abandon on this track, and Dylan punctuates the close of the song with a shout of "All right!"

"Highway 61 Revisited" offers situations similar to "Tombstone Blues," with a take on the Genesis story of Abraham, a slight at rock promoters who will stop at nothing to make money, and a play on Shakespeare ("Now the fifth daughter on the twelfth night").

"Desolation Row," an eleven-minute epic, offsets the frenzied lyricism of such songs as "Tombstone Blues," "From a Buick 6" and "Highway 61 Revisited" with grimness. Unlike "Highway 61 Revisited" or "Tombstone Blues," there is nothing humorous about the assorted characters of "Desolation Row." Ophelia; Einstein; Dr. Filth; Casanova: all become prisoners of this mad setting. Dylan's singing is so precise that each scene he presents in the song seems shockingly real.

But the first verse throws listeners for a loop: amidst this insanity, Dylan presents a picture of domestic bliss – "As lady and I look out tonight." Other surprises include mixing characters from Shakespeare, as Ophelia stands beneath Juliet's balcony, while Romeo winds up in the wrong place; the appearance of "Ezra Pound and T.S. Eliot /Fighting in the captain's tower," using imagism in this verse and throughout the song, showing the influence of both writers on Dylan; and a conclusion which offers a temporary respite from this horror, only to reveal that things are little better outside "Desolation Row."

The song is also concerned with evil. Dr. Filth is a sketchy character, but his name, and "his world / Inside of a leather cup" is enough to suggest his absolute diabolicalness. Verse eight, as Michael Gray observed, has an aura of the Kafkaesque to it (and a debt to Orwell):

At midnight all the agents
And the superhuman crew
Come out and round up everyone
That knows more than they do . . .
And then the kerosene
Is brought down from the castles.[37]

As with *Blonde on Blonde*'s "Sad-Eyed Lady of the Low-lands," "Desolation Row" provides a powerful conclusion to the album. But it does not overshadow what has gone before. The songs on *Highway 61 Revisited* achieve a totality, in the same way that *Bringing It All Back Home* and *Blonde on Blonde* do. The picturesque, endearing "It Takes a Lot to Laugh, It Takes a Train to Cry" is perfectly placed between the recklessness of "Tombstone Blues" and "From a Buick 6." "Queen Jane Approximately" is side two's equivalent of "Ballad of a Thin Man"'s confusion, recast in terms of romantic puzzlement. "Just Like Tom Thumb's Blues" posits a setting that becomes a lead-in to the atmosphere of "Desolation Row." From "Like a Rolling Stone" to "Desolation Row," Dylan is taking rock and roll in a new direction.

BLONDE ON BLONDE

RELEASED: JUNE 1966

Blonde on Blonde is Bob Dylan's magnum opus, a double album of fourteen songs recorded with an ace group of players. The music is the self-acknowledged apex (alongside *Bringing It All Back Home* and *Highway 61 Revisited*) of the "thin . . . wild mercury sound." The musicians for the Nashville sessions included Charlie McCoy, Kenny Buttrey, Joe South, Al Kooper and Jamie (Robbie) Robertson, and the hypnotic music that they make is astonishing both for its seamlessness and for the added momentum it gives to Dylan's lyrics.

It is hard to imagine *Blonde on Blonde* opening with anything other than "Rainy Day Women #12 & 35." The wheezy, circus-like atmosphere of the song testifies to the fusion between Dylan and his musicians. Lacing the chorus with an obvious drug reference, Dylan feeds off the rowdiness of his players, whose whoops, hollers and maniacal laughs fly in the face of schoolmarmish conventions about popular song.

References to drugs crop up throughout *Blonde on Blond*, although they are not nearly as devastating as the ravaged crux of "Just Like Tom Thumb's Blues." In "Stuck Inside of Mobile with the Memphis Blues Again," "the rain-man" gives the befuddled hero a toxic dose of alcohol. In "Pledging My Time," the narrator may be pledging his time to drugs, given that he can "feel all right" despite "a poison headache." The opening verse of "Visions of Johanna" contains a line about heroin ("And Louise holds a handful of rain"). And in "Just Like a Woman," the narrator mentions his ex-lover's use of amphetamine.

Tim Riley sights such lyrics as creating "new ground rules . . . that allow drug talk to surface as the counterculture's argot, a new mass idiom."[38] At times, Dylan plays with this taboo with such nonchalance ("Rainy Day Women") that even those who purport to be outraged have to admire his self-assurance. When Dylan takes the other extreme and explores the depravity of narcotism, he can make anyone quiver (as in the shocking way he strangles the words "shot" and "got" on the B-side live version of "Just Like Tom Thumb's Blues"). Other musicians soon followed suit; The Beatles were one of the first with *Sgt. Pepper's Lonely Hearts Club Band*'s "Lucy in the Sky with Diamonds," but their approach seems more labored. The Rolling Stones' 1971 album *Sticky Fingers* addresses the subject ("Sister Morphine"; "Dead Flowers"); what the Stones' take lacks in subtlety, it makes up for in edgy desperation. Never one to exhaust a topic, Dylan shuns drug talk in his post-*Blonde on Blonde* works, save for the booze-laden revelry of *The Basement Tapes*.

The double-edged nature of *Blonde on Blonde*'s drug songs reinforces the multi-dimensions of the album. Paul Williams reads "Rainy Day Women" as a message about enduring persecution, as one need not "feel so all alone."[39] "They'll stone you when you're playing your guitar" is a confident snicker about the audience's reaction to Dylan's post-Newport concerts with Levon and The Hawks in 1965. "Pledging My Time" is a derelict's plea for affection; the narrator's self-deprecating wit makes him a strangely like-able figure: "Won't you come with me, baby? / I'll take you where you wanna go. / And if it don't work out / You'll be the first to know." "Stuck Inside of Mobile" functions on the level of burlesque, and the joyful imagination that fuels the narrative makes a futile situation almost appealing.

"Stuck Inside of Mobile" is just one of many examples on *Blonde on Blonde* of Dylan's razor-sharp wit. "Fourth Time Around"'s deft comic touches (such as the chivalric fashion in which the narrator "gallantly" hands the girl his "very last piece of gum") parody both The Beatles' "Norweigan Wood" and traditional love songs, and the straight-faced opening verse cleverly hides the infantile merriment (temper tantrums and all) that follows. Compared to the faux Dylan-isms of John Lennon's "I Am the Walrus," or the petty barbs directed at Dylan on *The John Lennon Anthology*, "Fourth Time Around" proves that Dylan parodied The Beatles better than The Beatles parodied him.

In "Leopard-Skin Pill-Box Hat," Dylan builds each verse around a simple gag (the hat as an object of infatuation), giving the song charm. When Dylan performed it on his 1966 tour, it acquired a savage intensity that goaded the audience.

Dylan's jocularity added to his popularity in the 1960s. Most of his albums from the decade have their sustained moments of wit, and his interviews in the mid-1960s are tremendously amusing (and anything but set pieces). Dylan had a knack for exposing the foibles of others while letting his audience laugh along with him. *Don't Look Back*, and even the occasional moment in *Eat the Document*, shows Dylan having his way with his interlocutors, gleefully destroying any airs they might have. Together with *Highway 61 Revisited*, *Blonde on Blonde* is an extension of *Don't Look Back*'s comedic sensibilities.

As was the case with its electric predecessors (and even *The Freewheelin' Bob Dylan* and *Another Side*), *Blonde on Blonde*'s lighter songs are only part of the mix. *Blonde on Blonde* contains two of Dylan's finest love songs: "Just Like a Woman" and "Sad-Eyed Lady of the Lowlands." "Just Like a Woman" has been the focus of much ranting down through the years, mainly from those who see the song's title as a pillar of sexism. One writer went so far to accuse Dylan of practicing "hate-mongering."[40] The tenderness of the performance alone disproves any such reading of the song; Dylan sounds disconsolate over the end of the relationship, as when he sings "this pain in here," and when his voice breaks on the first "yes" in verse two. Dylan is not being sexist in the song – if he were, his singing would be angry and perhaps even patronizing towards the woman – instead, he is pointing out to his ex-lover that, even though she will not admit it, she, too, has been hurt by the separation ("you break just like a little girl"). The narrator even concedes in verse three that the woman had the upper hand in their relationship ("I was hungry and it was your world"), hardly something he would admit if his tone were sardonic. "Just Like a Woman" quickly became a staple of Dylan's live shows, and on *The Concert for Bangladesh* recording, Dylan tweaks the song's critics by singing "And she bakes just like a woman" in one chorus.

"Sad-Eyed Lady of the Lowlands" is a triumph of surrealism. Over eleven minutes long, it is one of the most famous of all album closers. Recorded at four in the morning and in one take, the song has a late-night, drugged-up, apocalyptic feel to it which makes it a kind of grand summation of the entire album.

Patrick Humphries, in his highly entertaining book *Absolutely Dylan* (which appeared in England under the wonderful title *Oh No! Not Another Bob Dylan Book!*), suggests Lord Palmerston's comments on the Schleswig-Holstein affair could apply to Bob Dylan talking about "Sad-Eyed Lady": "Only three people ever fully understood it-one is dead, one is mad . . . and I can't remember!"[41]

Like the *Shot of Love* outtake "Angelina," "Sad-Eyed Lady" functions within its own dreamscape. The imagery is breathtaking, be it the religious similes in the first verse ("your prayers like rhymes, /And your silver cross"), Dylan's description of the woman's features ("your eyes like smoke"; "And your flesh like silk, and your face like glass"; "the sunlight dims / Into your eyes where the moonlight swims"), or the bizarre language of verse three ("With your childhood flames on your midnight rug, / And your Spanish manners and your mother's drugs"). For all of the mythicizing in the lyrics, however, the song never seems sentimental, and "Sad-Eyed Lady"'s emotive qualities make it, in many ways, the quintessential Bob Dylan love song.

"Visions of Johanna" has the same mystical nature as "Sad-Eyed Lady." For *Biograph*, Cameron Crowe asked Dylan if he was with every word when he performed the song at his 1966 shows. Dylan replied:

> Oh yeah, I was probably with every word . . . because it meant so much to me. I could remember a song without writing it down because it was so visual. I still sing that song every once in a while. It still stands up now as it did then, maybe even more in some kind of weird way.[42]

This visualness is evident throughout the song, primarily in the graphic descriptions of the dingy apartment in the opening verse, and in the line "The ghost of 'lectricity howls in the bones of her face."

Dylan's main concern is with conveying the narrator's desperation, brought about by Johanna's absence. Acting as a foil to Johanna is Louise, who "seems like the mirror" (a line one writer misquoted as "seems like veneer"), which suggests her shallowness. Louise's presence starts to annoy the narrator, for he complains that "she just makes it all too concise and too clear / That Johanna's not here." By verse three, the narrator is so agitated that the mention of Johanna's name by the "little boy" provokes his anger. The "farewell kiss" that Dylan writes of is a metaphor that recurs throughout his songs (as in *Blood on the Tracks*) as a token of blissfulness and yearning. The narrator continues to be tormented by Johanna (his Madonna) until his despair consumes him, and he shuts out the physical world, save for the sounds of the rain and harmonicas playing.

"Visions of Johanna" and "Sad-Eyed Lady" are two of the supreme achievements in Dylan's songwriting career. But even songs on *Blonde on Blonde* that have received less attention throughout the years reveal a vitality that contributes to the album's stature. "Temporary Like Achilles" works a rejected lover's comeback into an offhand fusillade of snide remarks: "But is your heart made out of stone, or is it lime / Or is it just solid rock?" "Obviously Five Believers" pokes fun at reporters looking for Dylan to divulge the mysteries of his songs: "I got my black dog barkin' / . . . Yes, I could tell you what he means / If I just didn't have to try so hard." "Absolutely Sweet Marie" offers a handful of sound advice ("to live outside the law, you must be honest"; "a man can't give his address out to bad company"), and, in light of Dylan's July 1966 motorcycle accident, a strange prophecy:

> Well, I don't know how it happened
> But the river-boat captain; he knows my fate
> But ev'rybody else, even yourself
> They're just gonna have to wait.

Lyrics such as these might not be nearly as memorable if Dylan's singing didn't have such potent emotional accuracy. The ironic context "Absolutely Sweet Marie" comes to function in owes much to Dylan's sly vocal mannerisms and the mischeviousness with which he sings about his fate. As the tone of the album shifts from song to song, so too does Dylan's voice, balancing the cheeriness of "Fourth Time Around" with the seriousness of "Sad-Eyed Lady"; building to a comic pitch with "Rainy Day Women" and then following with the quirkiness of "Pledging My Time." The distinct delivery of the words to "Sad-Eyed Lady" and "Visions of Johanna" heightens the poetic nature of the lyrics.

Dylan's musicians read his shifts in feeling with astonishing ease. They always seem to know where Dylan is taking the song. Buttrey's omnipresent drumming and Kooper's organ work in "Visions of Johanna" create an atmosphere that the lyrics seem attuned to. As the song builds to its conclusion (beginning with "And Madonna . . ."), the band generates a tense excitement. In "Sad-Eyed Lady," the musicians lull the listener, and the slow tempo is part of the song's ethereal nature. "I Want You" is perhaps the performance which best exemplifies how well this group of players jelled. The whistling harmonica introduction, the doo-wop organ, Buttrey's drumming, Dylan's playful singing – all combine to make "I Want You" a marvelously catchy song. The instruments seem to wrap themselves around Dylan's words, so when Dylan slips up in verse four, the band carries him along, and the mistake almost sounds as if it were intended to be part of the song. On the album, Dylan's harmonica weaves throughout the music; as with his two previous electric records, he is helping to transform the harmonica into a rock instrument, taking it beyond its use in folk and blues.

Like *Highway 61 Revisited*, *Blonde on Blonde* sets a standard for musical competence. As Tim Riley wrote, *Blonde on Blonde* "confirms Dylan's stature as the greatest American rock presence since Elvis Presley."[43] The tight sound, range of the material and Dylan's singing on the record place it in the upper echelon of rock albums. Among rock's double albums, only The Rolling Stones' *Exile on Main Street* is its equal. And although Bob Dylan has gone on to make more masterful records, he has never again made an album that sounds quite like *Blonde on Blonde*.

THE BOOTLEG SERIES, VOLUME 4:
LIVE 1966,
THE "ROYAL ALBERT HALL" CONCERT

RECORDED: MAY 17, 1966 – RELEASED: OCTOBER 1998

If Dylan fans and critics were queried about the one Dylan concert they wished they could have attended, the overwhelming response would surely be Manchester, the Free Trade Hall, May 17, 1966. It was this show that featured a precise, majestic acoustic performance, followed by a passionate, tense electric set, in which the battle lines were drawn between the folk faithful and their former idol. The music Dylan and The Hawks (later The Band) created was raw, untamed and unforgettable.

For years, Dylan followers clamored for the release of this so-called "Royal Albert Hall" concert. In mid-1996, Columbia scheduled the album's release to commemorate the thirtieth anniversary of the tour. Predictably, Columbia canceled the set's release at the last minute, leaving fans to make do with bootlegs that could capture the intensity of the performances but could not overcome the technical limitations of pirated material. Finally, October 1998 saw the entire Manchester set released as *The Bootleg Series, Volume 4: Bob Dylan Live 1966, The "Royal Albert Hall" Concert*, a double-CD with liner notes by Tony Glover and recording information. The program sounds even more remarkable than it had on the bootlegs. The tape hiss is gone and the sound has been sharpened, while retaining the intimacy of the performance.

Each show on the 1965 and 1966 tours was in two parts: Dylan alone with just his guitar and harmonica, then with his band for the second half. Dylan was reportedly stoned during many of the acoustic sets on his Australian and European legs of the 1966 tour, but that's not the case here.[44] He seems focused on the material and committed to every word that he sings. The opener, "She Belongs to Me," has a varied tempo from the official release, and the words at the end of each line seem to hang in space ("Salute her when her birthday caalmsss"). "Fourth Time Around," a somewhat minor song on *Blonde on Blonde*, is every bit as strong as the other songs here, as Dylan enunciates every syllable. "Visions of Johanna" is very similar to the *Biograph* version from London's Royal Albert Hall (May 26), except it is sung with a slight drag on the words. "It's All Over Now, Baby Blue" had already appeared on *Biograph*. "Desolation Row" is simply spellbinding, with the last verse acquiring an eerie intensity. A sad "Just Like a Woman" follows, complete with magical guitar strum in the intro, and a lilt on Dylan's voice in the chorus. This is perhaps the surpassing acoustic performance of the European shows, five and a half minutes of pure bliss. The set closes with a similarly edifying "Mr. Tambourine Man."

The sound on the recording gives Dylan's voice an aura that enhances every line that he sings. More spectacular is the harmonica playing, truly the work of a virtuoso. During one stretch in "Mr. Tambourine Man," Dylan plays for well over a minute, until it sounds as if different instruments are involved. The harp weaves throughout the final solo of "Just Like a Woman." The introductory playing to "Fourth Time Around" gives the song a sadness that makes the lyrics seem less chastising. Dylan's harmonica work seems to foreshadow the electric second half; it's as if the manic energy brewing inside him is filtering through his harmonica solos before bursting out after the intermission. The audience is polite and attentive throughout act one, in part because some of the songs ("Fourth Time Around," "Visions of

Johanna" and "Just Like a Woman") were new to them. Indeed, his acoustic set makes few concessions to the folk crowd – all the songs come from his three recent "electric" albums.

For the electric sets, Dylan appeared with four-fifths of The Hawks (Robbie Robertson on guitar, Rick Danko on bass, Garth Hudson on organ, and Richard Manuel on piano) and, after a round of musical drummers following Levon Helm's departure, Mickey Jones. The Manchester amplified half begins with the sound welling up; even on record, the crowd's discomfort is palpable. Then comes the sonic blast of "Tell Me, Momma," Jones' drum rolls hurtling the song along with force. In "I Don't Believe You," superior to the Dublin version on *Biograph*, Dylan's harmonica meshes perfectly with the instruments. "Baby, Let Me Follow You Down" is recast as a rocker, Hudson's organ fast and frantic between verses. On "One Too Many Mornings," Rick Danko moved to the mike on the word "behind" in every chorus, adding a pained yet lovely inflection. Dylan's piano work in "Ballad of a Thin Man" alternates with Garth Hudson's squiggly organ figures. The Hawks seem to be experimenting with new sounds, with the fullest confidence in the end result. Dylan and his musicians are so attuned to each other that this music never veers off the road. Greil Marcus called it "the hardest rock 'n' roll anyone had heard, lifted by a lyricism that could turn contemplative in the middle of a storm – surrealistic dandy's blues subsuming moments of forgiving gentleness and unforgiving confrontation."[45]

All the while, Dylan's voice is the navigator. Awesome in its boldness and its splendor, Dylan's singing makes every word stand out as he takes his voice and his musicians to new heights. One can only marvel at what Dylan does with certain phrases: "Tell me, momma . . . / What's wrong with you this tiiimee?"; "You're right from your side / And I'm right from mine" in an anguished shout; "Something is happening / And you don't know what it is / Do you, Mister Jones?" with unrelenting fury.

The Manchester performance of "Just Like Tom Thumb's Blues" is outdistanced by the May 14 Liverpool version, released as a B-side to the "I Want You" single and now available only on the import set *Masterpieces*. The Band said it was the top performance of the entire tour,[46] and it may be just that. Robertson's guitar work is mind-bending, Hudson's organ playing is by turns both blissful and frightening, and Dylan's vocal channels exhaustion into emotion. Dave Marsh wrote that one could "make the case for rock and roll as a species of art using this record and nothing else."

Throughout the 1965-66 tours, Dylan had to contend with some audience members horrified by what they considered Dylan's apostasy, and ready to start a fight about it. A minority in the folk music crowd were vociferous in insisting that Dylan was a traitor for going electric. This dissension probably originated with reaction to *Another Side of Bob Dylan*. Irwin Silber, editor of the folk magazine *Sing Out!*, complained in his infamous, weepy "open letter" to Dylan that the "new songs seem to be all inner-directed now, inner-probing, self-conscious – maybe even a little maudlin or a little cruel on occasion."[47] The electric backing on *Bringing It All Back Home* only added to the controversy. And then, of course, came the Newport Folk Festival in July 1965. So much has been written about this event that the story need not be recounted here. Suffice to say that it is ironic that the Newport Folk Festival is remembered most not for any folk music it produced, but for the rock and roll that Dylan and his cohorts alchemized on stage that night. By the time the North American tour was in full swing in

October 1965, the folk crowd was up in arms. Everywhere Dylan and The Hawks went, people booed. "You get in this private plane, they fly you to a town, we got to this place, we play our music and people boo us," Robertson recalled. "Then we get back on the plane, we go to another town, we play our music and they boo us."[48] Levon Helm, disenchanted with the reaction, left at the end of November.[49] Forgetting the fact that Dylan's latest album, *Highway 61 Revisited*, had been entirely electric, audiences appeared shocked that Dylan would play with a band.

Manchester is the climax of this animosity. Dylan's opening volley is the introduction to "I Don't Believe You": "It used to be like that and now it goes like this." He ignores the slow hand-clapping before "Baby, Let Me Follow You Down," but by "Leopard-Skin Pill-Box Hat," Dylan is not about to back down from the audience's challenges, and he mumbles the song's title before the band attacks the song. Dylan meets the catcalls prior to "One Too Many Mornings" with purposeful babble, and then says, with mock hurt, ". . . if you only just wouldn't clap so hard." After "One Too Many Mornings," Dylan does "Ballad of a Thin Man," and a hush falls over the crowd as the song ends. What sounds like an expletive comes from an audience member, followed by laughter. Then, as Dylan strums his guitar, somebody shouts, "Judas!" (an unspeakably racist comment, as C. P. Lee has observed).[50] Dylan pauses and replies, his voice dripping with disgust, "I don't believe you." As Danko's loping bass comes in, Dylan sneers with ferocity, "You're a liar!," then turns and tells the band to "Play it f—— loud!" as the piano and organ chords strike up "Like a Rolling Stone." There is something about this dialogue that is absolutely amazing; hear it once or hear it a hundred times, it always, literally, sends shivers up the spine. And it makes all future audience-musician exchanges seem like superfluous prattle.

Eat the Document, a one hour film recorded during the 1966 tour, visually shows the hostility that was present at many of the concerts. As they file out of the Free Trade Hall, some people make comments to the camera.[51] "It was a bloody disgrace," snarls an angry, bespectacled young man. "He wants shooting, he's a traitor." "I wish he'd left that group in America," says another. Someone else adds, "He may think it's gimmicky but I think it was rubbish." One girl looks as if she is about to cry. Many of these remarks are interspersed with live performances, the point being that the anger present in the minority of the audience drove Dylan to take his music to a higher level. Dylan's singing on "Like a Rolling Stone" after the "Judas" incident could not be more intense. When the song ends, the crowd applauds, and Dylan groggily replies, "thank you," drained but victorious. A second of "God Bless America," perhaps a final poke at the European audience, ends the concert.

History has proven Dylan, not the hecklers, right. "He never caved in . . . and that was truly amazing," said Robertson.[52] Dylan knew that this was some of the finest live music being made, and that the folk crowd was refusing to acknowledge that an artist should be free to evolve musically and lyrically. Few musicians would get booed at every turn and still persevere with their artistic vision, making Dylan's accomplishment all the more impressive.

Live 1966 is not just a historical document. Decades later, the music still sounds tougher than any live show today. And even the best live rock albums (The Rolling Stones' devastating *Get Yer Ya-Yas Out*, The Who *Live at Leeds*, and a handful of others) can't quite measure up to the sustained intensity of *Live 1966*. After all, this is the maddest, most majestic music Bob Dylan – or anyone else – ever made.

CONCLUSION

1965 and 1966 are the years in which Bob Dylan became a legendary figure. By the time of his motorcycle accident in late July 1966, he had helped to revolutionize popular music and, as Joe Queenan later wrote, "had become arguably the most important figure in rock history – more important than Elvis because he wrote his own songs, full of musical imagination; more important than The Beatles because of his sway over John Lennon, his lyrics . . . and his bluesiness; more important than The Rolling Stones because, well, he was more important than The Rolling Stones."[53]

Dylan's influence on The Beatles is evident on many of their albums, but particularly on *Rubber Soul*, *Revolver*, and *Sgt. Pepper's Lonely Hearts Club Band*. The Beatles had perfected their amazing harmonies before these albums, but their lyrics for the most part remained of the "I love you, you love me" variety. By the time of *Rubber Soul*, their songs began to show more emotional complexity. With *Revolver*, *Sgt. Pepper* and the singles "Strawberry Fields Forever" and "Penny Lane," The Beatles' lyrics became multi-dimensional. "A Day in the Life" is perhaps their finest achievement, on par with any Dylan narrative.

The Rolling Stones produced their strongest work in the years after Dylan's "electric period," beginning with *Beggars Banquet* and peaking with their two greatest records, *Sticky Fingers* and *Exile on Main Street*. Their debt to Dylan appears in the lyrics to songs such as, among others, "Sympathy for the Devil," "Street Fighting Man," "You Got the Silver" (on which Keith Richards emotes like Dylan), "Live With Me" (modeled after "On the Road Again"), "Dead Flowers" and "Shine a Light," and the musicianship of *Highway 61*

Revisited and *Blonde on Blonde* is a probable influence on *Exile*'s remarkable sound.

Dylan made rock more forceful, more risqué. Certainly nobody had accomplished what Dylan did on tour in 1965-66, and with his albums of the time. Dylan made his voice the lead instrument, to the point where he became the metaphorical source for the music around him. "Before the electric tours of 1965 and 1966, 'rock' as such did not exist," wrote The Band's biographer Barney Hoskyns. "There was pop, there was rock 'n' roll, and there was R & B, but no one had ever fused all of these together with an avant-garde, anti-mainstream sensibility."[54] Although Hoskyns is talking about the connection between Dylan and The Hawks, and although this fusion had already occurred with *Highway 61 Revisited* (*Bringing It All Back Home* planted the seeds for this movement) Hoskyns' statement about creating a new kind of music is still applicable. Working with The Hawks on stage allowed Dylan to take this new music one step further, because playing it live before hostile audiences was tougher than playing it in the studio. With *Bringing It All Back Home*, Dylan began creating this music, and *Highway 61 Revisited*, *Blonde on Blonde*, and his tours brought together the elements of piano/organ, powerful drumming, intricate guitar work and an unprecedented new singing style to arrive at this sound.

Dylan had the attitude required to pull all this off, an unflagging sense of cool that allowed him to squash his detractors and look none the worse for doing so. One officially released document that captures Dylan on film at this time is *Don't Look Back*, made during Dylan's 1965 solo tour of England (recorded after the making of *Bringing It All Back Home* but before Dylan's appearance at Newport). D.A. Pennebaker's camera tracks Dylan into hotel rooms, on stage, and giving interviews. Every interviewer self-destructs when facing off with Dylan. "I don't believe in anything," he tells reporters at a press conference. "Are you cynical?" one replies. Later, he makes a student reporter and then a journalist for *Time* look absolutely foolish. Dylan shatters the veneer of superiority that the *Time* correspondent carries into the interview.

Don't Look Back's best trait may be that it doesn't try to make Dylan look like a saviour (unlike *Renaldo and Clara*, which pushes this conceit to the verge of megalomania). When a gaggle of girls stands outside his hotel room screaming, Dylan invites them up and then asks the teeny-boppers what they think of his music. "I don't like 'Subterranean Homesick Blues'" is one's petulant reply. "I have to give some work to my friends," Dylan says back to her. The scene mocks the adulation with which teens greeted rock stars (like The Beatles), and shows that such servility rarely translated into an understanding of the artist's work. (For a more recent example, consider how younger fans turned Bruce Springsteen's ironic comment on the American scene, "Born in the U.S.A.," into a jingoistic anthem).

The music in *Don't Look Back* is also noteworthy. In a hotel room, Dylan sings "Lost Highway" ("No, no, no! There's another verse," Bobby Neuwirth prods when Dylan thinks the song is finished). In a later scene, Dylan starts playing the piano and adds a layer of beautiful vocal harmony, a moment that has something of the spontaneity that occurs at the time *The Basement Tapes* were recorded. For the onstage footage, there are bits of "The Times They Are A-Changin'," "To Ramona," "Hattie Carroll," "Don't Think Twice," "Talkin' World War III Blues," "It's Alright, Ma," "Gates of Eden" and "Love Minus Zero."

The unreleased *Eat the Document* offers a glimpse of the workings of the 1966 tour. In one scene, an extremely tired Dylan sits in the back of a vehicle rubbing his eyes ("Do you suffer from sore eyes, groovy forehead or curly hair?," an acquaintance asks). Dylan's fast lifestyle during 1965-66 has been well detailed, but it is wrong to attribute Dylan's creative output at this time to the influence of drugs. Songwriting talent is inherent, and although his live performances may have been aided by drugs, the energy that is present in the shows is the product of determination.

Produced for ABC-TV but then canceled by the network, *Eat the Document* finally aired in 1971 in Manhattan for one evening and at the Whitney Museum of American Art in late 1972 for a two week run.[55] In 1998, it was revived and shown in New York City and Los Angeles. Like *Renaldo and Clara*, the film is all over the place, but the scenes in *Eat the Document* are more spontaneous than the stage-managing in the later film. There are a couple humorous scenes from press conferences, a singalong with Johnny Cash, and teasingly brief parts of most of the songs Dylan was performing on stage at the time. If hardly a great film, *Eat the Document* is still an interesting one, and worth searching out.

This manic period of Dylan's life ended rather abruptly. On July 29, 1966, in Woodstock, Dylan fell off his motorcycle. During his recovery period, as he would throughout his career, Dylan staked a new musical path.

PART IV

FROM BIG PINK TO NASHVILLE

BOB DYLAN'S GREATEST HITS

RELEASED: MARCH 1967

Fearing it would be some time before Dylan released another album, Columbia hastily assembled a "greatest hits" package and issued it in March 1967. Since most of the songs from Dylan's pre-accident period could have been included in this collection, this is simply the Dylan songs that were popularized as singles, either by Dylan himself or by another artist.

As such, *Greatest Hits* is only interesting because of the halo effect the cover photo achieves, and because it marks the first appearance of "Positively 4th Street" on an album. Addressed to a girl, Dylan's disgruntled folkie "fans," or the Greenwich Village crowd (Fourth street being located in the Village), "Positively 4th Street" is an eloquently nasty piece of writing. Dylan's self-assured singing and the taunting organ lend a force to "Positively 4th Street" which puts the song in a class all its own. Devoid of a chorus, each verse gains momentum, culminating in the most delicious put-down in the history of rock and roll:

Yes, I wish that for just one time
You could stand inside my shoes
You'd know what a drag it is
To see you

THE BASEMENT TAPES

RECORDED: 1967 – RELEASED: JUNE 1975

While the music world was breathlessly awaiting Bob Dylan's first appearance after his motorcycle accident, the man himself was quietly holed up in Woodstock, making music with The Band for most of 1967. At Dylan's home and in the basement of Big Pink (The Band's rented house), Dylan and The Band recorded an astonishing amount of material. In addition to the approximately forty original songs by Dylan, they covered folk, rhythm and blues, gospel, rockabilly and country tunes. Rick Danko once placed the number of songs recorded in the basement at a staggering 150, of which around 100 are available as official releases or in bootleg form.[56]

There's some confusion surrounding when exactly these sessions took place. Clinton Heylin has the time frame of June to November.[57] Levon Helm, in his autobiography, quotes Danko: "For ten months, from March to December 1967, we all met down in the basement and played for two or three hours a day, six days a week."[58] Helm, who rejoined The Band in late 1967, reports that Dylan actually recorded a bit more with The Band after the opening sessions for *John Wesley Harding*:

> Bob had left town in October to record his next album in Nashville. When he came back after Thanksgiving, we cut

"Nothing Was Delivered" and "Long Distance Operator," which Richard [Manuel] sang. I sang "Don't Ya Tell Henry," and we all worked on an unfinished song by Richard and Robbie [Robertson] called "Ruben Remus."[59]

Perhaps Greil Marcus offered the most sensible answer: "There is no common memory, let alone documentation, to provide the exact dates when Bob Dylan and the former Hawks began meeting to try their hand at old songs, or when old songs gave way to a long burst of mockery and novelty."[60]

Rejecting the psychedelic, often overblown music favored by their contemporaries, Dylan and The Band returned to earthy, traditional music, creating a sound which captured a range of musical styles, yet was at the same time unique. As Marcus writes in his liner essay: "[The music] sounds . . . like a testing and a discovery of memory and roots. *The Basement Tapes* . . . seem to leap out of a kaleidoscope of American music no less immediate for its venerability."[61] The songs Dylan wrote and recorded were used as demos for other artists (to name a few, Manfred Mann did "Quinn the Eskimo," "This Wheel's on Fire" was covered by Julie Driscoll, and The Band themselves used "Tears of Rage," "This Wheel's on Fire" and "I Shall Be Released" on their debut album *Music From Big Pink*), while the covers were done for pleasure, with no worries about fulfilling contractual obligations. Consequently, many of the songs have a loose, happy feel to them. The Band's harmonies are proof of the "spirit" (as Marcus calls it) that pervades these songs. On "Million Dollar Bash," the irresistible chanting in the chorus ("Ooh, baby; ooh-ee") steals the show from the amusing lyrics. "Goin' to Acapulco" gains its beauty as much from Dylan's singing as from The Band's accompaniment on the chorus, culminating in the "Yeah" which duets with Robertson's guitar. "Lo and Behold!," "Please, Mrs. Henry," "Yea! Heavy and a Bottle of Bread," "Nothing Was Delivered" and "Too Much of Nothing" benefit greatly from The Band's vocal assistance.

Another indication of the *joie de vivre* of these sessions is the bawdiness of many of the songs. In "Please, Mrs. Henry," an inebriated sop staggers around a party boasting about his drinking escapades and pleading with "Missus Henry" for sexual favors. Hudson's organ contributes a neat whistling sound after the chorus, and Dylan sounds like an affable drunk on some lines. "Yea! Heavy and a Bottle of Bread" is likewise a good party tune, punctuated by a very deep voice holding the word "bread" in the final line.

Dylan scatters sexual innuendo throughout the songs. Most listeners will have trouble deciphering what exactly Dylan is singing in the chorus of "Goin' to Acapulco" (it's either "some girl," "soccer" or "soft gut"), but few can miss hearing the male-oriented lines "And I'm just the same as anyone else / When it comes to scratching for my meat," no matter what *Lyrics* says he's singing.[62] Some of the lines in "Million Dollar Bash" are suggestive in nature ("Well, I'm hittin' it too hard / My stones won't take"), "Tiny Montgomery" features a "Three-legged man / And a hot-lipped hoe," and the unreleased "Get Your Rocks Off!" is a burlesque homosexuality tale. And then there is the scandalous, semi-original, and, unfortunately, still unreleased "All-American Boy," about a guitar hero who seduces groupies and contracts venereal disease.

But the humor in this material doesn't just come by way of lewd references. "Clothes Line Saga" is given a straight-faced reading, yet the song is loaded with delights: using "wild shirts" as a contrast to the laziness of the scene; Hudson's yawning organ; the absurdity of the situation when the neighbor blows his nose; the "whoo-hoo!" Dylan lets loose before the end of the song. "Lo and Behold!" is similarly engaging; no longer buying his lover trumpets or drums, Dylan's latest purchase is "A herd of moose / [Which] one day she could call her own." In "Yea! Heavy and a Bottle of Bread," Dylan bemoans "The poor little chauffeur . . . with a nose full of pus." "Tiny Montgomery" contains an odd assortment of animals ("One bird book / And a buzzard and a crow"; "Do that bird / Suck that pig . . . Go on out / And gas that dog" and "Don't Ya Tell Henry" recalls the story of Chicken Little.

When Marcus calls *The Basement Tapes* sessions "less a style than a spirit – a spirit that had to do with a delight in friendship and invention,"[63] he must have "Apple Suckling Tree" in mind. In the two verses, Dylan is just singing nonsense – "dummy lyrics," as they're called.[64] But the words are not important; what's important is the sound Dylan and these musicians create. Dylan' s mellifluous voice fills in where the words are slurred, and Dylan's jaunty piano and Hudson's organ provide added flavor to "Apple Suckling Tree." The sound of the chorus is that of a group of friends making feel-good music.

There is, however, serious material amongst this hilarity. A forerunner of "As I Went Out One Morning," "Tears of Rage" laments the corruption of the Founding Fathers' ideals of liberty and democracy in America. The second verse condemns those who would take advantage of such ideals for the purposes of self-aggrandizement:

> It was all pointed out the way to go
> And scratched your name in sand,
> Though you just thought that it was nothing more
> Then a place for you to stand.

Verse three sees greed as the root of the problem: "And now the heart is filled with gold /As if it was a purse." Dylan's anguished vocal makes the climax ("But, oh, what kind of love is this / Which goes from bad to worse?") even more powerful.

"This Wheel's on Fire" borrows its title from a passage in *King Lear* ("but I am bound / Upon a wheel of fire") and depicts the hectic time that preceded Dylan's accident:

> This wheel's on fire,
> Rolling down the road,
> Best notify my next of kin,
> If this wheel shall explode!

The musically thin "Too Much of Nothing" looks at the period of silence after the crash, which left many Dylan admirers "ill at ease." Some writers have seen the chorus as a reference to T.S. Eliot's first wife Vivienne, who went insane:[65]

> Say hello to Valerie
> Say hello to Vivian
> Give her all my salary
> On the waters of oblivion.

As great as the official album undoubtedly is, Robbie Robertson made some questionable decisions when assembling the material for release. Robertson, reportedly in an attempt to help The Band through financial straits,[66] interspersed eight songs by The Band. These songs, with the exceptions of "Don't Ya Tell Henry" and "Long Distance Operator" (and maybe "Ain't No More Cane") impede the flow of Dylan's recordings and sound out of place. Most of the songs were recorded for possible inclusion on The Band's debut album[67] and as such lack the feel of the true basement recordings.

Most listeners would surely have preferred "Quinn the Eskimo (The Mighty Quinn)" in place of "Orange Juice Blues (Blues For Breakfast)," "I Shall Be Released" instead of "Ruben Remus," or "I'm Not There (1956)" over "Yazoo Street Scandal." If Robertson really needed to include Band songs, he should have used "Ferdinand the Impostor," which sounds similar to "The Weight," and "You Say You Love Me," or gone way out on a limb and added one or two of Tiny Tim's songs with The Band, hilarious desecrations of "Be My Baby," "Memphis, Tennessee," "Sonny Boy," and the *piece de resistance*, a duet with an unidentified singer on Sonny and Cher's "I Got You, Babe."

Worse, Robertson neglected to include several Dylan originals, some of them masterpieces. The mysterious "Quinn the Eskimo" wouldn't appear until *Biograph*, while "I Shall Be Released," characterized by Richard Manuel's falsetto and Robertson's sublime guitar playing, wasn't released until *The Bootleg Series, Volumes 1-3*, although the version on *Greatest Hits, Volume II* brought the song the recognition that has made it a fan favorite.

The two most renowned unreleased songs from this period are "Sign on the Cross" and "I'm Not There." Sung in a strange, semi-oratorical voice, "Sign on the Cross" seems partly a prophecy of Dylan's evangelical stance in the late 1970s-early 1980s: "But I just would like to tell you one time / if I don't see you again, that the thing is, that the sign on the cross is the thing you might need the most." This phrase seems awkward on the page, but Dylan says it so compellingly that the underlying message comes through powerfully. The song's conclusion branches into a broader spirituality:

Oh, when your, when your days are numbered
And your nights are long,

You might think you're weak
But I mean to say you're strong.
Yes you are, if that sign on the cross,
If it begins to worry you.
Well, that's all right because sing a song
And all your troubles will pass right on through.

The only song that comes remotely close to "Sign on the Cross" is The Rolling Stones' "Far Away Eyes," which reads like a parody of the West Coast Christian ethos of the late 1970s but sounds like a remarkable expression of religious and romantic longing.

"I'm Not There" is even more amazing than "Sign on the Cross," one of the most unique performances a listener will ever hear. Greil Marcus has a quotation in his book *Invisible Republic* that refers to "I'm Not There" as maybe "the greatest song ever written";[68] perhaps it would be more accurate to call it the greatest song never written, since there are a lot of "dummy lyrics." The song is comparable to "Santa Fe" in that both songs don't really have lyrics (true, the words have been transcribed, but they don't make much sense, and often Dylan sings something different). Yet it doesn't matter that the lyrics don't all fit together, or that some words are not even words but sounds, because Dylan's voice brings a stunning immediacy to every line, so even if the listener can't comprehend what the singer is saying, he can feel what Dylan means. For instance, "Heaven knows that the answer she's don't call in no one / She's a wave, a sailing beauty, she's mine for the one" is a puzzling lyric, but with Dylan's voice pitched between heartbreak and hope, the lines sound glorious. Columbia's continued refusal to officially release "I'm Not There" and "Sign on the Cross" defies explanation.[69]

Other original songs lesser in stature but still worthy of release are "Get Your Rocks Off!," "All-American Boy," the jaunty farmyard blues "All You Have to Do Is Dream," complete with an intro that Dylan and The Band later used for "Like a Rolling Stone" at the Isle of Wight Festival, and "I'm Your Teenage Prayer," which features one of Dylan's most soaring vocals.

None of the covers Dylan recorded are on *The Basement Tapes*. This is unfortunate, since there are some fine interpretations, foremost among them "The Hills of Mexico," which Dylan cuts short, saying he's "just wasting tape" (although few would agree), "Bonnie Ship the Diamond," "Young But Daily Growing," "Ol' Roisin the Beau," "The Royal Canal," with Dylan pulling emotion out of every syllable, a gorgeous take of Eric von Schmidt's "Joshua Gone Barbados," and a stately "Bells of Rhymney." Dylan also used these sessions as an opportunity to explore his country roots: four Johnny Cash songs, "Belshazar," "Still in Town," "Big River" and a stomping "Folsom Prison Blues"; a good version of the Hank Snow hit "I Don't Hurt Anymore"; "Waltzing with Sin'; two Hank Williams favorites, a spoken "Be Careful of Stones that You Throw" and "You Win Again"; and the Ian and Sylvia country/folk songs "Four Strong Winds," "The French Girl" and "One Single River." More so than the official tracks, these covers anticipate the rustic slant of *John Wesley Harding* and *Nashville Skyline*.

There were excursions into other musical genres at these sessions. The plaintive gospel strain of "People Get Ready" is a precursor for the version in *Renaldo and Clara*. Hootenany melodies pervade "Down on Me" and "Baby Ain't that Fine." The blues of John Lee Hooker is here in the form of "I'm in the Mood" and "Tupelo." Traditional folk is represented in "See That My Grave Is Kept Clean," "Comin' Round the Mountain," "No Shoes on My Feet,"

"Come All Ye Fair and Tender Ladies," a minute of the Negro ballad "Po'Lazarus," which Dylan had sung at the start of his career, and "Johnny Todd." Dylan even makes a stab at falsetto in "Try Me Little Girl" (and comes up a mile short), and turns the children's song "See You Later, Alligator" into the merry amalgam "See You Later, Allen Ginsberg." Some of the songs come up later in Dylan's career, namely "People Get Ready," "A Fool Such As I" and "Spanish Is The Loving Tongue," not as good as the B-side but better than the farce on *Dylan*. Above all, these covers demonstrate Dylan's voluminous knowledge of song. More than any of his contemporaries, Dylan was fully aware of his antecedents. "When Dylan covers a song – or evokes one in his own compositions – cultural landscapes, sensual associations, and ethical lessons flood through him," observed Eric Weisbard. "Dylan, you feel certain, knows the roots of all of it."[70] And he knows how to separate the wheat from the chaff. In "Open the Door, Homer," Dylan derides a popular song from the 1940s entitled "Open the Door, Richard," and, in the process, consigns the banal hit single to the dust bin of musical history, the effortlessness of Dylan's vocal disguising the cutting nature of the lyric: "Open the door, Richard / I've heard it said before / But I ain't gonna hear it said no more."

The basement sessions are collected on the five volume bootleg set *The Genuine Basement Tapes*. The sound quality isn't great (volume three is in mono), but the set is well worth it for the revelations it contains. Maybe someday Columbia will release another double album set of these recordings, perhaps with originals on one disc and covers on the second.

This material has added historical value in that some of the songs appeared on the first bootleg album, *Great White Wonder*. Nowadays, bootlegging is big business, and no artist's work is bootlegged more than Bob Dylan's. Dylan has always despised bootlegging, and with good reason. He told Cameron Crowe, with a grain of exaggeration:

> The bootleg records . . . those are outrageous . . . If you're sitting and strumming in a motel, you don't think anybody's there, you know . . . it's like the phone is tapped . . . and then it appears on a bootleg record. With a cover that's got a picture of you that was taken from underneath your bed and it's got a strip-tease type title and it cost[s] $30. Amazing. Then you wonder why most artists feel so paranoid.

Despite the fact that most of the songs recorded in the basement have surfaced, there's still an element of mystery to those days in 1967. Only Bob Dylan and The Band know for sure what really went on in that basement. But the biggest mystery surrounding *The Basement Tapes* remains unsolved: why are the words to these songs printed, in *Lyrics*, between *New Morning* and *Pat Garrett & Billy the Kid*?[71]

JOHN WESLEY HARDING

RELEASED: DECEMBER 1967

If *The Basement Tapes* are the songs of a man making music for pleasure, then the songs on *John Wesley Harding* are those of a man offering hope in the form of parables which point the way back to basic moral and religious truths. While there are no explicit political statements in these songs, the lessons to be learned from them are inspiring.

The instrumentation on the album has been pared down to acoustic guitar, harmonica, bass, drums, and, on some songs, piano, giving *John Wesley Harding* a distinct sound. Charlie McCoy and Kenny Buttrey play with admirable ease.

McCoy's bass playing on, in particular, "John Wesley Harding" and "As I Went Out One Morning" is outstanding; Buttrey's drumming on "Dear Landlord" works off Dylan's lovely, understated piano playing. And Dylan's harmonica work has never sounded better (or been employed so effectively). Dylan's singing is calm and assured, reverberating through these rich, dense songs.

To describe *John Wesley Harding* as a "folk music" album is somewhat inaccurate – the record seems to blend folk, country, and rock, making it a truly remarkable album. The folk influence appears throughout, as many songs derive their antecedents from traditional material. The opening lines of "I Dreamed I Saw St. Augustine" are a cop from the popular ballad "Joe Hill' ("I dreamed I saw Joe Hill last night, / Alive as you and me"). In "As I Went Out One Morning," the first verse's "As I went out one morning / To breathe the air around Tom Paine's / I spied the fairest damsel" is a literal adaptation of the lines "As I went out one morning to breathe the morning air" in the folk song "Lolly-Too-Dum" and "As I was a-walking one morning for pleasure, / I spied a cow puncher a-riding along" in the cowboy tune "Git Along, Little Dogies." "As I Went Out One Morning" also recalls "Little Mohee" and the Irish folk song "As I Went A-Walking One Morning In Spring."

The "badman" ballad "John Wesley Harding" is rife with references to classic desperado stories. The title character (actual name John Wesley Hardin), who in real life was a cold-blooded killer (although, to be fair, Dylan does not seem to dispute this, he merely says that Harding "was never known / To hurt an honest man"), is modeled after the men of songs like "Billy the Kid," "Sam Bass," "Jesse James" and "John Hardy." Dylan writes that Harding "trav'led with a gun in ev'ry hand"; "John Hardy" includes the lines "John Hardy was a desp'rate little man, / He carried two guns ev'ry day." "Harding was a friend to the poor," Dylan says, mirroring these lines from "Jesse James": "Jesse James was a man; a friend to the poor"; "He stole from the rich and he gave to the poor." "Jesse James" is the most likely source for Dylan's song; James is name-checked in "Outlaw Blues," and Guthrie turned "Jesse James" into his song "Jesus Christ."

Hardin was no saint, to be sure, but Dylan seems to respect Hardin's compassion for the downtrodden. The role of the pariah in society is a key concept of the album. All the personages in these songs are, in some ways, outlaws, be it the joker and the thief in "All Along the Watchtower"; St. Augustine, a voice crying in the wilderness; the wicked messenger; the lonesome hobo, or the drifter. The hobo figure occurs frequently in Dylan's songs; in "Man on the Street" and "Only a Hobo" (inspired, no doubt, by "Hobo's Lullaby"), the "poet who died in the gutter" in "A Hard Rain's A-Gonna Fall," "the mystery tramp" and "Napoleon in rags" in "Like a Rolling Stone." In "I Am a Lonesome Hobo," the narrator leads a deceitful life, accumulates wealth, and then betrays his fellow man, leading to his downfall.

In verse three, the hobo emerges as an Ancient Mariner figure, urging others to avoid worship of false idols, and to judge oneself before pronouncing judgment upon others:

Live by no man's code,
And hold your judgment for yourself
Lest you wind up on this road.

Such words of wisdom appear throughout *John Wesley Harding*, but the messages are subtle enough to seem comforting rather than coercive. "Dear Landlord" is more than a plea to God; the song reassures listeners that everyone has a landlord in this life ("I know you've suffered much, / But

in this you are not so unique"), concluding with a verse
about individuality and mutual respect:

> Now, each of us has his own special gift
> And you know this was meant to be true,
> And if you don't underestimate me,
> I won't underestimate you.

The conclusion of "The Ballad of Frankie Lee and Judas
Priest" offers three morals: "one should never be / Where
one does not belong"; help one's neighbor with his spiritual
load; and human demands should not supplant the spiritual:
"And don't go mistaking Paradise / For that home across the
road."

Commensurate with the songs' overarching morality is
the streak of Judaeo-Christianity shot through *John Wesley
Harding*, proving to naysayers of Dylan's later, more overtly
religious albums that Dylan has always harbored Christian
beliefs. On the other hand, critics rightly point to *John
Wesley Harding* as evidence that some of the material on
Slow Train Coming, *Saved* and *Shot of Love* can be overbearing.[72] Greil Marcus said it well: "American piety is a deep
mine and, in the past, without following any maps, Dylan
has gone into it and returned with real treasures: *John
Wesley Harding* is the best example, but there are many
others. *Slow Train Coming* strips the earth and what it leaves
behind is wreckage."[73] The songs on *John Wesley Harding*
probe religion more opaquely, but even if one misses the
Biblical or Christian references, the songs engender a sense
of comfort. The Christianity of Dylan's later albums makes
him appear proselytizing. The best songs from those albums
– "Slow Train," "Precious Angel," "I Believe in You," "Covenant Woman," "In the Summertime," "The Groom's Still

Waiting at the Altar," "Caribbean Wind" and "Every Grain of Sand" retain an ambiguity that gives them wider appeal.

Dylan once dubbed *John Wesley Harding* "the first Biblical rock album," and there are references to the Bible scattered throughout the record.[74] In "All Along the Watchtower," Christ appears as the thief from Revelations, and verses three and four are drawn directly from Isiah. In "Drifter's Escape," the drifter is the classic martyr figure:

> And I still do not know
> What it was that I've done wrong.

The drifter's escape recalls Christ's escape from the Holy Sepulcher. "The Wicked Messenger" is mentioned in Proverbs, and the character is an Anti-Christ figure who brings evil.

Throughout, Dylan urges a religiosity as solace to the troubles plaguing the country, namely the quagmire of Vietnam and the racial problems at home. "I Dreamed I Saw St. Augustine" urges men to stake out their own spiritual path:

> No martyr is among ye now
> Whom you can call your own,
> But go on your way accordingly
> But know you're not alone.

The concluding lines present Dylan as frustrated with contemporary America for having lost its way.

In "The Ballad of Frankie Lee and Judas Priest," Judas Priest lends Frankie Lee money and, when Frankie spends it in a brothel, then takes his soul ("'Take your pick / Frankie Boy, / My loss will be your gain'"). Frankie succumbs to his earthly desires and dies of spiritual thirst, suggesting temptation is the road to ruin. The subject of "I Pity the Poor Immigrant" is an immigrant in the sense of being unnatural and morally and spiritually corrupt. The immigrant substitutes greed for faith: "falls in love with wealth itself / And turns his back on me." "As I Went Out One Morning" envisions liberty (in the guise of a fair damsel) in chains. "All Along the Watchtower" uses the fall of Babylon as a parable warning about the discord in the United States (in part borne out by the tumultuous year 1968 was to become).

John Wesley Harding proved to be an immensely popular album, and it made the point that music did not have to be excessive to be masterful, at a time when psychedelia was threatening to go too far. The Rolling Stones took their cue from Dylan, jettisoning the annoying gimmickry of the hopelessly dull *Their Satanic Majesties Request* for *Beggar's Banquet*. The Beatles retreated from the classic *Sgt. Pepper's Lonely Hearts Club Band* with the more traditional music of *The Beatles*. A tremendous confidence is there throughout the album, to the point that Dylan can conclude *John Wesley Harding* with two innocuous love songs, "Down Along the Cove" and "I'll Be Your Baby Tonight," and point the way to *Nashville Skyline*.

John Wesley Harding has a lot to offer, right down to the packaging. Some fans, by holding the cover photo upside down, discovered pictures of The Beatles in the tree bark (although, as the joke goes, if one holds the cover right-side-up, then turns it clockwise, the record falls out).[75] The liner notes make a good story, closing with Dylan proclaiming himself "a moderate man" who didn't lose his creativity or turn his back on what he believed in following his accident: "'Yuh didn't hurt yer hand, didja Frank?' . . . 'I don't believe so.'"

NASHVILLE SKYLINE

RELEASED: APRIL 1969

Confounding listeners once again, Bob Dylan returned to Nashville (both *Blonde on Blonde* and *John Wesley Harding* had been recorded there) and made an album of country music. With a smiling "Howdy, folks!" Dylan pictured on the cover and simple, happy songs, *Nashville Skyline* is an easy-listening, pleasurable record. The most shocking aspect of this material, however, is Dylan's voice. There isn't a trace of the nasally, madcap voice of old; instead, Dylan sings in a smooth baritone. Upon first dropping the needle, most listeners must have wondered who exactly was singing the first verse of "Girl from the North Country." Opinions differ on what Dylan did to bring about the change: was it natural, a break from cigarettes, or had Dylan been taking lessons in how to sing like a country crooner? Regardless, his voice is well suited to the songs on *Nashville Skyline*.

By themselves, these songs don't amount to much (except for "Lay, Lady, Lay" and "Tonight I'll Be Staying Here with You"). But taken together, the songs function wonderfully. As Paul Williams commented: "It [*Nashville Skyline*] creates and sustains a unique mood, from the first note on side one to the last note on side two. The whole is tremendously greater than . . . its parts."[76] Even the faltering duet with Johnny Cash on "Girl from the North Country" emanates a certain charm.

Lyrically, these songs are very modest. The imaginative imagery of Dylan's previous albums has been replaced by colloquial language. Still, that doesn't prevent Dylan from playing a few tricks. In "Lay, Lady, Lay," the narrator offers his love as a safe alternative to drugs: "Whatever colors you have in your mind / I'll show them to you and you'll see them shine." The song also provides a good example of Dylan's knack for reworking clichés: "You can have your cake and eat it too." "Country Pie" is fun, with Dylan inventing his own nursery rhyme:

Shake me up that old peach tree
Little Jack Horner got nothin' on me

"I Threw It All Away" occasionally lapses into triteness ("Love is all there is / it makes the world go' round"), but the organ work in the fourth verse easily redeems the lyrics. The jilted narrator of "One More Night" ("I had no idea what a woman in love would do!" [the joke being she's in love with another man]) may be the same person in "Tell Me That It Isn't True" who loses out to a "tall, dark, and handsome" stranger.

The musicians breeze through this material, providing many fine moments: the steel guitar on "Peggy Day"; the bongos and cowbells on "Lay, Lady, Lay"; the piano on "Tonight I'll Be Staying Here with You"; the smooth "Girl from the North Country."

Nashville Skyline proved to have a very important influence. Not only was Dylan turning away from the counterculture that was growing around him in Woodstock, he was actually bringing pop and country music together. Country music was unfairly derided as hick music; Dylan brought newfound popularity to country, making it more accessible to the pop crowd. *Nashville Skyline* inspired many artists who would help make country more commercial and less conservative, including The Nitty Gritty Dirt Band and Kris Kristofferson.

CONCLUSION

The music Bob Dylan made following his accident was a return to basic musical values, showing that music didn't have to be flashy to be effective. *The Basement Tapes* and *John Wesley Harding* are among Dylan's most durable works, and while opinions regarding *Nashville Skyline* differ, the album holds up better than much of the sound-alike material that passes for country music today.

By recording in Nashville, beginning with *Blonde on Blonde*, Dylan gave musicians of different genres a new setting in which to work. As Charlie McCoy explained in an interview in 1992:

> History will tell us that his coming here was one of the biggest things that ever happened to Nashville. At the time, nobody realized it, but it opened the door for all these other people to come down – the Byrds, Joan Baez, Buffy Sainte-Marie, and so forth. It was like, "Hey, if it's OK for Dylan then it must be OK down there." It was a great thing for the town.[77]

It is possible that Dylan would have made this type of music even if he hadn't crashed his motorcycle. Never one to stay in the same place for too long, Dylan must have disliked the manner in which rock was becoming too self-indulgent in 1967, as major artists were striving to outdo each other. But if 1967-69 was a successful period for Dylan, the following years would prove to be a time of uneven work and tentativeness.

PART V

ODDS AND ENDS

SELF PORTRAIT

RELEASED: JUNE 1970

All of Bob Dylan's musical turns during the 1960s were successful. Dylan opened the 1970s with another stunner; unfortunately, the finished product was, to say the least, a major disappointment. *Self Portrait* is a farcical double album; a haphazard collection of traditional songs, cover versions of songs written by artists (Paul Simon, Gordon Lightfoot) whose lyrics were modeled after Dylan's, live performances from Dylan's instantly forgettable performance at the Isle of Wight Festival in August 1969, and a smattering of unremarkable original material. There are twenty-four songs in all, very few of which are worth hearing. *Self Portrait* is almost unlistenable; as music critic Robert Christgau observed following the album's release, nobody plays more than one side at a time, a statement which still holds true today.[78]

The opening song, "All the Tired Horses," sets the tone for the album. Consisting of a female chorus chanting the lines "All the tired horses in the sun, / How'm I s'posed to get any ridin' done?" over and over again until the listener wants to scream, the orchestral arrangement of the song establishes the indifferent attitude which plagues *Self Portrait*. Much of the blame lies with Bob Johnston's production: the mixing is bad; the use of strings and horns misplaced; and some of the material recorded at the New York sessions was reportedly overdubbed down in Nashville with different musicians, and with Dylan absent.[79] Evidence of these flaws is everywhere: the squawking saxophone on the instrumental "Woogie Boogie"; the overwhelming accompaniment on "Belle Isle" and "Copper Kettle"; the creaky fiddle on "Blue Moon"; the bugles and brass on "Wigwam"; the lazy backup on "It Hurts Me Too"; the interchangeable arrangements of the two takes of "Alberta." The cuts from the Isle of Wight (with The Band) aren't much better; the musicians sound detached.

But even if the backup work was impressive, Dylan's voice is a blatant indication that he deliberately intended *Self Portrait* to be a terrible album. Dylan's singing is lifeless and uncommunicative; when the musicians do pick up the pace (as in "Let It Be Me"), Dylan continues to sing in the same lackadaisical fashion. As some writers have noted, on "I Forgot More Than You'll Ever Know," "Let It Be Me" and "Blue Moon," he sounds ready to sneeze; on others, such as "Alberta #1," "Take Me as I Am (or Let Me Go)," "Take a Message to Mary," and "It Hurts Me Too," he sounds as if he just doesn't care. The other big problem is that Dylan can't decide how exactly he wants his voice to sound: when he hits the line "And the women all were fast" in "Early Mornin' Rain," he slips into his *Nashville Skyline* voice; on "In Search of Little Sadie," he seems to be parodying his pre-*Nashville Skyline* singing style.

The three poorest performances on the album are "Blue Moon," "The Boxer" and "Like a Rolling Stone." "Blue Moon" is an obvious joke, as is "The Boxer," in which Dylan mimics both Paul Simon *and* Art Garfunkel. Dylan's "Lie-la-lie"'s are so laughable that it makes Simon and Garfunkel's decision to sing in tune commendable. And the live "Like a Rolling Stone" contains a staggering amount of slip-ups: forgetting the words, mumbling, omitting the third verse.

Of the other live cuts, only "Quinn the Eskimo" is palatable, providing one of the album's rare moments of excitement, when Dylan shouts "Well, that guitar now!" and Robbie Robertson tears into his solo. Dylan's voice is ramshackle on "She Belongs to Me," and the dreadful "harmonizing" during "Minstrel Boy" quickly does in the song.

Those commentators who have tried to defend *Self Portrait* often point to the variety of the traditional material and chalk the project up to writer's block.[80] Granted, Dylan wasn't producing many songs at the time, but it's highly unlikely he would have put together an album like *Self Portrait* as a response to his lack of original material – he would simply not put out any new product. The other difficulty with that interpretation is that the traditional material isn't cohesive in any way. The songs are mostly random oldies Dylan decided to record. Compare *Self Portrait* with *Good As I Been to You* or *World Gone Wrong* and the difference in intent becomes obvious. What upset critics even more about *Self Portrait* was Dylan's impish attempt to claim "Alberta," "It Hurts Me Too," "Belle Isle" and "In Search of Little Sadie" as his own (leading Michael Gray to herald "Belle Isle" as "a terrific parody of the Celtic ballad").[81]

The big question surrounding this mess is: why? The closest Dylan ever came to explaining what he was thinking at the time came in a 1984 interview for *Rolling Stone*:

> People need a leader. I didn't want that, though. But then came the big news about Woodstock, about musicians goin' up there, and it was like a wave of insanity breakin'

loose around the house *day* and *night*. You'd come in the house and find people there . . . at all hours of the day and night, knockin' on your door . . . I said, "Now, wait, these people can't be my *fans*. We moved to New York. Lookin' back, it really was a stupid thing to do . . . There'd be crowds outside my house. And I said: "I wish these people would just *forget* about me. I wanna do something they can't possibly like, they *can't* relate to . . .[Then] they'll go on to somebody else."[82]

For *Biograph*, Dylan added: "I was being bootlegged at the time and a lot of stuff that was worse was appearing on bootleg records. So I just figured I'd put all this stuff together and put it out, my own bootleg record, so to speak."[83]

In this context, *Self Portrait* may be viewed as a backlash against an invasion of privacy, privacy both as an artist and as an individual. Dylan's attempt to sabotage the bootleggers was based upon the theory that if the official releases were as bad as *Self Portrait*, then people would assume that the unreleased material would be even worse and not bother buying the bootlegs, thereby stemming the tide of bootleg records. The irony is that Dylan's plan failed, because many sought out bootlegged material as an antidote to *Self Portrait*.

Dylan's personal life was under attack at the time: those who perceived him as a savior were making pilgrimages to his home, while the likes of A.J. Weberman had begun harassing Dylan through the underground press.[84] When Dylan said he wanted to get some people off his back with the album, he must have been referring to the bootleggers, the A. J. Webermans, and those who complained that *Nashville Skyline* was a "sell out." No artist would want to isolate his mainstream audience, and that clearly was not Dylan's intent. Dylan later tried to ignore the album: there is no *Self Portrait* section in *Lyrics* (the songs are in the *Nashville*

Skyline chapter), and in the aforementioned *Rolling Stone* interview, he called the album a "joke."[85] Even the cover is a sham: Dylan's painting looks suspiciously like the glass collage of a clown that sits over the mantel in the cover photo for *Bringing It All Back Home*. For a lesser artist, *Self Portrait* would have been the end of their recording contract.

NEW MORNING

RELEASED: OCTOBER 1970

Within five months of *Self Portrait*, Dylan released *New Morning*, an album wherein domestic themes are juxtaposed with a quiet celebration of nature. Many of the tracks are love songs ("If Not for You," "Winterlude," "New Morning," "The Man in Me"); one is a hymn ("Father of Night"); others draw on personal experiences ("Day of the Locusts," "Went to See the Gypsy").

Most of the standouts are on side one: "If Not for You," "Day of the Locusts," "Time Passes Slowly" and "Went to See the Gypsy." "Day of the Locusts" is based on Dylan's controversial acceptance of an honorary doctorate in music from Princeton University in June 1970.[86] Dylan does a good job of establishing the mood surrounding a graduation ceremony and conveying a sense of the edginess young people feel before entering into the workforce.

"Went to See the Gypsy" is a parable about going to see Elvis. The narrator never gets to meet the gypsy, who flees with the dancing girl, but as the narrator leaves the hotel, he experiences a moment of epiphany when he comprehends the power Elvis could command as a performer:

> Outside the lights were shining
> On the river of tears,
> I watched them from the distance
> With the music in my ears.

"Time Passes Slowly" has a tranquil setting to it, evoking memories of Thoreau's retreat:

> We sit beside bridges and walk beside fountains,
> Catch the wild fishes that float through the stream,

Despite this idyllic scene, there's an undercurrent of restlessness in the final lines, which Dylan delivers with a strange sense of urgency:

> Like a red rose of summer that blooms in the day,
> Time passes slowly and then fades away.

It's as if Dylan isn't completely satisfied with his rural persona, and time is passing too slowly for him.

Dylan's affinity with nature, however uneasy it may be, gets played up in "New Morning." The picturesque opening verse personifies a pastoral paradise, with images of roosters, rabbits and country streams. Dylan plays with the time period in the quaint lines of the second verse:

> Can't you hear that motor turnin'?
> Automobile comin' into style

But, yet again, the sense of this lifestyle ending soon is present:

> The night passed away so quickly
> It always does when you're with me.

"Sign on the Window" features some beautiful piano work by Dylan, and Dylan again points the way to finding peace in nature. In the song's final verse, he makes an appealing withdrawal into the confines of domesticity:

> Build me a cabin in Utah,
> Marry me a wife, catch rainbow trout,
> Have a bunch of kids who call me "Pa,"
> That must be what it's all about

Of the other songs on *New Morning*, "Winterlude," "One More Weekend" and "The Man in Me" are mediocre; "If Dogs Run Free," "Three Angels" and "Father of Night" are horrible.

"Winterlude" is a dopey ditty about being in love; when Dylan sings "Winterlude, this dude thinks you're fine," his use of the word "dude" is likely to bring more chuckles than admiration. "One More Weekend" reads like a rewrite of "Honey, Just Allow Me One More Chance": "Come on down to my ship, honey, ride on deck, / We'll fly over the ocean just like you suspect" owes a debt to verse two of the earlier song; "Like a needle in a haystack, I'm gonna find you yet" mirrors "Honey, Just Allow Me One More Chance"'s lines "Well, lookin' for a woman / That ain't got no man, / Is like lookin' for a needle / That is lost in the sand." And Dylan's "la-la-la"'s in "The Man in Me" are way off pitch. Ironically, "The Man in Me" would eventually become one of the most well-known tracks on the album when it appeared as the main song in the Coen brothers' hilarious slacker film *The Big Lebowski*.

The closing song on side one, "If Dogs Run Free," suffers from Maeretha Stewart's excruciating scatting. As Dylan sings "It can cure the soul / it can make it whole," Stewart's background noises resemble the croaking of a frog.

Dylan gets so embarrassed by this ostentatious display that, as the song fades, he mutters "Forget it, baby." "Three Angels" and "Father of Night" aren't much better; in the former, Dylan's spoken intonations don't work; on "Father of Night," the rhymes are not particularly imaginative (fly/sky, night/white, wheat/heat), and Dylan sounds as if he has developed a lisp ("taketh," "teacheth").

Of the album's outtakes, "Working on a Guru," Dylan's limp parody of The Beatles' Maharishi infatuation, attracted some attention because it was recorded with George Harrison.

Ultimately, *New Morning* is an unsuccessful album. It lacks the coherence of *Nashville Skyline*, and although half of the songs are marvelous, there's something missing from this record. Paul Williams, in his excellent book *Performing Artist, Volume One*, finds a certain degree of inauthenticity in these performances: "[Dylan] goes through all the motions and touches all the bases, but leaves out Ingredient X."[87] Perhaps that's why *New Morning* is not an album Dylan fans find themselves returning to very often, and perhaps Dylan himself was unhappy about the results, which might explain why it would be three years before Dylan went into the studio again to put together a complete collection of original songs. *New Morning* is worth hearing, but its flaws become more pronounced with age, and the poorer tracks are, by Dylan's standards, very weak indeed.

BOB DYLAN'S GREATEST HITS, VOLUME II

RELEASED: NOVEMBER 1971

As was the case in 1967, Columbia needed a new Dylan product on the market, so they released a second *Greatest*

Hits package in time for Christmas 1971, this one a double album. *Greatest Hits, Volume II* consists of twenty-one songs, five of which were previously unavailable, and one that had only been released as a single earlier in the year ("Watching the River Flow").

Both "Watching the River Flow" and "When I Paint My Masterpiece" were produced by Leon Russell, who accompanied Dylan during his triumphant set at the Concert for Bangladesh in August 1971. "Watching the River Flow" features some blistering guitar work (especially in the introduction and after the third verse), and rollicking piano work from Russell. The song opens with a modest admission of writer's block: "What's the matter with me[?] / I don't have much to say." The likable "When I Paint My Masterpiece" also seems addressed to Dylan's flown muse, as the narrator travels to Rome in the hope of finding the inspiration to create his masterpiece.

"Tomorrow Is a Long Time" is taken from Dylan's April 1963 Town Hall Concert in New York City. The quiet intensity of Dylan's singing enhances the loveliness of the lyrics. This performance is a real treasure; an awe-inspiring moment.

The songs which close *Greatest Hits, Volume II* are superior reworkings (except for, perhaps, "I Shall Be Released") of songs from *The Basement Tapes* sessions. Recorded in October 1971 with Happy Traum alternating on bass, banjo and second guitar, and adding backing vocals, these are magical performances. Dylan's plaintive singing and passionate harmonica solo, and the universality of the chorus, quickly made "I Shall Be Released" a fan favorite. The version of "You Ain't Goin' Nowhere" included here makes up for what *The Basement Tapes* version lacks in energy: the wonderful new lyrics, delightful upbeat melody, harmonica playing, and harmonizing on the chorus makes this performance an absolute masterpiece, full of heart and charm. The final gem, "Down in the Flood," gains its allure from the brilliant abrupt opening and the strumming during each verse. These three songs alone make *Greatest Hits, Volume II* a must-have for both casual and die-hard Dylan fans.

Whereas the songs on Dylan's first *Greatest Hits* collection were his more recognizable hits, *Volume II* contains only two album singles ("Lay, Lady, Lay" and "Tonight I'll Be Staying Here with You"). The sequencing of the songs was done by Dylan, and, as a result, the songs flow together smoother than on the earlier collection. Despite coming from different sessions, none of these songs sound out of place. *Greatest Hits, Volume II* remains the best introduction to Bob Dylan's work.

PAT GARRETT & BILLY THE KID

RELEASED: JULY 1973

Playing the appropriately titled Alias in Sam Peckinpah's film *Pat Garrett and Billy the Kid*, Dylan also provided the music. Dylan's role in the movie isn't much, and he delivers his lines badly, but he does appear in one of the film's more entertaining scenes, reading labels off tin cans in a deadpan manner while Garrett brutally murders Holly and Harris.

The musical score is arguably the best thing about the picture. The soundtrack may, at first, sound inconsequential, but the music begins to grow on one upon repeated listening. Only two new Dylan lyrics are on the album: the elegiac "Knockin' on Heaven's Door," which became a hit single due to its lush musical setting and memorable chorus, and "Billy," an outstanding western ballad written as an overview to the poignant story of Billy's betrayal by Garrett. Another original, the hootenany-style "Goodbye Holly," was left off the album. There are three takes of "Billy" on the album: "Billy 1" and "Billy 7" incorporate three verses each (one of which, from "Billy 7," is not in *Lyrics*); "Billy 4" is almost complete. The nuances in each version, be it the harmonica solos in "Billy 1," Dylan's tough yet sensitive delivery of "Billy 4," or the sense of impending doom in "Billy 7," make these performances special.

All of the instrumentals are strong, one of which – "Final Theme" – is extraordinary. The stately "Final Theme" is, as Ellen Willis once noted, appropriate as music for both weddings and funerals.

Jonathan Cott described *Pat Garrett & Billy the Kid* as "a kind of beautiful, rough-hewn, mostly instrumental mantra album from the mythical Old West;"[88] and the music conjures up an era in America's past in a way that few of the soundtracks to westerns can.

DYLAN

RECORDED: AT THE SESSIONS FOR *Self Portrait* AND *New Morning* (1969-1970).
RELEASED: NOVEMBER 1973

Dylan's decision to sign a recording deal with Asylum Records after his contract with Columbia had expired prompted the good folks at CBS to slap together, without Dylan's permission, a bizarre collection of cover versions. Some of the songs were recorded for, but left off of, *Self Portrait*; others were done as warm-ups at the *New Morning* sessions. *Dylan*, as the album was plainly titled, was intended to lure Dylan back to Columbia; when critics got word of

Columbia's malevolent intentions, the end result was probably more harmful to Columbia than to Dylan.[89]

Dylan isn't quite the abomination writers usually portray it as; the songs aren't so much offensive as they are worthless. The only song which might have held up, "Lily of the West," falls apart due to the synthetic female backup singers, who also hamper "Sarah Jane," "Mr. Bojangles" (in which Dylan duels with them on the word "dance"), "Big Yellow Taxi," and a ludicrous arrangement of "A Fool Such As I." The other Presley standard Dylan tackles is "Can't Help Falling in Love." Dylan's wheezy singing (also prevalent on "The Ballad of Ira Hayes" and "Mary Ann") prompted one wag to suggest that Dylan comes close to discovering the Lost Chord.[90] "Spanish Is the Loving Tongue" pales in comparison with the heartfelt solo piano take Dylan released as a B-side of "Watching the River Flow" (this version is available on *Masterpieces*). The version on *Dylan* includes a break that sounds like the Mexican Hat Dance and a second half which bears no resemblance to the sluggish opening (upon first hearing, it sounds like two separate songs). To top it all off, the mixing is dire. The only gracious thing to be said for *Dylan* is that, unlike *Self Portrait*, it isn't a double album.

CONCLUSION

1971-72 were years of relative inactivity for Bob Dylan, which suggests that he was searching for a medium in which he could balance his personal life with his art. Dylan spent a lot of time in the studio in 1970, but in 1971 he went into the studio only briefly. In November, he released a topical song, "George Jackson," a dubious ode to the black activist and armed robber who had been killed in prison. The Big

Band version of the song has the feel of a gospel spiritual. The acoustic take is straight-forward and moving.

1971 saw the publication of Dylan's ill-fated "novel" *Tarantula*. The book had been slated for release in 1966, but publication was halted due to Dylan's accident. Bootleggers hawking copies on the streets of New York forced Dylan's hand in 1971, but *Tarantula* proved hardly worth the wait. *Tarantula* is an amalgamation of images, ideas and personages (some real, some fictional), with an almost total disregard for narrative structure, save for a letter at the end of each chapter. The result is an uninteresting stream of consciousness muddle.

In 1973, his work during the filming of *Pat Garrett & Billy the Kid* got Dylan's creative juices flowing again, and by 1974 he had returned to touring.

1970-mid-1973 is a minor period in Dylan's career; there was, however, one live performance which stands out. On August 1, 1971, Dylan appeared at the Concert for Bangladesh and stole the spotlight. The show was Dylan's first appearance on stage in two years. With George Harrison on second guitar, Leon Russell on bass and Ringo Starr on tambourine, Dylan's set proved to be one of the highlights of his career. Singing in a style that had never sounded so good, Dylan opened with the suitable "A Hard Rain's A-Gonna Fall." "It Takes a Lot to Laugh, It Takes a Train to Cry" and "Blowin' in the Wind" followed, both songs featuring enchanting harmonica playing. The audience erupted on "Mr. Tambourine Man" (inexplicably absent from the film), and Dylan concluded with an amazing version of "Just Like a Woman," with Russell and Harrison leaning into the microphone to sing on the chorus. The transcendent moment came when Dylan sang "Ain't it clear that – I . . ." and his voice echoed throughout Madison Square Garden on the "I." Dylan wasn't trading on his past but reinventing these songs. Before the camera cut away from him after the last chords of "Just Like a Woman," Dylan turned his head and basked in the glory of the performance as the crowd gave him a thunderous ovation. Dylan had reminded his audience that, despite the ups and downs of recent years, he could still dominate.

PART VI

THE RENAISSANCE

PLANET WAVES

RELEASED: JANUARY 1974

The recording of *Planet Waves* in November 1973 marked the beginning of a sustained period of work for Bob Dylan. With The Band providing backup, the album has a consistency that Dylan's albums since *Nashville Skyline* largely lacked. Dylan's voice sounds stronger and more committed to the material than on *New Morning*.

The domesticities of *Planet Waves* are more convincing than those of *New Morning*. The opener, "On a Night Like This," is a sexy, laid-back song about a fling with an old acquaintance. As with some of the songs on *New Morning,* the setting is a cabin in the woods, isolated from society. The homey scene in verse three works as a metaphor for the passion of the moment:

    Build a fire, throw on logs
    And listen to it hiss
    And let it burn, burn, burn.

The setting of "Never Say Goodbye" is similar:

    Twilight on the frozen lake
    North wind about to break

On footprints in the snow
Silence down below.

He associates the woman the song is addressed to with nature. In "Something There Is About You," the woman helps summon up memories of the narrator's past:

Thought I'd shaken the wonder and the phantoms of my
    youth
Rainy days on the Great Lakes, walkin' the hills of old
    Duluth . . .
Something there is about you that brings back a
    long-forgotten truth.

The first line has negative connotations, but these are quickly dispelled as the narrator warms to these latent recollections. On *New Morning*, Dylan's explorations of love and nature occasionally sound forced (as Michael Gray writes in his discussion of the album: "You don't render a vision of happiness by insisting that you're happy"); on *Planet Waves*, these themes are developed more subtly and, ultimately, more effectively.

This is true of "Forever Young," a father's benediction to his children that never sounds overwrought. In an interview for the Dylan fanzine *The Telegraph*, Allen Ginsberg singled out "Forever Young": "I've heard ["Forever Young"] sung round camp fires, not recognizing it was Dylan, and [people would say], 'Oh my God, that beautiful old favorite is Dylan?!'"[91] "Forever Young" is a simple yet skillful song, with lyrics that are instantly memorable. On the slow version, Dylan sings the chorus with passion, giving the song its anthemic quality.

Planet Waves is most successful in balancing lighter songs with a more serious examination of relationships. *Planet Waves* invites comparisons to *New Morning*, but part of the album functions as a precursor for *Blood on the Tracks*. "Dirge," with Dylan playing stunning piano, is the type of lyric that Dylan hadn't written for a while. As a goodbye to a lover, the song works in a put-down that recalls the acerbic farewell of "Positively 4th Street": "You were just a painted face on a trip down Suicide Road." In verse one, the stage becomes a metaphor for the end of the relationship: "The stage was set, the lights went out all around the old hotel." The theater reappears in verse two, wherein Dylan makes reference to "Lower Broadway." The crux of the song comes with the fourth and sixth verses, as the protagonist searches for companionship ("In this age of fiberglass I'm searching for a gem"; "The naked truth is still taboo"), while reflecting on the mysteries of life: "The crystal ball up on the wall hasn't shown me nothing yet." "Dirge" seems almost like a prelude to "Idiot Wind."

"Wedding Song," a solo acoustic take, is a similarly arresting performance. Some of the lines are laudatory to the point of triteness ("I love you more than ever, more than time and more than love"), and "I love you more than money" isn't much of a compliment, but verse five contains a remarkable expression of individuality and forgiveness:

> The tune that is yours and mine to play upon this earth,
> We'll play it out the best we know, whatever it is worth,
> What's lost is lost, we can't regain what went down in the
>   flood

Verse six follows up on this theme, in which Dylan appears to be directly addressing his audience:

> It's never been my duty to remake the world at large,
> Nor is it my intention to sound a battle charge

The song's most striking lyric, "In the courtyard of the jester which is hidden from the sun," uses Dylan's recurring clown image ("A Hard Rain's A-Gonna Fall," "Like a Rolling Stone," "All Along the Watchtower"), perhaps a character along the lines of The Fool in Shakespeare, a man who knows more than people give him credit for. Stranger is the line "Eye for eye and tooth for tooth, your love cuts like a knife," the only moment of real anger in the song.

Despite the strength of "Dirge" and "Wedding Song," there are some awkward lines in *Planet Waves*, indicating Dylan hadn't quite returned to the peak of his songwriting powers. "My dreams are made of iron and steel" is cold, and "Hold on to me so tight / And heat up some coffee grounds" is ridiculously unromantic.

Time, unfortunately, has not been kind to *Planet Waves*. The Band's competence notwithstanding, the record sounds dull on occasion. The playing is curiously cautious, as if The Band was just warming up for the 1974 tour. Perhaps a few more takes would have given the album a bit more vitality. Nonetheless, *Planet Waves* works as part of a trilogy with *Blood on the Tracks* and *Desire*.

BEFORE THE FLOOD

RELEASED: JUNE 1974

Before the Flood is the souvenir album of Bob Dylan's important 1974 North American tour, a tour which marked his return to the concert circuit after an eight year absence. Using almost the same sidemen who had backed him in 1966, Dylan revamped his old songs in front of full houses from coast to coast. The press greeted the tour with euphoria, glad to see Bob Dylan back on the road after a long layoff.

Unfortunately, *Before the Flood* (which is actually a souvenir album of the Los Angeles shows, given that only one of the songs ["Knockin' on Heaven's Door"] is from a concert other than the three shows at the L.A. Forum that concluded the tour) is largely unsatisfying. Dylan gives the songs a speedy delivery that tends to make them all sound the same. As Patrick Humphries complained, "[Dylan is] shouting the lyrics as if to ensure that everyone in the vast arenas [can] hear them."[92] Dylan rushes through the songs with little variation in his voice, often screaming the last word of each line. Dylan keeps pace with The Band by yelling instead of falling back into the music. One could almost shuffle Dylan's singing among the tracks on side one and get the same results. Only on "Knockin' on Heaven's Door" does Dylan sound slightly relaxed, perhaps because the song is from earlier in the tour.

The instrumentation sounds a bit muddied and over-loud at times, but The Band's playing stands out in spots on side one: Robbie Robertson's searing guitar work gives "Most Likely You Go Your Way (and I'll Go Mine)" force; the country chords of the original version of "Lay, Lady, Lay" are transformed into a rock beat; the organ sweep of "Ballad of a Thin Man" salvages the song, which otherwise goes nowhere.

The acoustic trio which opens side three almost atones for Dylan's grating electric set. "Don't Think Twice, It's All Right" is something else entirely, a performance that, by itself, is worth the purchase price of the album. Dylan hits the notes perfectly, as when his voice trails off on the word "right" in the chorus. He sings the song like a man still upset over losing this woman. In the two harmonica solos (after verses three and four), Dylan bends the notes so as to give the song a whole new level of meaning.

The harshness of "Just Like a Woman" has been criticized, but it is actually one of the better vocal performances on *Before the Flood*.[93] Dylan wrings the emotion out of the song, letting his voice shift with an abruptness that keeps the listener waiting to see the next direction the song will take. The sorrowful harmonica playing at the end is tantamount to the closing moments of the *Blonde on Blonde* version.

"It's Alright, Ma (I'm Only Bleeding)" is one of the few songs in which shouting the final word of a line works: Dylan is still pointing his finger at society's problems. And the phrase "But even the president of the United States / Sometimes must have / To stand naked," which draws some timely applause, says more about the morality of Watergate than any number of editorials written on the subject,

Of the final electric songs, "All Along the Watchtower" becomes a sizzling rocker, and "Like a Rolling Stone," which deserves to be the closer, opens with Robertson's guitar chords teasing the audience the way they had eight years earlier on the same song, albeit with a different effect upon the crowd. Then comes a single note from Garth Hudson's organ, then Richard Manuel's piano, and the song soars. "Blowin' in the Wind," which follows, is anti-climactic, coming off as little more than a crowd-pleaser.

The more likable material in *Before the Flood* is on the second record, but most people will undoubtedly prefer the originals. Dylan later expressed dissatisfaction with the tour, telling Cameron Crowe that "I was just playing a role on that tour . . . I was playing Bob Dylan and The Band was playing The Band . . . it was an emotionless trip."[94] Levon Helm voiced similar sentiments in his autobiography: "I sometimes had a funny sensation: that we were acting out the roles of Bob Dylan and The Band, and the audience was paying to see what they'd missed many years before. We all felt that way, including Bob . . . it just wasn't a very passionate trip for any of us."[95] Granted, Dylan and The Band avoid being nostalgic by reworking these songs, but perhaps their feelings get in the way of the later shows. Side one of *Before the Flood* sounds like the work of men anxious to get a tour over with. This music can never hold up to comparisons with the later shows from the 1966 tour, when Dylan and The Band (minus Levon Helm) were taking the songs into a new musical realm. For most of *Before the Flood*, Dylan doesn't give the songs the sensitive treatment they deserve, and the arrangements suffer accordingly.

BLOOD ON THE TRACKS

RELEASED: JANUARY 1975

Regarded by many as the finest album of the 1970s, *Blood on the Tracks* is an astonishing work of art. Consisting of ten songs, the record has an emotional force unprecedented for a music album. The lyrics are brilliant, using a wide range of narrative techniques.

The musical accompaniment is similar to that on *John Wesley Harding*: subtle, precise instrumentation designed to enhance the effect of these songs. Dylan's singing comes from the heart, bringing forth deep human feelings.

The original sessions for *Blood on the Tracks* took place in New York in September 1974; Dylan rerecorded some of the songs ("Tangled Up in Blue," "You're a Big Girl Now," "Idiot Wind," "Lily, Rosemary and the Jack of Hearts" and "If You See Her, Say Hello") in Minnesota in December, giving the album a bit more spark. The musicians from the two sessions are different, but all the songs sound of a piece.

Critics like to make a big deal about Dylan having recently separated from his wife at the time the songs were written, but that fact adds nothing to one's appreciation of this material. In his book *Hard Rain*, Tim Riley makes a good point regarding narrow autobiographical interpretations: "The most banal way to read Dylan songs is to link them up with his life, as though he had no greater ambition than to record his autobiography . . . his songs inhabit personas."[96] Dylan, in the *Biograph* notes to "You're a Big Girl Now," is indignant about the matter:

> "You're a Big Girl Now" well, I read that this was sup-posed to be about my wife . . . I mean it couldn't be about anybody else but my wife, right? . . . I don't write confes-sional songs . . . well, actually I did write one once and it wasn't very good – it was a mistake to record it and I regret it . . . back there somewhere on maybe my third or fourth album.[97]

The song in question has to be "Ballad in Plain D," and the reason the song is such a failure is that it comes across as autobiographical and impersonal – people can't relate to the characters. Every listener can, in some way, identify with the personages in *Blood on the Tracks*, for Dylan is, in John Bauldie's words, "universalizing the feelings of love and loss."[98]

A stronger source of inspiration for the songs was an art teacher named Norman Raeben, under whom Dylan studied for a while in 1974.[99] Not much is known about this man, but, according to Dylan, "He taught you [about] putting your head and your mind and your eye together – to make you get down visually something which is actual . . . He looked into you and told you what you were." From Raeben, Dylan also learned how to write songs with "no sense of time," and how to make songs "like a painting where you can see the different parts but then you also see the whole of it." Indeed, the songs on *Blood on the Tracks* are not constrained by any specific time frame, and repeated listenings reveal separate, unique aspects of each song, without losing the entire picture.

Dylan said he worked to achieve these effects on "Tangled Up in Blue," and the song blends past and present so that each scene comes to life, beginning with the instantly identifiable opening sequence, in which the narrator wakes in the morning thinking about an old love:

> Early one mornin' the sun was shinin',
> I was layin' in bed
> Wond'rin' if she'd changed at all
> If her hair was still red.

This provides a backdrop to the narrator's musings; verse two shuffles forward to their separation, and verse three concerns his life after this woman (with a joke about having "a job in the great north woods" until "one day the ax just fell"), when she still figures quite prominently in his thoughts:

> I seen a lot of women
> But she never escaped my mind, and I just grew

Dylan juggles the time frame again in verse four, going back to where the opening lines of verse two leave off. The narrator recalls his first encounter with this woman, leading up to Dylan's eternal meditation on the force of great writing:

> And every one of them words rang true
> And glowed like burnin' coal

Pourin' off of every page.
Like it was written in my soul from me to you.

In the next verse, the protagonist moves in with the woman and her husband during a time when "There was music in the cafes at night / And revolution in the air" (possibly a reference to the 1960s). In the final verse, the time is later in the narrator's life, with him still thinking about this woman, trying to recapture a happier period. It's likely that he will never get to this woman, but the song strikes an emotional chord in listeners, showing a man's omnipresent memories of a lover who may have been the right person. In the song, Dylan blends past, present and future, as the different stages in the life of one man converge.

Cameron Crowe calls "Tangled Up in Blue" "one of [Dylan's] best story songs";[100] the same may be said for "Lily, Rosemary and the Jack of Hearts," a masterful, lengthy narrative that anticipates many of the songs on *Desire*. With a country beat and a western setting, "Lily, Rosemary and the Jack of Hearts" is the tale of a mysterious outlaw who comes into town, seduces the ladies, and leaves with a fortune, but not before Big Jim has been killed and Rosemary is set to be executed. Again, the element of memory comes to the forefront of the narrative: the song closes with Lily "thinkin' about the Jack of Hearts" and, presumably, wondering if she will ever see him again.

The stories of "Tangled Up in Blue" and "Lily, Rosemary and the Jack of Hearts" both tend to hinge on fate, a theme that becomes the focus of the encounter in "Simple Twist of Fate." It's unclear who this woman is: is she a long-time love, a more recent lover, a one-night stand, or a hooker? Tim Riley argues that she is a prostitute, and parts of the song lend credibility to that hypothesis (they check into a hotel, the narrator "Hunts her down by the waterfront docks where the sailors all come in").[101] But the romantic setting of the opening verse (the park) suggests new-found love, and the hotel may be strange because they aren't familiar with the area. The narrator's unsettling reaction to the woman's flight seems too deep for someone to experience over a hooker, implying that this may have been a lengthy relationship on the rocks and now finished (unless he's associating this woman with an old love, which might account for these feelings):

> He woke up, the room was bare
> He didn't see her anywhere.
> He told himself he didn't care, pushed the window open
>   wide,
> Felt an emptiness inside to which he just could not relate.

Oblivious of everything around him ("He hears the ticking of the clocks"), he goes looking for her, but his search proves futile. As in "Tangled Up in Blue," the narrator feels this is the woman for him, but fate intervenes.

On *At Budokan*, Dylan gives the conclusion new lyrics, suggesting more than just a one-off encounter (too bad the *Budokan* performance is irredeemably shabby). Dylan sings:

> People tell me it's a crime
> To remember her for too long a time.
> She should have caught me in my prime, she would have
>   stayed with me
> Instead of going back out to sea, leaving me to meditate
> Upon a simple twist of fate.

"If You See Her, Say Hello" is another song about a past love. Some writers have compared this to "Girl from the North Country," and although this is true to the extent that the lament is addressed to an unnamed companion, the milder reminiscences in the earlier song contrast quite strikingly with the narrator's agonized recollections in "If You See Her, Say Hello."[102] One cannot imagine Dylan singing "our separation . . . pierced me to the heart" in "Girl from the North Country." The overwhelming impression left by "If You See Her, Say Hello" is sorrow (indicated by the pain in Dylan's voice when he sings "And I've never gotten used to it, I've just learned to turn it off"), with just a tinge of bitterness: "If she's passin' back this way, I'm not that hard to find / Tell her she can look me up if she's got the time."

Still, the wounded party admits to some of his weaknesses: "Either I'm too sensitive or else I'm gettin' soft." This is something the cocky young narrator of Dylan's early years rarely did, and it is a measure of his development as a songwriter that many of these songs seem poignant and, at times, accepting. When Dylan sings "oh" in "You're a Big Girl Now," he taps into a panorama of human emotions. He gets the same effect by stretching certain words in "Simple Twist of Fate" (straight, relate, etc.).

Many of the themes and images in *Blood on the Tracks* coalesce in "You're A Big Girl Now." The mood vacillates between anguish and vague hope:

> I can change, I swear, oh
> See what you can do.
> I can make it through,
> You can make it too.

The metaphor of the rain figures most prominently in "You're a Big Girl Now," as Dylan builds on its use in "Tangled Up in Blue," "Buckets of Rain" and "Shelter from the Storm." The narrator in "You're a Big Girl Now" begins by using a dichotomy of the elements as an example of the extremes in the feelings of him and his ex-lover: "And I'm back in the rain, oh, / And you are on dry land." One writer saw Dylan as possessing a "Shakespearean sense of rain"; Dylan uses rain to indicate a tremendous emotional shift, a change that can be either positive (as in "Buckets of Rain," where it seems to offer the promise of renewal) or negative (as in "You're a Big Girl Now").[103]

In "Shelter from the Storm," the narrator gains a temporary respite from the emotional and physical maelstrom he finds himself in. This quiet, driven acoustic song has an almost otherworldly setting, at times resembling a scene from another era (a lonely, desolate plain).

The wanderer in "Shelter from the Storm" is truly an Everyman figure (as are the other characters in the album), a battered, scarred man who is ultimately saved. In verse four, the narrator enumerates a Job-like series of disasters:

> I was burned out from exhaustion, buried in the hail,
> Poisoned in the bushes an' blown out on the trail,
> Hunted like a crocodile, ravaged in the corn.

He associates his struggles with those of Christ's ("She walked up to me so gracefully and took my crown of thorns"; "In a little hilltop village, they gambled for my clothes"). Dylan follows this line with a chilling twist: "I bargained for salvation an' she [not "they"] give me a lethal dose." The implication is that she lowers the relationship on a spiritual level, that he expected her to offer more than shelter, and her rejection is somehow sinful.

Nevertheless, his appreciation for her actions is genuine, and he concludes with a wish that he could do things differently.

The narrator's experiences have resigned him to fate: "nothing really matters much, it's doom alone that counts." This is the theme of "Idiot Wind," eight minutes of vehemence, with Dylan's singing at its angriest, and organ work that gives Dylan's words added vengeance.

Dylan begins the song with a swipe at his critics, likening the rumors the press plants to a far-fetched story about shooting "a man named Gray," stealing his wife, and inheriting a fortune when she dies. Dylan then goes on to scoff at those who considered him "washed up": "Even you, yesterday you had to ask me where it was at, / I couldn't believe after all these years, you didn't know me any better than that." "You had to ask me where it was at" recalls the bewildered journalist in "Ballad of a Thin Man," who asks "'Is this where it is?'" But even a superstar as cool as Dylan knows the demands of being a public figure can be staggering at times: "I haven't known peace and quiet for so long I can't remember what it's like."

The title for the album comes from verse seven in "Idiot Wind": "Down the highway, down the tracks, down the road to ecstasy." The final verse suggests a victory (albeit a hollow one), as the narrator achieves freedom through catharsis:

> I been double-crossed now for the very last time and now
>   I'm finally free,
> I kissed goodbye the howling beast on the borderline
>   which separated you from me.

But the song encompasses so much more than just a broken relationship. "Idiot Wind" functions as a postlude to an era, a time when Vietnam had been lost and Nixon's resignation had snuffed out the waning idealism of the 1960s ("Idiot wind, blowing like a circle around my skull, / From the Grand Coulee Dam to the Capitol"). For, a dozen years later, the answer is still blowin' in the wind.

As a source for the song, Macbeth's soliloquy, which depicts life as "a tale / Told by an idiot, full of sound and fury / Signifying nothing,"[104] has been invoked. This derivation is clearly apparent in the final chorus, as Dylan switches from "you" to "we," making the attack less personal and more universal.

Not all the material on *Blood on the Tracks* is as damning as "Idiot Wind." The up-tempo "You're Gonna Make Me Lonesome When You Go," with its breezy harmonica introduction, is not as somber as its title might suggest. Sung in a spirit reminiscent of "You Ain't Goin' Nowhere" (the *Greatest Hits: Volume II* version), this is another Dylan song wherein the narrator links his love with nature: "Flowers on the hillside, bloomin' crazy, / Crickets talkin' back and forth in rhyme, / Blue river runnin' slow and lazy." The song culminates in a farewell pledge to cherish the memories:

> But I'll see you in the sky above,
> In the tall grass, in the ones I love.

The album's final song, "Buckets of Rain," seems conciliatory in tone. The simple, brief lines help *Blood on the Tracks* end on a positive note, and there is even a bit of imagistic language – "Little red wagon / Little red bike" – that resembles William Carlos Williams' famous poem "The Red Wheelbarrow." The concluding words are soothing:

> Life is sad
> Life is a bust
> All ya can do is do what you must.
> You do what you must do and ya do it well.

Commenting on the thematic unity of *Blood on the Tracks*, Dylan said of the songs: "you've got yesterday, today and tomorrow all in the same room";[105] on the album, Dylan captures how experiences recur in man's consciousness and shape the present and future actions of an individual. These are songs haunted by the past.

Dylan's intention to create songs that are like paintings is an attempt to put the various stages of life on a canvas, so each part becomes important. And, in the process, these songs bring out the feelings people have as they live these experiences.

On *Blood on the Tracks*, Dylan realized everything he had set out to accomplish with the album, making the record one of his greatest achievements.

DESIRE

RELEASED: JANUARY 1976

As follow-ups go, *Desire* is to *Blood on the Tracks* what *The Basement Tapes* and *John Wesley Harding* are to *Blonde on Blonde*: very different lyrically and musically from its predecessor, but a masterpiece in its own right. Many of the songs on *Desire* are stories, skillfully crafted narratives that reveal Dylan's command of the ballad form. *Desire* also marked the first time Dylan had done extensive writing with a collaborator. Jacques Levy had frequently worked with Roger McGuinn, and, liking their material, Dylan suggested to Levy that they do some writing together. According to Levy, the results were impressive: "It was just extraordinary, the two of us started to get hot together . . . we'd finally got to a point where we both recognized what the right idea was and what the right words were and whether it came from him or me it doesn't make a difference."[106] On the album, only "One More Cup of Coffee (Valley Below)" and "Sara" were written by Dylan alone.

With *Desire*, Dylan began to experiment with a different musical style. Scarlet Rivera's exquisite violin playing makes the album unique in Dylan's catalogue, and it gives *Desire* a big band sound, despite featuring only Rivera, Rob Stoner on bass, Howie Wyeth on drums and Dylan on guitar and harmonica (although other musicians play on "Romance in Durango" and "Hurricane"). Emmylou Harris adds some pleasant harmonies throughout, and, after *Desire*, Dylan uses female backup singers regularly (but without the same degree of success). The majority of the songs were recorded in one take, with the music as spontaneous as on the Dylan albums of the 1960s. On the playful "Mozambique," Wyeth's backdoor drum roll (Rob Stoner told Bob Spitz that Wyeth hadn't realized Dylan was doing a take) is proof of this spontaneity.[107]

The anguish that rings throughout *Blood on the Tracks* has echoes in *Desire*, but *Desire*, with one exception, deals less with the sense of loss and more with devotion. "Mozambique" seems almost flippant on the page, but Dylan avoids doggerel by playing off Harris' backing, giving the lyrics a certain alluring simplicity. (The fact that the country drifted into civil war not long after the song's release makes "Mozambique" unintentionally ironic).

"Isis" and "One More Cup of Coffee" both praise impenetrable figures. In "Isis," the narrator's machismo ("As we rode through the canyons, through the devilish cold, / I was thinkin' about Isis, how she thought I was so reckless") inhibits his true feelings for his bride, which come forth in the final verse, but only after his quest for material possessions fails:

Isis, oh, Isis, you mystical child.
What drives me to you is what drives me insane.

As in "Isis," the woman in "One More Cup of Coffee" (a gypsy) possesses a certain hold over the narrator. Her heart "is like an ocean / Mysterious and dark," and she ignores her suitor:

> But I don't sense affection
> No gratitude or love
> Your loyalty is not to me
> But to the stars above.

These two songs have parallels to "She Belongs to Me" and "Love Minus Zero / No Limit."

In "Romance in Durango," the woman is the devoted heroine, even taking the hombre's gun while he lies dying.

"Oh, Sister" emphasizes reincarnation and the need for faith, making *Slow Train Coming* seem like the logical extension of these feelings:

> We grew up together
> From the cradle to the grave
> We died and were reborn
> And then mysteriously saved.

When Dylan does attempt to recapture the greatness of *Blood on the Track*," love songs, the result is somewhat disappointing. "Sara" is intermittently mundane, lacking the restraint that Dylan so often shows when he pays homage to females.

"Sara" is most effective as a tableau, as in verse five (which offers a hint of mysticism):

> How did I meet you? I don't know.
> A messenger sent me in a tropical storm.
> You were there in the winter, moonlight on the snow
> And on Lily Pond Lane when the weather was warm.

One of Dylan's foremost strengths as a songwriter is in his use of setting. In *Rolling Thunder Logbook*, Sam Shepard talks about this aspect of Dylan's art:

> One thing that gets me about Dylan's songs is how they conjure up images, whole scenes that are being played out in full color as you listen. He's an instant film-maker. Probably not the same scenes occur in the same way to everyone listening to the same song, but I'd like to know if anyone sees the same small, rainy green park and the same bench and the same yellow light and the same pair of people as I do all coming from "A Simple Twist of Fate." Or the same beach in "Sara" or the same bar in "Hurricane" or the same cabin in "Hollis Brown" or the same window in "It Ain't Me, Babe" or the same table and the same ashtray in "Hattie Carroll" or the same valley in "One More Cup of Coffee."[108]

Unsurprisingly, Dylan was forced to defend the use of his wife's name in the song. In a 1978 *Rolling Stone* interview, Dylan danced around the question of the song's literalness:

> . . . when people say 'Sara' was written for 'his wife Sara' – it doesn't necessarily have to be about her just because my wife's name happened to be Sara. Anyway, was it the real Sara or the Sara in the dream? I still don't know.[109]

Critics further questioned Dylan's claims in "Sara" that he wrote "Sad-Eyed Lady of the Lowlands" in the Chelsea Hotel (he is said to have written the song in Nashville while recording *Blonde on Blonde*), and that he had overcome his drug problems at this time.[110]

The controversy engendered by "Sara" is minor compared to the brouhaha "Hurricane" and "Joey" touched off.[111] "Hurricane" is based on the case of black boxer Rubin

"Hurricane" Carter, who had been imprisoned in 1967 for the murder of three whites in a bar in Paterson, New Jersey. Dylan visited Carter in prison, wrote a song about him, and staged two benefit concerts for him during the Rolling Thunder Revue, helping lead to an unsuccessful retrial in 1976 (Carter was freed in 1985 and the charges were dismissed).

Sticking up for those accused of crimes invariably smacks of cliquishness; nonetheless, Dylan's sympathy for Carter is not feigned, as some have charged (otherwise, why would Dylan go to so much trouble for Carter?). "Hurricane" is certainly involving, although Dylan tends to tailor the story to suit his purposes (as he had with his tale of armed robber George Jackson, which conveniently neglects to mention that Jackson was shot during a bungled prison escape). In "Hurricane," the dialogue between the police and Arthur Dexter Bradley seems like the product of Dylan's imagination. Dylan and Levy slip up slightly in verses four and five, when one of the dying victims says Carter "'Ain't the guy!,'" yet the preceding verse states that "this man could hardly see."

Regardless of the controversial nature of the lyrics, "Hurricane" is an incredible musical performance, with Dylan doing some topnotch singing, Wyeth's drumming playing off Dylan's vocal tricks, and the guitar strumming between the lines adding to the action as the drama unfolds.

"Joey" deals with even touchier subject matter. Popular culture has always exercised a certain fascination for legendary hoodlums: Billy the Kid, John Wesley Hardin, Pretty Boy Floyd, Jesse James, Bonnie and Clyde: their lives have been adapted from their viciousness into a bastardized version of the Robin Hood saga, so the line between fact and fiction becomes blurred. Joey Gallo should be so lucky to earn such mythopoeic immortality.

Along these lines, Dylan is writing about a contemporary bad guy. Gallo was the leader of one of New York's crime families; he was reportedly responsible for the deaths of at least two adversaries, and he spent nine years in prison for extortion. Like George Jackson and, years later, Mumia Abu-Jamal, Gallo garnered sympathy from the literati by passing himself off as a "cultured" criminal victimized by "The System." In "Joey," Dylan tries to make Gallo seem like a gentleman who was an unwilling participant in his henchmen's misdeeds. This misplaced sentimentality leads to some puzzling lyrics: "There was talk they killed their rivals, but the truth was far from that" – crime boss Albert Anastasia was snuffed out by Gallo, and Gallo may have been behind the killing of mafioso Joe Colombo; "It always seemed they got caught between the mob and the men in blue" – Gallo's gang *was* part of the mob; and verse five in its entirety (deciding not to kill hostages hardly gives cause for admiration). When critics learned of Gallo's less-than-angelic past, they unloaded on Dylan, as slaters like Lester Bangs had strong words about the song (although, in this case, Bangs also appeared to have some sort of personal vendetta against Dylan).[112]

But only Bob Dylan could salvage a song about a nefarious gangster. On the strength of the performance, "Joey" cannot easily be dismissed. Dylan's singing and Rivera's violin playing give the song a sense of dignity, and the chorus acquires a mournfulness as Dylan and Harris duet. And for all of the song's lyrical trappings, the climax is rendered with a touch of drama:

> One day they blew him down in a clam bar in New York
> He could see it comin' through the door as he lifted up his fork.
> He pushed the table over to protect his family

Then he staggered out into the streets of Little Italy.

As with "Isis," "Hurricane," "Romance in Durango" and "Black Diamond Bay," "Joey" is a narrative with an effortless flow. Allen Ginsberg calls "Black Diamond Bay" "a short novel in verse," and his phrase may be applied to the aforementioned songs.[113] The construction of "Black Diamond Bay," in particular, is perfect, as individual calamities build up to one giant catastrophe at the end.

The real greatness of *Desire* lies in the execution of these narratives, as Dylan and the band give the songs a musical backdrop that is altogether appropriate (the pulse of "Hurricane"; the south-of-the-border feel of "Romance in Durango"; the passion of "Sara"). In fact, the performances are so good that *Desire* overcomes moments of questionable taste and emerges as one of Dylan's best records.

HARD RAIN

RELEASED: SEPTEMBER 1976

Released as a souvenir of the Rolling Thunder Revue, *Hard Rain* is culled from two of the final shows on the tour (Fort Worth, Texas and Fort Collins, Colorado). Five of the tracks are from the Colorado show, which was taped for a television special by the same name.

The band's core are holdovers from *Desire*, with a few more guitarists (including Mick Ronson, who had played with David Bowie) and some piano work by Howie Wyeth and T-Bone Burnett.

Rob Stoner, who plays bass on the songs, calls *Hard Rain* "an extraordinary snapshot – like a punk record or something. It's got such energy and such anger."[114] *Hard Rain* is a remarkable live album; parts of it are as wild and as daring as anything from the 1966 tour, a grand symphony of sound that uncovers new layers of meaning in these songs.

An interesting aspect of the album is how well the songs fit together: they sound as if they were written specifically for this record. Dylan's penchant for reworking his songs results in new, exciting versions of standards like "Maggie's Farm" and "Lay, Lady, Lay," and a different approach to the *Blood on the Tracks* material.

Often, individual instrumental parts move to the forefront. The introductions to these songs are fabulous: the strumming that precedes "Maggie's Farm," "One Too Many Mornings," "I Threw It All Away" and "Idiot Wind" is impressive, and the opening sequences to "Stuck Inside of Mobile with the Memphis Blues Again" and "Shelter from the Storm" are absolute classics. The guitar intro to "Stuck Inside of Mobile" has a dream-like quality to it, and the awe-inspiring blend of guitars that inaugurates "Shelter from the Storm" stands as one of the single greatest instrumental moments on a Dylan record. Unfortunately, the compact disc version of *Hard Rain* drowns out many of these introductions with unnecessary crowd noise. Usually, this is merely a minor flaw, but the omission of the guitar note that opens "Shelter from the Storm" is a frustrating oversight. This music deserves to stand on its own, and, for that reason, the lp and cassette versions of *Hard Rain* are preferable to the compact disc.

As a singer, Dylan is in complete command, bending and stretching words and notes. As with the best Dylan records, the musicians interact with Dylan with breathtaking adroitness. For instance, before the last line of each verse in "Maggie's Farm," Dylan pauses, plucks his guitar a bit, and then comes charging back in with the band. In "One Too Many Mornings," he holds the word "laid," working with

Scarlet Rivera's violin. On "Oh, Sister," Dylan sounds delirious when he sings the bridge, letting the word "saved" echo into silence before the guitar chords chime in. The musicians are with Dylan all the way, and, as Paul Williams observed, their technique "transforms every sound into a grace note."[115] The stop-start pauses throughout the song are there for strategic effect: they keep the band alert and ready for any sudden shift in momentum.

As noted, the flexibility of these arrangements imparts new meaning to the lyrics. "One Too Many Mornings" includes the coda "I've no right to be here / If you've no right to stay / Until we're both one too many mornings / An' a thousand miles away," emphasizing the finality of the relationship. Dylan omits the middle section of "Stuck Inside of Mobile," but his delivery of the chorus is brilliant vocal work, amplifying the song's sense of desperation. The lead-up to "Oh, Sister" is a funny moment: drunks in the audience holler at Dylan to do "Lay, Lady, Lay"; instead, he delivers a moving take of "Oh, Sister" and follows, with trademark Dylan slyness, with a boisterous, rewritten version of "Lay, Lady, Lay." Steven Soles and Rob Stoner help out vocally, and Dylan replaces the suavities of the original lyrics with an unabashed pick-up line: "Forget this dance, let's go upstairs / Let's take a chance, who really cares."

Hard Rain reaches its zenith with an incredible version of "Shelter from the Storm," featuring a guitar riff that explodes between verses. On *Blood on the Tracks,* Dylan sings the song like a man thankful for the refuge he has found. Here, the delivery is of someone furious about everything he has gone through to get to this point, and he turns away from this woman and blasts his tormentors. Dylan sings "they" instead of "she" in the line about receiving "a lethal dose," thereby strengthening the Christ analogy. Despite leaving out verses two and eight, verse six comes after verse nine, an intelligent bit of sequencing.

"I Threw It All Away" sounds as new as a *Desire* song, and "You're a Big Girl Now" generates as much pain as the *Blood on the Tracks* take. In "Idiot Wind," Dylan takes the feelings (hostility/ disgust) of the *Blood on the Tracks* version to " a manically gleeful, cathartic extreme" (as John Bauldie wrote).[116] Several of the rewrites are important: "One day you'll be in the ditch" becomes the even more savage "in the grave"; "Visions of your chestnut mare" is now the rancorous "Visions of your smoking tongue"; and "I been double-crossed now for the very last time and now I'm finally free" emerges as "now I finally see" (i.e. the true nature of this woman). And Dylan's singing on this track is unparalleled.

"Idiot Wind" is a fitting closer to this rewarding album. Sadly, *Hard Rain* has not been fully appreciated, and it probably never will be. As Paul Williams emphasized (in his book *Performing Artist: The Middle Years*), the reasons people don't like this album are: they expect these songs to sound a certain way, they are upset because certain performances were not included on the album, they don't listen to it enough, and, one might add, they expect these performances to be polished (as if Dylan has ever wanted to deliver pat arrangements).[117]

Full of inventive singing and bold music, *Hard Rain* captures the Rolling Thunder Revue in all its ragin' glory.

CONCLUSION

The years 1974-76 saw Dylan regain the level of popularity he had sustained during the 1960s. *Planet Waves*, although inferior to *Blood on the Tracks* and *Desire*, was his first complete album of original songs since *New Morning (Pat*

Garrett & Billy the Kid being primarily instrumental), and it reached number one in America. The 1974 tour with The Band received rapturous acclaim from fans and the press, bringing Dylan back to the forefront of popular music. *Blood on the Tracks* did even better: the critics hauled out the inevitable cliché "Dylan's best album since *Blonde on Blonde*" (the cliché is now "Dylan's best album since *Blood on the Tracks*"), and many selected it as album of the year. Upon the album's release, *Rolling Stone* devoted their entire reviews section to the record, printing a hodgepodge of comments (some negative) from rock critics throughout the country, and two lengthy essays by Jon Landau and Jonathan Cott, both of which wound up having next to nothing to do with the album.[118] *The Basement Tapes* came out in June 1975 and was enthusiastically received, and *Desire*, which went on to become Dylan's biggest selling album, achieved the rare feat of reaching number one on both sides of the Atlantic. Sandwiched between the release of *Desire*, the Rolling Thunder tours garnered more praise. When the second part of the Rolling Thunder Revue ended in May 1976, Dylan had successfully completed nearly three years of creative activity. Following the tour, Dylan dropped out of public view (save for a closing performance with The Band at The Last Waltz in November), not returning until 1978, another hectic year. Since 1974-76, Dylan has not yet enjoyed the critical and commercial success of these years.

Dylan's failed attempt at filmmaking, *Renaldo & Clara*, comes out of the Rolling Thunder period. At nearly four hours, the movie is a difficult viewing experience, mainly because the editing is horrendously choppy, and because the people involved are musicians, not actors. The difference in quality between the music (the concert footage is outstanding, and the accompanying music to the scenes is often fascinating, notably an odd yet gorgeous rendition of "People Get Ready," part of "Sad-Eyed Lady," and a wonderful performance of "One Too Many Mornings") and the dramatic sequences is immeasurable. Many of the film's scenes – Ronnie Hawkins seducing a groupie; Steven Soles berating Ronee Blakley; Clara (Sara Dylan) and Renaldo (Dylan) fondling on a bed while Joan Baez watches – are not merely bad, they're vulgar. Even when Dylan's intentions seem modest, as in the group's visit to an Indian village, or a sing-along with an elderly lady, things fall apart quickly: the former becomes a "God amongst the common man" scenario; in the latter, Baez's feigned enthusiasm for the crone's singing exposes the incident's superficiality, and, in an unbelievably tasteless scene, the woman tries to hawk copies of a tape she made.

Dylan seems to have headed into this project unaware of the complexities of putting a movie together. Shooting dozens of hours of film is one thing; trying to form it into a coherent whole is quite another. Dylan's cut-and-paste approach means that he fills the movie with references to himself, all the while trying to give the appearance that he's making an updated *Don't Look Back*: condescension masquerading as hipsterism. *Renaldo & Clara* is like one long improvisation that only Dylan and his entourage (or maybe just Dylan himself) are privy to. The film remains a hollow memento of the Rolling Thunder Revue.

PART VII

JOURNEY THROUGH DARK HEAT

STREET LEGAL

RELEASED: JUNE 1978; REMIXED AND RE-RELEASED JULY 1999

Street Legal is, in Jonathan Cott's words, "one of Dylan's most passionate, questing and questioning records."[119] The songs delve gloomily into man's consciousness: Dylan's dark night of the soul.[120] The lyrics are among the most complex and fascinating that Dylan has ever written.

For the album, Dylan chose a sound close to what the lyrics were trying to convey: raw, edgy, nervy music that demands a lot of the listener. The sound is full band: three guitars, drums, bass, keyboards, percussion, saxophone, violin, mandolin and a trio of female voices; aiming at an *Exile on Main Street*-style blend but coming up short. The music gets a bit muddy at times, and although Dylan's voice is strong, he often doesn't enunciate clearly, slurring words. On the whole, however, the arrangements work, and it's clear that Dylan structured the music to fit the difficult lyrics.

In 1999, Dylan sanctioned a remix of the album. The resulting sound is sharper and louder, bristling with an energy that shames the original mix. Ian Wallace's drums are more pronounced, "Changing of the Guards" gets a new intro and an extra forty-five seconds, there is more separation among the instruments, and Dylan's vocals have a clarity previously absent. It is worth buying, and worth reconsidering *Street Legal* in this context.

"Señor (Tales of Yankee Power)" is the most agreeable track on the original mix, a restrained performance with a crisper sound than the other cuts, which might explain why it's the only song from these sessions to appear on *Biograph*. An overt political statement, "Señor" is part of Dylan's recurring theme of a directionless America. The opening verse queries post-Vietnam America as to the course it will take:

> Señor, señor, can you tell me where we're headin'?
> Lincoln County Road or Armageddon?

In verse two, the narrator wonders where democracy is hiding, and he later senses the emergence of the Far East into the picture ("I can . . . smell the tail of the dragon"). The bridging verses are somewhat confusing, but the first is almost a throwback to "As I Went Out One Morning," and the second refers to the futility of Vietnam and the broken dreams of the soldiers. The final verse makes reference to Jesus' repudiation of the moneychangers, and shows the narrator's utter confusion:

> Señor, señor, let's overturn these tables,
> Disconnect these cables.
> This place don't make sense to me no more.

Likewise, "New Pony," a searing blues number, has a certain air of despondency about it, except here it's a witchy woman who's giving the narrator trouble. The pony and the woman are linked metaphorically, and the narrator sees their fates as intertwined. Nevertheless, an attraction lingers, and temptation overcomes the singer:

> Well, come over here pony, I, I wanna climb up one time
>   on you
> You're so nasty and you're so bad
> But I swear I love you, yes I do.

The other songs on the album that deal with relationships all tend towards ambivalent feelings. "Baby, Stop Crying," "Is Your Love in Vain?," "True Love Tends to Forget" and "We Better Talk this Over" are infused with a pessimism that dampens the narrator's pleading. Many of the lines in these songs are despairing ("Go get me my pistol, babe, / Honey, I can't tell right from wrong"; "Every day of the year's like playin' Russian roulette"; "Eventually we'll hang ourselves on all this tangled rope"). Some writers interpreted parts of *Street Legal* as reflecting a streak of misogyny, and some lines are certainly provocative.[121] On "Is Your Love in Vain?," the narrator questions whether the woman's affection is sincere or fake: "Do you love me, or are you just extending good-will?" The manner in which Dylan bleated out the line "Can you cook and sew, make flowers grow[?]" had feminists furious; Dylan was awkwardly saying that a woman should offer a man comfort and support. Despite his skepticism, the narrator can't help but give in to the woman: "All right, I'll take a chance, I will fall in love with you." "We Better Talk This Over" is a gruff farewell, but the narrator does emerge as a sympathetic character; his expression of dismay and anger is more genuine than the self-pitying musing that spoils "Is Your Love in Vain?"

The cornerstones of this album are "Changing of the Guards," "No Time to Think" and "Where Are You Tonight? (Journey Through Dark Heat)." All three have an apocalyptic fervor and are as harrowing as anything Dylan has ever written. The band can't quite pull off the tricky arrangement of "No Time to Think" (on both mixes), but the song captures the state of a man on the brink. Life and death intermingle in the song, and the word play stresses how everything becomes jumbled in this condition. The references to Judas' betrayal ("In the Federal City you been blown and shown pity, / In secret, for pieces of change"; "Betrayed by a kiss on a cool night of bliss") imply that the song's protagonist has been deceived, as revealed in verse seven:

> Your conscience betrayed you when some tyrant waylaid
>   you
> Where the lion lies down with the lamb.
> I'd have paid the traitor and killed him much later
> But that's just the way that I am.

Parts of the song seem directly connected to "Changing of the Guards," especially verses three ("The empress attracts you") and fifteen ("The bridge that you travel on goes to the Babylon girl / With the rose in her hair"). "Changing of the Guards" is just as challenging as "No Time to Think," but it holds up better musically, with some striking guitar embellishments and a neat fade-in.

"Changing of the Guards" incorporates a vision of warfare and destruction. Dylan once said that *Street Legal* "has to do with an illusion of time," and this is shown particularly in a song like "Changing of the Guards," wherein past, present and future seem to become one.[122] The opening verse seems medieval in nature, as a shepherd laments sixteen years of warfare. In the following verses, a strange woman appears, desired by both the narrator and the captain. Verse four contains the sinister lines, "I seen her on the stairs and I couldn't help but follow, / Follow her down past the fountain where they lifted her veil." Dylan is quoted as saying, "Once you see what's under the veil, what happens to you? You die, don't you? Or go blind."[123] This appears to set the stage for the tumult that follows.

In verses five and six, the narrator witnesses the effects of the battle ("I rode past destruction in the ditches") on "the endless road." In the cataclysmic finale, religious fervor creeps into the lyrics: "Eden is burning, either get ready for elimination / Or else your hearts must have the courage for the changing of the guards."

The struggle between good and evil is shown on a more personal level in "Where Are You Tonight?": "I fought with my twin, that enemy within, 'til both of us fell by the way." In the penultimate verse, the narrator gives in to temptation, and his subsequent violent reaction shows his desperation:

> I bit into the root of forbidden fruit with the juice
>   running down my leg.
> Then I dealt with your boss, who'd never known about
>   loss and who always was too proud to beg.

In the gut-wrenching conclusion, the narrator finds salvation:

> There's a new day at dawn and I've finally arrived.
> If I'm there in the morning, baby, you'll know I've
>   survived,
> I can't believe it, I can't believe I'm alive,
> But without you it doesn't seem right.

Dylan's move into evangelical Christianity makes more sense in the context of these songs. The final verse in "Where Are You Tonight?" speaks of redemption, and the opening line

("There's a long-distance train rolling through the rain")
foreshadows *Slow Train Coming*. "Where Are You Tonight?" is the story of a man rescued from despair. In
"Changing of the Guards," Dylan spurns his critics and
prepares for his own personal changing of the guards:

> Gentlemen, he said,
> I don't need your organization, I've shined your shoes,
> I've moved your mountains and marked your cards . . .
> . . . your hearts must have the courage for the changing
>   of the guards.

BOB DYLAN AT BUDOKAN

RECORDED: FEBRUARY 28, MARCH 1, 1978

RELEASED IN AMERICA: APRIL 1979 (RELEASED IN JAPAN IN
NOVEMBER 1978)

Originally intended to be a Japanese-only release, *Bob Dylan
at Budokan* was eventually issued in America in April 1979,
after the album had been extensively bootlegged. All tracks
come from the February 28 and March 1 shows in Tokyo,
and, because Dylan and the band were still trying to find
their footing at these early shows, the record is a poor
souvenir of the 1978 world tour.

Most of the songs have been radically altered, and,
judging by the work of the band, Dylan was still developing
the arrangements. The band, very close to the one that did a
decent job with the tough *Street Legal* songs, sounds unex-
cited, as if they were backing a lounge singer and not Bob
Dylan. Songs such as "Ballad of a Thin Man," "Shelter from
the Storm" and "Just Like a Woman" are insufferably dull.
Others get bizarre new arrangements: "Don't Think Twice,
It's All Right" and "Knockin' on Heaven's Door" done

reggae; "Blowin' in the Wind" as a lullaby; "It's Alright, Ma (I'm Only Bleeding)" as mind-numbing hard rock. Occasionally, Dylan and the band are out of synch, as is the case with "The Times They Are A-Changin'" and "Like a Rolling Stone." The low point of the album is an unlistenable rewrite of "Going, Going, Gone." Steve Douglas' flute, saxophone and recorder playing doesn't help matters; Paul Williams said Douglas "sounds as though he's just had his creativity squelched by his boss and decided to get back at him by playing the most hackneyed, irritating little riffs he could come up with."[124]

Dylan's singing is frequently apathetic. He delivers almost every song the same way, which tends to rob songs such as "Simple Twist of Fate," "Oh, Sister" and "I Shall Be Released" of their emotion.

Worse is the insincere patter between songs. Many critics accused Dylan of "going Vegas" with this tour, and although, in reality, Dylan was experimenting with a different sound (as Richard Williams observed), some of the comments Dylan makes between songs lend credibility to the "Vegas" theory.[125] For instance, he introduces "Simple Twist of Fate" as "a simple love story. Happened to me." And he spoils "The Times They Are A-Changin'" before the song even starts, responding to the audience's request for an encore by saying, "You're so very kind, you really are. We'll play you this song. I wrote this about fifteen years ago. It still means a lot to me. I know it means a lot to you too."

At Budokan does have its moments: the bright harmonica playing as the introduction to "Love Minus Zero / No Limit"; the conga sound in "One More Cup of Coffee (Valley Below)"; the violin in "All Along the Watchtower"; and a slow version of "I Want You." Still, this overpriced double album is way too long (one hundred minutes) to sustain the interest of most listeners, and the majority of the

songs are available in superior form on *Before the Flood* and
Hard Rain.

CONCLUSION

After his divorce in 1977, Dylan released the miserable
Renaldo & Clara in January 1978. The film was reviled by
critics and saw only limited theatrical distribution.

Frustrated by the reaction to *Renaldo & Clara*, Dylan hit
the road in 1978 as a relief from his critics and his domestic
troubles. The shows in England were greeted with hysteria
by fans and the press; the American critics, still sour towards
Dylan after *Renaldo & Clara*, disliked the concerts and gave
Street Legal a critical drubbing.

As the tour was winding to a close, Dylan was fighting
the flu and was generally unhappy.[126] He decided his life
needed a change.

PART VIII

SIGN ON THE CROSS

SLOW TRAIN COMING

RELEASED: AUGUST 1979

By April 1979, Bob Dylan, born a Jew, had fully embraced Christianity.[127] The songs on *Street Legal* suggested the possibility of renewal through faith, and Dylan received spiritual encouragement throughout 1978 from band members David Mansfield, Steven Soles and Helena Springs, and from his girlfriend, Mary Alice Artes. During a show in San Diego in November 1978, someone tossed a silver cross on stage, and Dylan picked it up. A couple of days later, while examining the cross in his hotel room in Arizona, Dylan said that he sensed Jesus Christ's presence. Inspired by the experience, Dylan enrolled in Bible school in California in early 1979. In April, he wrote the songs for *Slow Train Coming* (except for "Do Right to Me, Baby," which he had penned in December) and recorded the album in May.

The new album came as a profound shock to everyone. Some of the songs relied heavily on the Bible, and many were wrathful denunciations of America's spiritual and political position. Others had an Old Testament apocalyptic slant to them. The rest were personal testaments.

To get his beliefs across, Dylan worked with producer Jerry Wexler to create a smooth, rhythm and blues-style album. With Mark Knopfler on guitar and Pick Withers on drums, *Slow Train Coming* has a nice, easy-listening sound to it that makes the often dour lyrics more palatable. Dylan's voice sounds sharper than it had in 1978, and "Gotta Serve Somebody" earned Dylan a Grammy award for Best Male Vocal (incredulously, his first Grammy – which speaks volumes about the irrelevance of the Grammy Awards in the 1960s and 1970s, during which numerous artists, including The Rolling Stones, never won a Grammy).

Because of the clean production, the first side of *Slow Train Coming* sizzles. "Gotta Serve Somebody" isn't a strong song lyrically, but the drums, organ and female chorus work well with Dylan's singing. In "I Believe in You," the guitar chords and gentle instrumental breaks complement Dylan's heartfelt, devotional vocal performance.

"Precious Angel" and "Slow Train" form the heart of this album; Ron Rosenbaum said that they "would be classic Dylan songs even if they were about the Dalai Lama."[128] Knopfler plays some hot guitar chords on the title track, and Barry Beckett's keyboard work is first-rate.

"Slow Train" is a contemporary attack on America. In verse three, Dylan decries foreign control of the country; America is losing its way as greed becomes the prime motivator in society. The line about "Sheiks walkin' around like kings, wearing fancy jewels and nose rings" has more to do with avarice than Zionism. The next verse continues on the theme of "the home of the brave" selling itself out. In verse six, Dylan wonders why so many people are starving in the world with the resources available to distribute food, and he laments the corruption of certain ideals:

> People starving and thirsting, grain elevators are bursting
> They talk about a life of brotherly love, show me
>   someone who knows how to live it.

Dylan also decries what he views as the failing spiritual values of America. Verse five adopts the "devil as man of peace," metaphor as a condemnation of hypocrites. Meanwhile, the slow train – the second coming – is "up around the bend."

The chorus to "Precious Angel" could be sung by a church choir, but the lyrics are more frightening than those to "Slow Train." When Dylan rails against non-believers in verse three, he incorporates a terrifying vision of the end:

> Can they imagine the darkness that will fall from on high
> When men will beg God to kill them and they won't be
>   able to die?

Verse six has an epic sweep to it, encompassing the Exodus of the Jews from Egypt and the Last Judgment:

> But there's violence in the eyes, girl, so let us not be
>   enticed
> On the way out of Egypt, through Ethiopia, to the
>   judgment hall of Christ.

To hear Dylan pronounce the word "Christ," there can be little doubt of his commitment.

Parts of the song don't measure up lyrically to the above lines: verse four downplays other religions and attacks women who don't give their husbands spiritual guidance, and for those listeners who weren't going to church on a regular basis, Dylan kindly reminded them that "Ya either got faith or ya got unbelief and there ain't no neutral ground." The discomforting aspect of the last line is that, as Rosenbaum implied in his article about the album, it shows a hint of "cult brainwashings."[129] The same may be said of "Gotta Serve Somebody," as Dylan makes the only choice between the devil and the Lord – saying, in truth, that there is no choice. In the single "Trouble in Mind," Dylan voices strange sentiments, attacking those who "Put their faith in their possessions, in their jobs or their wives." Since when is putting faith in one's wife a repudiation of one's religious beliefs? And since when does one have to choose between one's wife and one's faith? Rigid fundamentalists can be intolerant of those who don't ascribe to their beliefs, and they often adopt the stance that a person is sinful unless he or she belongs to their sect (the "brainwashing" that Rosenbaum speaks of). Greil Marcus compared Dylan to the religious fanatics who hector people at airports.[130] Looking at the aforementioned lyrics, it's not hard to see why many people took umbrage at the brand of Christianity propounded by Dylan on *Slow Train Coming.*

The key problem with this album, though, isn't lyrics like these, the trouble is that Dylan's slow train runs out of steam by side two. With the exception of "When He Returns," these songs are nowhere near as impressive musically as their counterparts. The arrangements to "Gonna Change My Way of Thinking," "Do Right to Me, Baby (Do Unto Others)" and "When You Gonna Wake Up?" are similar, nearly interchangeable. These songs are polished but tiresome. Only the horns on "When You Gonna Wake Up?" add some variety.

The lyrics themselves are weak: "When You Gonna Wake Up?" and "Do Right to Me, Baby," are, like "Gotta Serve Somebody," "glorified lists" (in Marcus' phrase).[131] "Do Right to Me, Baby," built around the golden rule, is, at best, unimaginative, and, at worst, downright lazy. The almost-reggae "Man Gave Names to All the Animals" is even poorer: another list, this one, in Patrick Humphries' words, "a spiritual Dr. Dolittle."[132]

The writing in "When He Returns" gets careless in spots as well: "He unleashed his power at an unknown hour that no one knew," for instance. Nonetheless, Dylan delivers an unbelievably moving vocal performance over Barry Beckett's dramatic piano playing, and the lyrics gain extra force as a result.

The song is part of Dylan's role of "prophet of doom" that he adopts throughout the album, as Dylan warns society to alter its ways. Such preachiness can be tiresome, but the fine production makes *Slow Train Coming* a musical success.

SAVED

RELEASED: JUNE 1980

If *Slow Train Coming* is Dylan's "fire-and-brimstone" album, then *Saved* is his "praise the Lord" album. These songs speak more of personal struggle and deliverance. "Saved" and "What Can I Do for You?" give thanks to the Lord; "Covenant Woman" concerns a person who helped the narrator find Christ. "Solid Rock" and "In the Garden" are based on the teachings of the New Testament. Only "Are You Ready?" follows in *Slow Train Coming*'s apocalyptic footsteps.

Saved marks Dylan's first foray (on record) into full-fledged gospel, in the tradition of Dylan's late 1979 and early 1980 Christian-songs-only concerts. Much of the gospel material on *Saved* is hit-and-miss: the title track, for example, is pretty chaotic, the clashing cymbals and off-kilter drumming burying the zippy piano runs. With the emphatic female backup singers added, the result is a wash of noise.

"Solid Rock" succeeds where "Saved" failed, mainly because Tim Drummond's bass riff gives the full-force gospel sound its foundation. On *Biograph*, the song is digitally remastered, giving it a tad more energy.

The devotionals on side one – "Covenant Woman" and "What Can I Do for You?" – are dignified. Spooner Oldham's organ playing helps make "Covenant Woman" a fine love song, and the lyrics shine: "I've been broken, shattered like an empty cup, / I'm just waiting on the Lord to rebuild and fill me up" is a fascinating metaphor, and "You know that we are strangers in a land we're passing through" has an element of spiritual wonder to it.

"What Can I Do for You?" starts out clumsily ("You have given me eyes to see"), but the lyrics get more interesting as the song progresses. The final verse finds the narrator reaching personal salvation:

Well, I don't deserve it but I sure did make it through.
What can I do for You?

The track is also notable for, as Michael Gray wrote, "out of nowhere, the most eerie, magnificent harmonica work Dylan has done since the stoned, majestic concerts of 1966."[133]

There are echoes of Dylan's past in "Pressing On" as well: Dylan sings "Shake the dust off of your feet, don't look back," and his voice breaks into a chuckle on "don't look back." The song features a glorious piano introduction and determined singing, but the latter part of the song gets too noisy, with some unnecessary warbling by the singers.

"In the Garden" is quieter; the music tends to enhance the lyrics, which skirt the gospels to offer a brief, compelling view of Christ. During his 1986 tour with Tom Petty and the Heartbreakers, Dylan often performed the song, introducing it with a rap in which he referred to Jesus as his hero.

The final songs on the second side, "Saving Grace" and "Are You Ready?," are duds. The arrangement of "Saving Grace" is not that bad, but it never really gets going, and the lyrics get strident ("There's only one road and it leads to Calvary"). In "Are You Ready?," the interminable chanting of the title becomes oppressive; Dylan has never been one to write repetitive songs, making "Are You Ready?" one of his weaker offerings. Dylan handled the Armageddon question much better in "When He Returns," and verse two suggests that people are selfish if they are not Christian:

> Am I ready to lay down my life for the brethren
> And to take up my cross?
> Have I surrendered to the will of God
> Or am I still acting like the boss?

Halfway through the song, however, Dylan confronts doubts about his own faith, saying "Am I ready? Hope I'm ready," providing a respite from the smugness that hinders much of his evangelical material.

The album's standout performance is its least ambitious one: a sweet reading of the country standard "A Satisfied Mind," complete with some soulful humming by Dylan and his singers.

Like *Slow Train Coming*, *Saved* mixes good and bad; unlike *Slow Train Coming*, there are no masterpieces on the album. But Dylan seems to have softened his tone a bit, as *Saved* contains no really scathing attacks on society. Unfortunately, the sound is a distinct comedown from the quality of *Slow Train Coming*. Many of these songs worked better on stage. When Dylan and his band clicked, they delivered magnificent music that uplifted rather than condemned. An unreleased song from this period, "Ain't Gonna Go to Hell for Anybody," provided one of the most satisfying moments at Dylan's 1980 concerts. Beginning with a solo backup singer chanting the title, the song rose to a rollicking, enthusiastic pitch. Another new song, "Coverdown Breakthrough," had similar power. A concert album was reportedly considered in place of *Saved* but not released, by order of Columbia brass.[134]

The worst thing about *Saved* is its cover: a gaudy, Michelangeloesque painting of a hand reaching down from the heavens to touch, implicitly, only those who buy the record. Apparently, Columbia didn't care much for it either: for the compact disc format, the original cover was replaced with the drawing on the inside sleeve of Dylan playing the harmonica.

SHOT OF LOVE

RELEASED: AUGUST 1981

Shot of Love is a more secular album than *Slow Train Coming* and *Saved*, as none of the songs are explicitly evangelical. The sound is quite different from that of the previous two albums; although most of the cast from *Saved* is present, *Shot of Love* is a rock record, with more guitar interplay and less use of female backup singers.

Of the songs that rock hardest, only "Shot of Love" and "The Groom's Still Waiting at the Altar" are exemplary rock songs. The title track includes a slashing guitar riff between verses, and the chorus is well synchronized. "Shot of Love" is one of Dylan's angriest songs, addressing the devil as the invisible enemy:

Why would I want to take your life?
You've only murdered my father, raped his wife,

Tattooed my babies with a poison pen,
Mocked my God, humiliated my friends.

"The Groom's Still Waiting at the Altar" speaks of warfare and destruction: "Cities on fire, phones out of order, / They're killing nuns and soldiers, there's fighting on the border." The bulk of this earthy rocker, however, is personal in nature; a man left stranded at the altar and wondering what exactly he did wrong.

The rest of the material with a big band sound isn't quite as successful. "Trouble" is a clunker, the album's poorest track and a victim of poor sequencing (sandwiched between "In the Summertime" and "Every Grain of Sand"). The song isn't properly mixed either; at one point, the "yeah" of a female singer gets turned up horrendously high in the mix. "Watered-Down Love" has enjoyable lyrics ("Won't sneak up into your room, tall, dark and handsome"), but there's something missing from the song that hinders it, perhaps it's because the band isn't giving a totally committed effort. Dylan messes up on the second line of verse four, and the band can't compensate for the error. "Dead Man, Dead Man" is a savage character attack on a man numbed by greed, and Dylan gets off a terse, brilliant critique of violent political ideologies ("What are you tryin' to overpower me with, the doctrine or the gun?"), but, musically, the song is unremarkable, and the line "Ooh, I can't stand it" gets slurred, so it sounds like Dylan is singing, "Who can stand it?"

The arrangement of the chorus to "Property of Jesus" has punch; unfortunately, the lyrics are drenched in self-pity. Lines like "Stop your conversation when he passes on the street, / Hope he falls upon himself, oh, won't that be sweet" sound ridiculous, and the song's vindictiveness never reaches into the same territory as the classic Dylan put-downs of old.

"Lenny Bruce," a hyperbolic ode to the late comedian, has shortcomings lyrically and musically. Dylan's piano playing sets up the song, but he doesn't take advantage vocally, as evidenced when Dylan sings the line about riding with Bruce in a taxi. Dylan's other tributes to outlaw figures were, to some degree, restrained; here, Dylan makes the mistake of elevating Bruce to the role of martyr. Dylan even goes so far as to compare him to Christ ("Lenny Bruce moved on and the ones that killed him are gone"). Dylan expects listeners to believe that Bruce was a hero because he "Never robbed any churches nor cut off any babies' heads." Tim Riley, in *Hard Rain*, comments on the absurdity of that statement: "Needless to say, plenty of other people are not guilty of those same crimes, and praise by omission has never been the highest form of flattery."[135]

Since "The Groom's Still Waiting at the Altar" was only added to *Shot of Love* years after the album's original release, the album might be easy to shrug off if it didn't include two of Dylan's greatest songs, "In the Summertime" and "Every Grain of Sand." Among other things, these tracks showcase Dylan's adroitness as a harmonica player: the solos sound as if they are being played by a Negro bluesman.

"In the Summertime" opens with a timeless evocation of tranquillity and innocence:

> I was in your presence for an hour or so
> Or was it a day? I truly don't know.
> Where the sun never set, where the trees hung low
> By that soft and shining sea.

Verse two eloquently conveys the oneness of two people in love ("I got the heart and you got the blood"), and offers the prospect of universal salvation, indicating a shift away from the rigid "us and them" mentality of *Slow Train Coming* and

Saved: "Then came the warnin' that was before the flood / That set everybody free." In the third verse, the narrator pledges everlasting love:

> And I'm still carrying the gift you gave,
> It's a part of me now, it's been cherished and saved,
> It'll be with me unto the grave
> And then unto eternity.

"In the Summertime" hints at a celebration of the glory of God's nature; "Every Grain of Sand" is a timeless paean praising the wonders of creation. Dylan, in the *Biograph* notes, says: "That was an inspired song that came to me . . . It wasn't really too difficult. I felt like I was just putting words down that were coming from somewhere else."[136]

Building on Blake's poem "Auguries of Innocence" (which begins, "To see a world in a grain of sand, / And a heaven in a wild flower"), Dylan's understanding of God's universe (the earlier version of the final verse, as heard on *The Bootleg Series*, reads, "I am hanging in the balance of a perfect, finished plan") shows how everything in life has meaning: "In the fury of the moment I can see the Master's hand / In every leaf that trembles, in every grain of sand."

Ultimately, the entire album isn't as assured as "In the Summertime" and "Every Grain of Sand." The record sounds uneven, and, with the exception of "Shot of Love" and "The Groom's Still Waiting at the Altar," it comes across as a tentative return to rock and roll.

CONCLUSION

Dylan's evangelical phase stands as the most controversial period of his career and, unlike his other moves, the furor surrounding it has not abated. At the time of its release, *Slow Train Coming* immediately divided fans and commentators. Long-time admirers differed in their opinions; some, like Robert Shelton, felt that Dylan was "mistaking his role of misunderstood combatant for past similar roles in which he was simply running too far ahead of the consciousness of his audiences."[137] Others, like *Rolling Stone* publisher Jann Wenner, praised the record; Wenner opined that, "in time, it is possible that it might even be considered [Dylan's] greatest [album]."[138] He was wrong, of course, but the positive press helped sales, and the album proved a surprising commercial success.

Unfortunately, *Saved* and *Shot of Love* were resounding flops, critically and commercially, which suggests that many people didn't like what they heard on *Slow Train Coming*. Dylan's concerts in late 1979 and early 1980 consisted entirely of new material, and Dylan began delivering sermons to his more audible critics in the audience. Some of his fans didn't seem to notice that, on many nights, as in a series of shows in Toronto in April 1980, Dylan and his band were making white-hot gospel. By the end of his 1981 tour, Dylan's popularity was suffering. James Wolcott, with his usual malevolent brilliance, joked that Dylan's fundamentalist stance was "the most damaging conversion since the Jewish cabalistic messiah Sabbatai Zevi bowed to the blade and embraced Islam in 1666."[139] But, in the same article, Wolcott admits that Dylan has always "played the role of mystic bard," and he cites "Like a Rolling Stone" and "Ballad of a Thin Man" as evidence that Dylan "has always been a man of the Old Testament," accusatory and "quick to scourge."[140] Dylan's knowledge and understanding of the Bible manifests itself throughout his career, from 1962's "Long Ago, Far Away" to *John Wesley Harding* to *Blood on the Tracks* to *Street Legal* to *Infidels*. It appears that, in

1978-1981, Dylan needed Christ more than he ever had.
Dylan attempted to illustrate this point with a parable about
Leadbelly at a November 1980 concert:

> [Leadbelly had] been out of prison for some time when he
> decided to do children's songs. And people said, "Oh my!
> Did Leadbelly change?" Some people liked the old songs,
> some people liked the new ones. Some people liked both
> songs. But he didn't change. He was the same man.[141]

After 1981, Dylan never really abandoned Christianity, he
merely reintegrated Christianity into his songs and softened
his stance. There were reports in 1982 that Dylan had
returned to Judaism, but Dylan probably never fully abandoned his Jewish roots. In the *Biograph* notes to "Every
Grain of Sand," he explains: "I like to keep my values
scripturally straight though – I like to stay a part of that stuff
that don't change."[142]

Slow Train Coming, *Saved* and *Shot of Love* are average
albums in Dylan's catalogue, but, regarding the larger issue,
fundamentalist Christianity seems to be the logical out-
growth of Dylan's reading of the Bible. Bart Testa, writing
in *Maclean's*, offered a reasoned assessment of Dylan's new
evangelical material:

> Dylan's Christianity is largely an extension of his long-
> term self-image as a holy outlaw . . . Dylan [is] claiming
> just one more American folk idiom, down-home Protes-
> tant evangelism, for his showbiz persona. This is no issue
> of Dylan's sincerity, though, for his self-image has always
> been national poet, outlaw, prophet, and moral con-
> science. Christ has always had a place in Dylan's chorus.
> If anything, His guest spot at the main microphone is just
> a bit overdue.[143]

PART IX

SURVIVING IN A RUTHLESS WORLD

INFIDELS

RELEASED: NOVEMBER 1983

After a two year absence, Dylan returned to the music scene with a powerful new album of originals. *Infidels*, under the guidance of Mark Knopfler, is probably Dylan's best-produced record. Dylan's dabblings with hit producers during the 1980s had mixed results, but *Infidels* stands as the high point of this experimentation. Dylan's singing never gets drowned out by the band, and the players forge a unified, sharply defined sound.

One would be hard pressed to put together a session band better than this one: Knopfler and ex-Rolling Stone Mick Taylor on guitar, Dire Straits' Alan Clark on keyboards, and master players Sly Dunbar on drums and Robbie Shakespeare on bass. All these songs have their musical merits: Knopfler's guitar solo on "Jokerman"; the gentle accompaniment to "Sweetheart Like You"; the weaving harmonica in "License to Kill"; the overriding guitar riffs in "Man of Peace"; the delicate piano notes in "I and I"; the harmonica/guitar duet before the final verse of "Don't Fall Apart on Me Tonight." "Neighborhood Bully" and "Union

Sundown" are fiery rock songs straight out of *Highway 61 Revisited.* "License to Kill" is the only underproduced track.

Dylan's singing is more expressive than on any album since *Desire.* The vocal inflections of old have returned as in the strong singing in "Jokerman" (particularly on the chorus), the way in which Dylan sings "What's a sweetheart like you do-oin' in a dump like this?," or his pronunciation of the word "followed" in "Man of Peace." At times driven ("Jokerman," "Neighborhood Bully"), at times plaintive ("License to Kill"), at times tender ("Sweetheart Like You," "Don't Fall Apart on Me Tonight"), Dylan's voice is as flexible as ever.

Lyrically, the songs are characterized by tight imagery and dense symbolism. "Jokerman" is a prime example, layered with rich, evocative lines. The music video works as a fine companion to the song (the same can't be said for the "Sweetheart Like You" video), as the lyrics are superimposed over pictures of famous works of art, making for an involving viewing experience.

The video only serves to heighten the mystery of who the Jokerman is. Aside from the Christ analogy in the opening lines ("Standing on the waters casting your bread"), the song casts the Jokerman as a mystical, devilish figure who is removed from things on earth. Verse three attributes superhuman qualities to the Jokerman: "You're a man of the mountains, you can walk on the clouds, / Manipulator of crowds, you're a dream twister" (the video shows a picture of Hitler at this point). The fourth verse gives the impression of the Jokerman as representative of physical perfection, but the civil disorder in verse five and the violent, frightening nature of verse six implies that the Jokerman is most likely an evil being who can manifest himself in various forms.

"Man of Peace," in its entirety, concerns the devil's various incarnations. The song's source is the Bible, which tells of Satan "transformed into an angel of light" (II Cor 11:14). As in "Jokerman," Dylan uses the snake as the classical symbol of evil, here signifying imminent apocalypse:

> Well, a howling wolf will howl tonight, a king snake will crawl,
> Trees that've stood for a thousand years suddenly will fall.
> Wanna get married? Do it now,
> Tomorrow all activity will cease.

With "Jokerman" and "Man of Peace," Dylan channels his Christian concerns into less dogmatic lyrics. Parts of *Infidels* recall *Slow Train Coming*'s condemnations of modern America. In verse three of "Jokerman," Dylan intones: "you're going to Sodom and Gomorrah / But what do you care?" In the same verse, Dylan lashes out at greed: "You look into the fiery furnace, see the rich man without any name." This denunciation of the quest for earthly riches becomes one of the prevailing themes of the album. In "License to Kill," Dylan laments that man "wants it all and he wants it his way."

"Union Sundown" is the most severe attack on corporate America. Dylan complains that America has become corrupt by selling out to cheap labor in foreign countries, and, because of globalism, has regressed to a neo-colonial system of exploitation. In a 1984 *Rolling Stone* interview, Dylan expanded upon this idea:

> Right now, it seems like in the States, and most other countries, too, there's a big push on to make a big *global* country – one big country –where you can get all the materials from one place and assemble them someplace else and sell 'em in another place, and the whole world is just all one, controlled by the same people, you know?[144]

Dylan then goes on to compare the situation depicted in "Union Sundown" with what happened in Hibbing, Minnesota, while he was growing up:

> . . . actually, it's just colonization. But see, I saw that stuff firsthand . . . And eventually, they said, "Listen, this is costing too much money to get this out. We must be able to get it someplace else." Now the same thing is happening, I guess, with other products.[145]

The Dylan of "Union Sundown" voices the same sentiments as the young Bob Dylan who portrayed the decline of Hibbing twenty years earlier. In "North Country Blues," Dylan writes:

> They say that your ore ain't worth digging.
> That it's much cheaper down
> In the South American towns
> Where the miners work almost for nothing.

Dylan manages to lend wit to "Union Sundown," be it the wry irony of a Chevrolet built in Argentina, or the opening of the song, as the narrator checks his possessions in the hope of finding something that bears the label "made in the U.S.A." (as Dylan puns in the chorus). At least the narrator is willing to admit that he, too, is at fault for buying these goods, answering the charge of self-righteousness on Dylan's part.

Dylan's distaste for modern technology provokes, in the same song, a somewhat strained critique of the United States' exploration of outer space. Dylan fears that the role of the American farmer will be reduced as the move continues to find cheaper means of production:

They used to grow food in Kansas
Now they want to grow it on the moon and eat it raw.

Similarly, "License to Kill" attacks the spread of technology when serious problems on earth (such as starving farmers) remain unsolved: "Oh, man has invented his doom, / First step was touching the moon." The "actor in a plot" in "License to Kill" may be President Reagan, whose (aborted) Star Wars program represented technology at its most misguided. "License to Kill" also appears to advocate gun control, for the license to kill is both technology that is used for violent means and the right to own guns which potentially leads to violent crimes.

Another facet of *Infidels* is Dylan's concern with the Middle East, specifically the land of Dylan's forefathers, Israel (cast as the "neighborhood bully," usually a pejorative term). The song is perfectly in keeping with Dylan's lifelong affinity with the underdog. "Neighborhood Bully" touches upon the Exodus, the creation of the state of Israel from "the crumbs of the world," and the condescending attitude of most nations towards Israel ("Not supposed to fight back, and have thick skin, / Supposed to lay down and die when his door is kicked in"; "Well, he's surrounded by pacifists who all want peace . . . They lay and they wait for this bully to fall asleep"), and castigates those who ascribe to racial stereotypes about Israel as a state that "just likes to cause war."

Additionally, the lyrics sometimes take on a majestic quality, as with the opening lines of verse eight, which recall the final verse of "Precious Angel":

Every empire that's enslaved him is gone,
Egypt and Rome, even the great Babylon.
He's made a garden of paradise in the desert sand.

Two love songs, "Sweetheart Like You" and "Don't Fall Apart on Me Tonight," round out the album. In "Sweetheart Like You," Dylan takes an ancient pick-up line and spins it into his musings on life, love and power. Some writers see the song as chauvinistic, particularly verse three, which reads:

> You know, a woman like you should be at home,
> That's where you belong,
> Taking care of somebody nice
> Who don't know how to do you wrong.

But Dylan's compassionate singing hardly sounds sexist, and the following line, "Just how much abuse will you be able to take?" places the entire verse in a different context.

The two bridging verses are significant: the first echoes "Like a Rolling Stone"'s "do you want to make a deal?" line ("You could be known as the most beautiful woman / Who ever crawled across cut glass to make a deal"); the second implies that power corrupts ("Got to be an important person to be in here, honey, / Got to have done some evil deed") and works off the magnificent final verse:

> They say that patriotism is the last refuge
> To which a scoundrel clings.
> Steal a little and they throw you in jail,
> Steal a lot and then they make you king.

The chorus to "Don't Fall Apart on Me Tonight" has the same tenderness that invests "Sweetheart Like You," but the song seems closer in spirit to "I and I." In verse three of "Don't Fall Apart on Me Tonight," Dylan speaks of the demands fame has placed on him:

But it's like I'm stuck inside a painting
That's hanging in the Louvre,
My throat starts to tickle and my nose itches
But I know that I can't move.

In "I and I," the narrator refuses to talk about his past ("Besides, if she wakes up now, she'll just want me to talk / I got nothin' to say, 'specially about whatever was"), and he concludes that "I've made shoes for everyone, even you, while I still go barefoot." But he does admit that his journeys have been fruitful (with an eye to Frost's "The Road Not Taken"). "Took an untrodden path once, where the swift don't win the race, / It goes to the worthy, who can divide the word of truth."

Like *Slow Train Coming* and *John Wesley Harding, Infidels* points to a lack of faith in America. The songs on the record manage to sound old themes while examining current issues. It is unfortunate that Dylan chose to exclude "Blind Willie McTell" and "Foot of Pride" from the album, because they encapsulate the themes of corruption and spiritual decay as well as any of the other songs. The smooth love song "Someone's Got a Hold of My Heart" and the gentle hymn "Lord Protect My Child" (perhaps not released on *Infidels* because Dylan felt the lyrics were too similar to "Forever Young") were also worth including on the record. These omissions notwithstanding, *Infidels* remains Dylan's best work of the 1980s.

REAL LIVE

RELEASED: NOVEMBER 1984

A few months after the release of *Infidels*, Dylan launched a brief European tour with a slimmed-down band of mostly mediocre musicians (save for the masterful Mick Taylor on guitar). *Real Live*, ostensibly the souvenir album for the tour, shows Dylan playing it safe, as only "Tangled Up in Blue" and "Masters of War" have been significantly reworked.

The majority of the electric cuts on *Real Live* pale in comparison to the originals. The playing of the band ranges from ragged to momentarily impressive; Taylor's flashy guitar work is the one commendable aspect of this band, although his playing never reaches the heights of his Rolling Stone days. But the recording is poor; the sound of the band often gets buried in the background, and the songs tend to plod along. Too often, Dylan's vocals are clipped and hurried, quite a letdown after his singing on *Infidels*. The obligatory renditions of "Maggie's Farm" and "Ballad of a Thin Man" are perfunctory; "Masters of War" and "Tombstone Blues" (with Carlos Santana, who opened for Dylan during the tour) are palatable but hardly classics, unexciting if not uninspired. "License to Kill" and "I and I" are somewhat more energetic than the versions on *Infidels*, and Dylan sears some of the lines in "I and I" ("Into the *narrow* lanes") with gusto.

Nevertheless, the acoustic songs cannot be ignored. "Girl from the North Country" is nice but a little flat; Dylan never really lets his emotions burst forth as he does in "It Ain't Me, Babe" and "Tangled Up in Blue." There is a delightful moment during "It Ain't Me, Babe" when Dylan turns the chorus over to the audience and they chant their way through the "No, no, no" part, followed by rapturous applause. The two harmonica solos top off the performance.

The song which ultimately makes *Real Live* worth hearing is "Tangled Up in Blue." Dylan solos on the song, playing the guitar well and doing some fine singing. The new lyrics (Dylan, in the *Biograph* notes: "On *Real Live* it's more like it should have been . . . the imagery is better and more the way

I would have liked it than on the original recording") put greater focus on the woman's ex-lover (not the man "four times her age," but the "he" in verse six of the *Blood on the Tracks* take). The subject encounters a series of misfortunes after his separation from this woman ("He nearly went mad in Baton Rouge / He nearly drowned in Delacroix"); his destiny is never resolved.

The narrator's relationship with this woman isn't as pronounced as it is in the Minnesota version; only at the end does he reveal that "We always did love the very same one." In the early version, the narrator's life becomes intertwined with the fate of his companions ("And when finally the bottom fell out / I became withdrawn"). On *Real Live*, he senses disaster and acts accordingly: "When it all came crashing down / I was already south." In the conclusion, the narrator is "still headin' towards the sun /Tryin' to stay out of the joints," and his search is not for this woman but for "someone among the women and men / Whose destiny is unclear." The crowd responds enthusiastically to the new lyrics; audibly cherishing the moment. If only Dylan had put together a live album of tracks as remarkable as "Tangled Up in Blue" is; that would have made a strong souvenir album, instead of the bar band session that *Real Live* resembles.

CONCLUSION

1983 marked another major creative songwriting period for Dylan. In April, he wrote nearly twenty songs, the majority of which are now available to the public (on *Infidels* and *The Bootleg Series*). *Infidels* was generally well received by the press, except for some writers who didn't like the album's political content, and the record stayed on the American charts for six months.[146]

The European press gave good reviews to the 1984 concerts. With *Infidels* and the tour, Dylan managed to regain some of his critical and commercial stature.

PART X

HAS ANYBODY SEEN MY STYLE?

EMPIRE BURLESQUE

RELEASED: MAY 1985

Empire Burlesque, an album consisting largely of nondescript love songs, is Dylan's attempt to keep current with modern production values. With the help of dance mix specialist Arthur Baker, Dylan added over dubs of synthesizers, horns, percussion, echoes and backing vocals to the original arrangements. The result is a frumpy, abrasive sound that doesn't suit the work of a man, who, in 1984, had criticized the automated approach to recording ("everything is just machine orientated").

The tracks are drawn from various studio sessions, albeit with some big-name players (Mick Taylor, Ron Wood, Jim Keltner, Al Kooper, the Heartbreakers). Baker gives *Empire Burlesque* a unified sound, but he brings the rhythm section jarringly forward in the mix, and the additional layers of noise are merely a distraction. For instance, the unnecessary orchestral sounds in the second and final verses of "Emotionally Yours" mar the performance, for Dylan sings the song in a devotional manner that atones for the lyric's maudlin sentiments. Dylan should have done the song straight, with piano and organ the predominant sounds. The pounding drumming and squawking horns upset "Seeing the Real You at Last," and the ending to "Never Gonna Be the Same Again" is unlistenable. "Clean-Cut Kid" has an annoying hip-hop sound to it, with Ron Wood playing an awful guitar part. Dylan's singing on this track doesn't help matters: he strains to hit the notes and comes up short. "I'll Remember You" is a pretty song, but there's a weird echo effect on the vocals.

"When the Night Comes Falling from the Sky" and "Dark Eyes" are fine songs lyrically, but they are poorly performed. By the middle of "When the Night Comes Falling," Dylan sounds as bored with the song as most listeners will be. "Dark Eyes" is a melodic nightmare; as biographer Clinton Heylin observed, Dylan sings as if he's been drinking heavily.[147]

Although the bulk of the album is unattractive, Baker occasionally puts his ministrations to good use. "Tight Connection to My Heart (Has Anybody Seen My Love)" is fantastic, with a smooth gospel feel and emphatic backing on the chorus by the female singers, and "Something's Burning, Baby" smolders with an erotic charge.

In addition to the misplaced production, most of the songs have problems lyrically. The writing shows signs of laziness: many lines are stolen from old movies, as if Dylan had just sat through a Humphrey Bogart marathon before writing the lyrics.[148] "Seeing the Real You at Last" stitches in lines from *The Maltese Falcon* ("I don't mind a reasonable amount of trouble"), *Key Largo* ("Didn't I take chances?"), and *The Big Sleep* ("At one time there was nothing wrong with me / That you could not fix"). "I'll Remember You" works in the lines "There's some people that / You don't forget, / Even though you've only seen'm / One time or two" from *The Big Sleep*, and "When the Night Comes Falling" borrows from *The Maltese Falcon* throughout ("Don't look for me, I'll see you" is one line). These quotations might have worked better in the songs if Dylan had done a bit of paraphrasing.

The ballads on *Empire Burlesque* are limpid: "I'll Remember You" and "Emotionally Yours" are sappy, and "Never Gonna Be the Same Again" includes the dubious, and quite laughable, lines:

> Sorry if I hurt you, baby,
> Sorry if I did.
> Sorry if I touched the place
> Where your secrets are hid.

The topical material also has its limitations. Dylan can't decide whether he wants "Clean-Cut Kid" to be a condemnation of the system that can send innocent kids to Vietnam ("He bought the American dream but it put him in debt / Only game he could play was Russian roulette") or an amusing series of anecdotes ("He went to Hollywood to see Peter O' Toole / He stole a Rolls Royce and drove it in a swimming pool"). Worse is the tired moralizing in "Trust Yourself": "Don't look to me for answers, folks," Dylan seems to be saying.

The second side has stronger writing. "When the Night Comes Falling" has a cinematic opening ("Look out across the fields, see me returning") and a brilliant eighth verse:

> For all eternity I think I will remember
> That icy wind that's howling in your eye.
> You will seek me and you'll find
> Me in the wasteland of your mind.

"Something's Burning, Baby" is a sharp chronicle of a relationship on the rocks, with a couple of great Dylan lines

("Even the bloodhounds of London couldn't find you to-day"; "I've had the Mexico City blues since the last hairpin curve"). The pained "Dark Eyes" makes a strong closer.

On the whole, *Empire Burlesque* isn't a particularly bad album; it's an album with an identity crisis. The lyrics are sometimes bland, sometimes imaginative, as unpredictable as the music itself. Dylan's flirtation with an ultramodern sound doesn't suit his image as a spontaneous studio worker, and he is clearly uncomfortable with the proceedings (after the album's release, Dylan told *Time* that "playing with a synthesizer is not really as much fun as playing with an instrument").[149] As Greil Marcus maintained, *Empire Burlesque* is "Clunk not funk."[150]

BIOGRAPH

RELEASED: NOVEMBER 1985

A lush, five-record boxed set, *Biograph* is a monumental tribute to the man who has had perhaps the most pervasive influence on popular music. Containing fifty-three songs, eighteen previously unreleased, *Biograph* also includes song-by-song comments from Dylan himself and a thirty-five page booklet prepared by Cameron Crowe in which the normally recondite Dylan does a phenomenal amount of talking.

The set allows old fans to renew their love for Dylan, and enables people just becoming familiar with Dylan to understand what all the fuss is about. Most listeners will want to play these records over and over again, to hear the live "Isis," "Caribbean Wind" and "Up to Me" on the same record, or to hear classics such as "Lay, Lady, Lay," "Like a Rolling Stone" and "Mr. Tambourine Man" in pristine sound quality.

Of course, it is easy to find fault with a set as expansive as this one: there are too many songs from *Planet Waves* and not enough from *Blood on the Tracks*, *Desire* and *Street Legal*; there are no songs from the Concert for Bangladesh or Dylan's 1978 world tour; some of the outtakes from *Infidels* might have been added once the original aim of honoring "twenty years of Dylan" had been missed; and the notes should list the backing musicians on each track. But everybody has their own ideas about how they would assemble a set like this, and considering the daunting task he faced of distilling hundreds of hours of music into a three-and-a-half hour career retrospective, compiler Jeff Rosen did a commendable job.

Biograph is intended as an overview of Dylan's career, showing how the various musical styles he has absorbed are present throughout twenty years of work. Sequencing the songs chronologically might have encouraged people to skip over certain periods, thereby undoing the whole purpose of the project. A newcomer to Dylan's work, listening to this set, would experience difficulty in pinpointing the songs that come from one time period and those that come from another. "The Groom's Still Waiting at the Altar" sounds like a product of the same session that yielded "Tombstone Blues."

Critics charge that the individual sides on *Biograph* don't reveal thematic links between songs; that the selection is random.[151] While that may be true of sides five, seven and nine, the other sides reveal a distinct pattern. Side one includes happier love songs; side two contains topical material from Dylan's early years; the cuts on side three are rock songs, from the tenuous rockabilly of "Mixed-Up Confusion" to the full-blown force of "Like a Rolling Stone"; side four mainly includes imagistic songs; the sadder; end-of-a-relationship love songs are on side six; side eight, except for

"Just Like a Woman," is playful; side ten songs are spirituals or religion-oriented. At times, the sequencing is amusing: putting "Tangled Up in Blue" and "It' s All Over Now, Baby Blue" side by side, or having the ending of "Can You Please Crawl Out Your Window?" ("You gotta lotta nerve to say you are my friend / If you won't come out your window") lead into "Positively 4th Street."

For a change, Dylan is being honest with an interviewer in discussing this material. The song notes reveal that Dylan remembers where and when he wrote most of his songs, and what he was thinking or trying to say at the time of composition. Sometimes, Dylan uses the conversation with Crowe as a springboard to talk about his views on life. The opportunity to discuss "Every Grain of Sand" prompts a fascinating sermon from Dylan ("Everything is crooked now and the signs all point you the wrong way – it's like we're living at the time of the Tower of Babel, all our tongues are confused"; "Did you ever hear that to conquer your enemy, you must repent first, fall down on your knees and beg for mercy?").[152] In the *Biograph* booklet, Dylan contributes some very private photos and talks about his musical roots, his learning processes, and his hostility towards the use of music in advertising (which only makes his decision, in 1993, to sell Richie Havens' version of "The Times They Are A-Changin'" to an accounting firm that much harder to fathom). To promote *Biograph*, Dylan also granted *Time* an interview, providing some interesting comments ("I was the same 20, 30 years ago that I am now. My values haven't changed") that deserve to be read alongside the *Biograph* booklet.[153]

The real gold in this collection, though, is the unreleased songs. Listeners will thrill to hear the stunning "I'll Keep It with Mine," the overlong but nonetheless compelling "Percy's Song," the hymnal "Lay Down Your Weary Tune,"

Dylan's deadpan delivery in the original version of "Quinn the Eskimo," the "mm, mm" sounds Dylan makes in the early take of "You're a Big Girl Now," the goosy "Baby, I'm in the Mood for You" (a companion to "Honey, Just Allow Me One More Chance"), and the rough grace of the demo version of "Forever Young."

The live versions of "Isis," "Visions of Johanna" and "It's All Over Now, Baby Blue" are strong enough to make most listeners forget about the album versions (no small feat). Cameron Crowe states that "Visions of Johanna" has an otherworldly quality to it, and the same may be said for "Baby Blue," with Dylan's insistent guitar strumming and the way in which his voice echoes on certain words ("home"; "follow you"). Listening to these two songs makes one think of Dylan's quote in the booklet: "I always thought that one man, the lone balladeer with the guitar, could blow an entire army off the stage if he knew what he was doing."[154]

The Rolling Thunder version of "Isis" has an orgiastic instrumental blend near the end of the song, with a fabulous, half-crazed delivery of the final verse.

Three of the unreleased songs – "Abandoned Love," "Caribbean Wind" and "Up to Me" – are as good as anything Dylan has ever done in his career. "Abandoned Love," from the *Desire* sessions (left off in favor of "Joey," for some strange reason), is one of Dylan's loveliest, and saddest, songs. Scarlet Rivera's blissful violin playing and the work of the female backup singer (especially on the line "Whose gods are dead and whose queens are in the church") could hardly be improved upon, and Dylan's singing is astonishingly beautiful, conveying the despair the narrator feels at not being able to free himself from this woman. The language resembles that of a nineteenth century English novel ("I come back from the town from the flaming moon / I see you in the street, I begin to swoon"), but, like a skilled author,

Dylan never lets the romanticized language slip into bathos. The concluding lines are heart-rending in their poignancy:

> Won't you descend from the throne, from where you sit?
> Let me feel your love one more time before I abandon it.

"Caribbean Wind," not included on *Shot of Love* because Dylan was having trouble deciding which lyrics to use ("I think there's four different sets of lyrics to this . . . I had to leave it"), has a similar emotional effect.[155] The hissing sounds during the introduction are spooky, and the listener can hear the desperation in Dylan's voice as the story unfolds. The female backing is perfect: when Dylan sings "She had chrome brown eyes that I won't forget as long as she's gone," the female singer harmonizes on the word "gone" and carries Dylan's voice, as if the sounds the singer is making come from the heart of Dylan. It is one of the most sublime moments in Dylan's recording career.

In the tradition of "Changing of the Guards," "Caribbean Wind" is about a man who sees everything collapse around him. Dylan makes the narrator's confusion palpable: "flies buzzin' my head, / Ceiling fan broken, there's a heat in my bed." Verse five is one of Dylan's finest lyrics (with a smart reworking of the old joke about shooting the messenger):

> Atlantic City by the cold grey sea
> Hear a voice crying "Daddy," I always think it's for me,
> But it's only the silence in the buttermilk hills that call.
> Every new messenger's bringing evil reports
> 'Bout armies on the march and time that is short
> And famines and earthquakes and train wrecks and the
>   tearin' down of the walls.

An early version of the song, recorded in October 1980, is rough but strangely chilling, with the emphasis more obsession than dread. In its only live incarnation, at the Warfield in San Francisco in November 1980, the song took on a more overtly religious tone than in the other versions. Hopefully, Columbia will some day release the song in all its fascinating versions.

"Up to Me" is from the *Blood on the Tracks* period. In the song, remembrances of a past love are interspersed with Dylan's personal reminisces of his career. In verse two, Dylan speaks openly about his refusal to play by the rules of others:

> If I'd thought about it, I never would've done it, I guess I
>   would've let it slide,
> If I'd paid attention to what others were thinkin', the
>   heart inside me would've died.

The final lines make a fitting summation of Dylan's career:

> If we never meet again, baby, remember me,
> How my lone guitar played sweet for you that old-time
>   melody.
> And the harmonica around my neck, I blew it for you,
>   free,
> No one else could play that tune,
> You knew it was up to me.

KNOCKED OUT LOADED

RELEASED: JULY 1986

A random collection of leftovers from *Empire Burlesque* and assorted studio sessions, *Knocked Out Loaded* finds Dylan with very little to say for himself. Three covers, three collaborations, and two feeble originals make up the album. Seemingly a cast of thousands plays on the record. Dylan himself described *Knocked Out Loaded* as "all sorts of stuff. It doesn't really have a theme or a purpose."[156] Not exactly a great sales pitch.

The fact that there are different musicians on every track gives the album no cohesion whatsoever. The abysmal mixing means that instruments are either obscured or too prominent, and the sound is fuzzy. The female gospel singers have lost what little charm they had to begin with; there are too many of them (five to six per track), and they sing as if they're trying to upstage Dylan.

Knocked Out Loaded isn't a total washout: Dylan's version of Herman Parker Junior's (whom Dylan cites in the *Biograph* booklet as an influence) "You Wanna Ramble" rumbles along at a good clip, as does "Got My Mind Made Up."[157] Steel drums aside, "Precious Memories" is decently performed, and Dylan sounds more relaxed on "Under Your Spell" than on the other songs.

But "Maybe Someday" and "Driftin' Too Far from Shore" are flat and lifeless, and the addition of a children's choir to "They Killed Him" transforms an already weak song into a farce. Dylan could have chosen a better song of Kristofferson's to cover: the lyrics, a rehash of "Abraham, Martin and John," are just plain weak (was Christ really "on the road to glory"?).

The overrated "Brownsville Girl," an eleven-minute song written with Sam Shepard, gave Dylan a reason to put *Knocked Out Loaded* together. But, as a writer for *The Nation* complained, the ballad is "so thoroughly lacking in musical and narrative drama that it just trudges along without making much of an impact."[158] The concept (having a man watching a movie flash back to his travels with a woman throughout the southern United States) is relatively original, and Dylan tosses off some good lines ("She said even the swap meets around here are getting pretty corrupt"; "I didn't know whether to duck or to run, so I ran"), but the pace is so lacklustre that, unlike "Lily, Rosemary and the Jack of Hearts," "Brownsville Girl" is not a song that people will find themselves returning to very often. Worse, the sound of the chorus is terrible, with creaky saxophone and trumpet parts and overloud female backing. The original version, entitled "New Danville Girl," featured more restrained accompaniment.

What makes *Knocked Out Loaded* most disappointing is that Dylan reportedly had the opportunity to put together a stronger album. One outtake from the *Empire Burlesque* sessions, a moving take of Allen Toussaint's "Freedom for the Stallion," would have been the best cover by far if it had been used on *Knocked Out Loaded*. Al Kooper later said that, at the sessions he played on, Dylan "cut a lot of stuff for that album that was great, but he didn't use it."[159] In *Rolling Stone*, Mikal Gilmore spoke of "blues-infused rock and roll with a startling force and imagination . . . gritty R&B, Chicago-steeped blues, rambunctious gospel and raw-toned hillbilly forms" recorded at the Topanga Canyon sessions. [160] Gilmore writes in the same article that, two weeks later, Dylan's enthusiasm had cooled, and that lack of inspiration is painfully evident throughout *Knocked Out Loaded*.[161]

DOWN IN THE GROOVE

RELEASED: JUNE 1988

Another assortment of songs, *Down in the Groove* is similar in layout to its predecessor. The musicians vary from track to track, the songs seem patched together, and the production is poor. But frivolity can be fun, and *Down in the Groove* manages to be a delightful, feel-good album. *Down in the Groove* captures the spirit that *Knocked Out Loaded* was aiming for but failed to achieve. The musicians rock with abandon on tracks like "Let's Stick Together," "Sally Sue Brown" and "Ugliest Girl in the World." The backup singers are used more effectively than on *Knocked Out Loaded*, letting their harmonies tinge the songs rather than overwhelm them. It is also nice to see that Dylan has regained his sense of humor, something which had appeared only sporadically since the 1960s.

On the opening track, "Let's Stick Together," Dylan's voice is playful and carefree, and the song is set to a grungy guitar riff. Madelyn Quebec's keyboard playing enhances "When Did You Leave Heaven?". The male backing on "Sally Sue Brown" adds thrust, although the song lumbers a bit. Old friends Eric Clapton and Ron Wood help out on "Had a Dream About You, Baby," but Dylan's clothespin-on-the-nose vocal gets slightly trying.

"Death Is Not the End" is thrown in from the *Infidels* sessions, and it's an inspirational song and performance. Dylan's vocal has fire, climaxing on the glorious lines:

Oh, the tree of life is growing
Where the spirit never dies
And the bright light of salvation shines
In dark and empty skies.

The second side is patchy but has its moments. "Ugliest Girl in the World," co-written with Grateful Dead lyricist Robert Hunter, is a riot; it sounds as if it could have been written at the time of *The Basement Tapes*. Brimming with comic touches, the song tells of a man who confronts his inexplicable attraction to a woman who cracks her knuckles, snores in bed, walks with a hop, and just "ain't much to look at."

"Silvio," also written with Hunter, has the musical feel of a traditional folk song, as do some of the lyrics:

> Going down to the valley to sing my song
> Gonna sing it loud and sing it strong
> Let the echo decide if I was right or wrong.

"Ninety Miles an Hour (Down a Dead End Street)" adds a male gospel pair that recalls the backup on "Yea! Heavy and a Bottle of Bread," and the various vocals blend comfortably. Dylan's singing is well timed, as in the conclusion: "Ninety miles an hour down a dead (pause) end (pause) street"

Dylan's version of the old shanty "Shenandoah" is one of the finest recordings of the song, with a rolling melody, superb female backing and a gorgeous harmonica opening.

Another standard, "Rank Strangers to Me," concludes the album. Dylan imbues "Rank Strangers" with a real sense of sadness, his voice "answered by an arching, echoing bass, as if it were coming from the depths of a dream" (in Richard Williams' words).[162] The song is a slice of Americana, and the lyrics remind one of "Rip Van Winkle."

It doesn't matter that the songs on *Down in the Groove* don't hang together thematically. Nor does it matter that the album is far from a creative masterpiece. The fun Dylan and the musicians have is infectious. *Down in the Groove* is a throwaway album, but an enjoyable one nonetheless.

DYLAN & THE DEAD

RELEASED: FEBRUARY 1989

Dylan's affiliation with the Grateful Dead in July 1987 had the potential to be an inspired meeting of two musical legends. After all, Dylan and the Dead had a few things in common: Jerry Garcia had appeared on stage with Dylan before (in 1980 and 1986); the Dead had covered some of Dylan's songs throughout the years ("When I Paint My Masterpiece"); both have a flair for releasing mediocre live albums; and Garcia and Dylan evidently had the same barber (for the California shows, Dylan grew a beard, à la Garcia, to complement his big hair [seen on the album sleeve; one writer said Dylan looks like he has a raccoon living in his hair]).[163]

Unfortunately, the shows proved to be monotonous affairs, and the *Dylan & the Dead* album is a woeful souvenir. Dylan is the chief culprit; his singing is harsh and slurred. There is not a single song on the album during which Dylan does not fumble over the words at some point. There is nothing really wrong with forgetting the lyrics on stage (even Dylan cannot be expected to remember all the words to all his songs), but there is no need to put such mistakes onto vinyl. "Gotta Serve Somebody" is such a disaster that it is guaranteed to make listeners cringe. Things get so bad that, at one point, Dylan sings, "Take all your troubles, give 'em to the blind."

Dylan does not click with these musicians, he just gets them down in the hole that he's in. Conversely, Garcia and company don't help much when Dylan gets in trouble vocally. Dylan's old tricks of changing chords or altering the melody during songs is too much for the Dead to handle. The pace to this material is slow, making "Queen Jane

Approximately" tedious and "All Along the Watchtower" and "Knockin' on Heaven's Door" retreads. "Joey" is an embarrassment: Dylan and the Dead strip the song of its delicacy, and the band falls behind in the chorus. The Dead's inappropriate vocal backing on the songs is a lame attempt to atone for what their musical accompaniment lacks.

In the past, Dylan usually prodded his musicians to play at their highest level, but he's not concerned with doing that here. And even when the Dead sound momentarily inspired, Dylan hijacks the attempt with his irritating singing. For instance, the lonesome guitar introduction to "I Want You" is a classic, and the music on the song is competent, but Dylan sings with no sense of subtlety ("I want *choo*").

Aside from "I Want You"'s opening sequence, there's not much on *Dylan & the Dead* that makes the album worthwhile. The comic art cover, however, is crudely appealing. But the whole exercise smacks of cynicism. Releasing an album almost two years after the tour seems like a stopgap measure, and putting the album in both names meant that both Deadheads and Dylan fans put out money for a record that is unrepresentative of both artists' work. Given its contents, it's not surprising that *Dylan & the Dead* was D.O.A.

CONCLUSION

The inconsistency that affects much of Dylan's later work is nowhere more evident than in the years 1985-88. Some critics touted *Empire Burlesque* as a "comeback" album, but few of the songs written by Dylan during this time prove very lasting, and writer's block sets in until *Oh Mercy*. Alongside *Empire Burlesque*, *Knocked Out Loaded* and

Down in the Groove show Dylan searching for some sort of cogent style.

Nevertheless, Dylan kept a high profile in 1985, promoting *Empire Burlesque* with a handful of music videos, and appearing at Live Aid and at Farm Aid (the latter event inspired by Dylan's comments at Live Aid that Americans should supply economic aid to the American farmers, who were experiencing financial difficulties).[164] *Biograph* was a great success in the United States, sparking a flood of boxed sets onto the market.

In 1986 and 1987, Dylan toured the world with Tom Petty and The Heartbreakers. Dylan has a lead role in the 1987 film *Hearts of Fire*, a turkey if there ever was one. His co-star, the pubescent-looking Fiona, is not a singer (nor an actress, for that matter), and her chirpy vocals make up most of the film's live footage. Dylan's musical contribution is small and insignificant, but he does get to live out every rock star's dream of trashing a hotel room. Released in England for a week, the film never made it into American theaters. Since then, Dylan has made one more film appearance, a gratuitous cameo in *Backtrack*, featuring Jodie Foster as an artist of some sort who falls in love with her stalker, Dennis Hopper (happens all the time).

In 1988, Dylan did an excellent U.S. tour. With G.E. Smith leading the way on guitar, Dylan and the band stormed through sets. Dylan's work as a member of the Traveling Wilburys (George Harrison, Tom Petty, Roy Orbison and Jeff Lynne) on the wonderful *Volume One* boosted his critical stock at a much-needed time (after the bad reviews of *Knocked Out Loaded* and *Down in the Groove*), only to have the release of *Dylan & the Dead* lower it again.

The erratic output by Dylan over these years and his cavalier attitude towards releasing records during this time makes it one of the least satisfying periods of his career, although the release of *Biograph* and the 1988 tour are the highlights.

PART XI

SERIES OF DREAMS

OH MERCY

RELEASED: SEPTEMBER 1989

Realizing he needed to close out the decade with a strong album, Dylan enlisted the help of producer Daniel Lanois, who had previously worked with U2 and Robbie Robertson. Lanois' meticulous care makes *Oh Mercy* one of Dylan's cleaner sounding records. Steeped in a backwoods aura reminiscent of the recording location (New Orleans), *Oh Mercy* has, in Lanois' words, a "blazing strangeness around it."[165] Dylan's raspy but gentle singing has been pushed to the foreground, allowing the session men to play at a nice, easy pace without sounding like they are competing with Dylan for the spotlight. The sound throughout *Oh Mercy* is agreeable: the guitar shuffle of "Political World"; the soft country sounds of "Where Teardrops Fall"; the tranquil nighttime sounds in the introduction to "Man in the Long Black Coat"; Dylan's piano work in "Ring Them Bells" and "Disease of Conceit."

Dylan even took the time to write original material for the album, something he hadn't done since 1985. Still, a couple of the songs are weak. Dylan comes across as self-righteous in "Disease of Conceit," and the tone is preachy. "Political World" has some dubious lyrics ("We're living in a time when men commit crimes" – Has there ever been a time when men haven't committed crimes?), but the bulk of the song is thought-provoking ("Wisdom is thrown into the jails").

Some of the songs recall Dylan's past work. In "Everything is Broken," Dylan dashes off a list of fractured goods ("Broken hands on broken plows, / Broken treaties, broken vows, / Broken pipes, broken tools, / People bendin' broken rules")/ and the song moves at a spirited pace. Richard Williams dubbed it "a 'Subterranean Homesick Blues' for fretful forty-somethings."[166]

"The Man in the Long Black Coat" harkens back to "Lily, Rosemary and the Jack of Hearts." "The Man in the Long Black Coat" is not an extended narrative like the earlier song, but its sinister title character is something of a Jack of Hearts figure, sweeping into a small town and stealing the hearts of the women, and arousing fear in the hearts of the men.

The man's appearance prompts a sermon from the local preacher, who says that "every man's conscience is vile and depraved, / You cannot depend on it to be your guide." Dylan's response is perhaps an unconscious dig at his evangelical period: "it sticks in the throat."

Another aspect of the song that is a throwback to the *Blood on the Tracks* period is Dylan's use of time. The past and present seem to merge in the song. The opening verse, for instance, appears to be set after the man has left the scene, but the final verse tells of "Tree trunks uprooted," immediately linking the line up with the first verse ("African trees / Bent over backwards by a hurricane breeze"), as if the man's arrival is connected with this phenomenon.

The relationship songs are just as interesting. As in "You're Gonna Make Me Lonesome When You Go," the narrator of "Where Teardrops Fall" connects his lost love with the natural world: "the soft winds," "the flickering light," "the turning of twilight," "the shadows of moonlight," the sun coming up. Despite the shedding of tears, the prevailing mood of the song is happiness.

Side two's "Most of the Time" is a much sadder song. Recollections of a woman haunt the narrator, and the song is made particularly tragic by his awareness of the irony of his statements. Dylan sings "Most of the time" as a painful afterthought to his disavowal of any love he still harbors for this woman, so when he says "I don't even think about her / Most of the time," the listener knows that these memories are tearing him apart. The narrator does admit openly that "I don't run and hide / Hide from the feelings that are buried inside," and one can be sure that the narrator knows every scene by heart.

In "What Was It You Wanted?," the narrator sees the woman as a Judas figure: "What was it you wanted, / When you were kissing my cheek?" The following lines have chilling Biblical overtones, suggesting the seizure of Christ after His betrayal:

Was there somebody looking
When you gave me that kiss?

Dylan blurs reality and illusion in the song, so after his encounter with this woman, the narrator asks her, "Who are you anyway?" and "Are you talking to me?," a strange twist on a slightly eerie scenario.

The narrator of "What Good Am I?" seems a very compassionate figure, supporting his lover through trying times. But the song is not just about being true to a woman: it is sure to make people think of Dylan's lifelong fight against injustice. When Dylan sings the lines, "What good am I? / If I know and don't do / If I see and don't say" and, in the same verse, "If I turn a deaf ear to the thunder in the sky," it brings back memories of "Blowin' in the Wind." This is a song about one man's courage, something Dylan talks about in "Political World" ("Courage is a thing of the past").

Oh Mercy also contains two songs with a hymnal quality to them. "Ring Them Bells" is similar to "Chimes of Freedom": Dylan hears the bells as tolling for the oppressed, the poor, the forsaken. Further, "Ring Them Bells" recalls the apocalyptic slant of Dylans' late 1970s material: "Ring them bells / For the chosen few / Who will judge the many / When the game is through." The final verse juxtaposes the soothing nature of the bells with a scene wherein "the fighting is strong / And they're breaking down the distance / Between right and wrong." The bridge in the final song, "Shooting Star," follows along similar lines:

> Listen to the engine, listen to the bells
> As the last fire truck from hell goes rolling by
> All good people are praying.

Nevertheless, the song (Dylan's wish upon a star) is comforting, a bedtime prayer for an old love ("Seen a shooting star tonight, and I thought of you"), and a wish for the future ("Tomorrow will be another day").

The most promising aspect of *Oh Mercy* is not its musical content, but the fact that it proves Dylan still capable of writing first-rate songs. *Oh Mercy* arrived in stores just in time to remind people that, nearing fifty, Dylan could compete with any of his contemporaries.

And yet, as he had with *Infidels*, Dylan left some first-rate material off the finished product, namely "Dignity," "Series of Dreams" and "Born in Time." Both "Dignity" and "Series of Dreams" are vibrant, superbly performed songs. "Born in Time" featured perhaps the most perfectly realized production by Lanois, and an assured vocal performance by Dylan that stands as one of his best of the last two decades and reveals how weak the raspy take on *Under the Red Sky* really is. These three songs would have made *Oh Mercy* the masterpiece that many heralded it as upon its release.

UNDER THE RED SKY

RELEASED: SEPTEMBER 1990

After the critical success of *Oh Mercy*, Dylan again wrote new songs for the follow-up. Unfortunately, the lyrics to *Under the Red Sky* are amongst the weakest Dylan has ever written, simple little ditties with not much in the way of profundity.

Dylan relied upon the production duo of Don and David Was to bring the sound up to contemporary standards. The Was brothers give the record a polish without losing the ruggedness that is Dylan's trademark. The producers have brought in some big names: George Harrison, Jimmie and Stevie Ray Vaughan, Kenny Aronoff, Al Kooper, Elton John, and even David Crosby (on backing vocals on two songs).

But no number of superstar guests can compensate for the fatuity of the lyrics. In the past, Dylan could write commonplace lines and make them seem fresh and vigorous (as he did on *Nashville Skyline*, *New Morning* and parts of *Planet Waves*). Here, some of the lyrics are so astonishingly banal that it's difficult to imagine Dylan writing them. The Dylan of, say, the *Nashville Skyline* period would never have rendered a conclusion as limp as the one to *Under the Red Sky*'s "10,000 Men":

Ooh, baby, thank you for my tea!

Baby, thank you for my tea!
It's so sweet of you to be so nice to me.

Earlier in the same song, Dylan sings the ludicrous lines:
"Hey! Who could your lover be? / Let me eat off his head so
you can really see!"

The opening track, "Wiggle Wiggle," sounds an omi-
nous note for the rest of the album. While Slash of Guns 'n'
Roses plays some laconic guitar chords, Dylan rattles off
lines such as "Wiggle, wiggle, wiggle like a bowl of soup, /
Wiggle, wiggle, wiggle like a rolling hoop" and "Wiggle,
wiggle, wiggle like a pail of milk." Those lines alone must
have cost Dylan a few admirers.

Most of the songs come across as nursery rhymes. Some
people insist that the title track is a splendid fable, but the
story never gets sufficiently developed. All Dylan seems to
be singing about is the man in the moon coming to earth and
drying the rivers up.

Even worse than "Under the Red Sky"'s lines like "One
day the little boy and the little girl were both baked in a pie,"
or the childish numbers rhyming of "2*2," is "Cat's in the
Well," which begins: "The cat's in the well, the wolf is
looking down / He got his big bushy tail dragging all over the
ground." The statement in the bridge that "The world's
being slaughtered and it's such a bloody disgrace" is uncon-
vincing: it's as if Dylan has to throw in a serious comment to
try to make up for the song's triviality.

"Handy Dandy" is the type of title that typifies much of
Under the Red Sky's content. The bridging verses are clever,
but Dylan uses "sugar and candy" four times as a cheap
rhyme for "Handy Dandy" (not to mention the organ piece
ripped off from "Like a Rolling Stone," complete with Al
Kooper playing the part).

Even "God Knows," on first listen one of the better songs, has its flaws ("God knows everything"; "God knows there's a Heaven").

There are the occasional bright spots on *Under the Red Sky*. "Unbelievable" has an ear-splitting guitar intro, and the song became the album's only single. "They said it was the land of milk and honey, / Now they say it's the land of money. / Who ever thought they'd ever make that stick?" is a delightful lyric, and the lines "Kill that beast and feed that swine, / Scale that wall and smoke that vine, / Feed that horse and saddle up the drum" would fit in "Tiny Montgomery."

"T.V. Talkin' Song" is the other keeper, notable for the joke "Sometimes you gotta do like Elvis did and shoot the damn thing out," and the irony of the narrator watching the day's events on television, the object of such scorn throughout the song.

Dylan's singing is far too inconsistent to arouse much enthusiasm for the other lyrics. "Born in Time," as shown by the *Oh Mercy* take, has the potential to be a lovely song, but Dylan's voice is croaky; and he has a lot of trouble pronouncing the word "revealing." In "10,000 Men," his voice seems to fade out at the end of each line. In "God Knows," Dylan's singing in the last three verses gets flooded over by the music, and he raises his voice to be heard. During "Handy Dandy," his singing starts to splutter on the words "sugar and candy." On the whole, Dylan doesn't sound very devoted to this material.

There are those writers who contend that the nursery rhyme lyrics in *Under the Red Sky* are somehow deep comments on the state of the world, but there's really little evidence of such insight on the record. Dylan's use of kiddy images and descriptions never move beyond their baseness to take on a stronger meaning. The individual lines don't build upon each other to enhance the songs: they're flat and one-dimensional.

Dylan once spoke of doing a children's album (probably in jest but who can say for sure?) *Under the Red Sky* is as close as he has come to doing one.[167]

THE BOOTLEG SERIES, VOLUMES 1-3 [RARE AND UNRELEASED], 1961-1991

RELEASED: MARCH 1991

To commemorate Bob Dylan's fiftieth birthday, Columbia finally decided to release some of the rare Dylan material that they had been sitting on for ages. *The Bootleg Series, Volumes 1-3 [Rare and Unreleased], 1961-1991* offers a more extensive survey of Dylan's unreleased recordings than *Biograph*. With fifty-eight songs from throughout his career included, *The Bootleg Series* functions as a sketchy map for Dylan's development as an artist.

Volume One reminds one of the incredible pace at which Dylan was absorbing, writing, and recording when he first appeared on the music scene. From Negro spirituals ("No More Auction Block") to ancient folk ballads ("House Carpenter") to traditional vignettes ("Moonshiner"), many of these songs underscore the wide ranging material that Dylan learned on the Dinkytown and Greenwich Village circuits.

Some of Dylan's own compositions reveal his derivative powers. "Man on the Street" borrows the melody of an American frontier song; "Rambling, Gambling Willie" has its roots in an old Irish ballad; "Walls of Red Wing" is melodically linked to a Scottish folk song.

The Guthrie influence is pervasive throughout the early material. "Hard Times in New York Town," which uses the tune and verse structure of "Down on Penny's Farm," a southern folk song, reads like a Guthrie ballad, as shown by the sixth verse:

> I'll take all the smog in Cal-i-for-ne-ay,
> 'N' every bit of dust in the Oklahoma plains,
> 'N' the dirt in the caves of the Rocky Mountain mines.
> It's all much cleaner than the New York kind.

"Talkin' Bear Mountain Picnic Massacre Blues" and "Talkin' John Birch Paranoid Blues" reflect Dylan's ability to use the talking blues format that Guthrie had mastered. The gloriously evocative conclusion to "Let Me Die in My Footsteps" captures a vision of American nature as powerfully as Guthrie ever could:

> Go out in your country where the land meets the sun
> See the craters and the canyons and where the waterfalls
>   run
> Nevada, New Mexico, Arizona, Idaho
> Let every state in this union seep deep down in your soul.

Likewise, the uplifting "Paths of Victory" shows Dylan's eye for details of the natural world, and reveals a strong belief in the individual spirit.

But the signature composition has to be "Last Thoughts on Woody Guthrie," a poem that spans five pages of text and, despite some initial hesitancy on Dylan's part, gets recited at breakneck speed. After enumerating various societal ills, Dylan finally makes reference to his hero in the hagiolatrous conclusion:

> You can either go to the church of your choice
> Or you can go to Brooklyn State Hospital

You'll find God in the church of your choice
You'll find Woody Guthrie in Brooklyn State Hospital

And though it's only my opinion
I may be right or wrong
You'll find them both
In the Grand Canyon
At sundown.

Many of Guthrie's songs exalted nature, and so Dylan actually sees not only God in the twilight of the Grand Canyon,
but Guthrie as well. Dylan implies that, like the Grand
Canyon, Guthrie is an American icon.

The topical songs on *The Bootleg Series* continue the
Guthrie tradition of social awareness, but many assume a
more universal quality ("The Times They Are A-Changin',"
"When the Ship Comes In"). "Let Me Die in My Footsteps"
isn't simply a condemnation of the Cold War mentality that
fosters a climate of fear in the land of the free, it's an attempt
by an individual to counter this atmosphere and, furthermore, a celebration of the beauty of America in striking
contrast to the destruction a nuclear war would bring.

"Talkin' John Birch Paranoid Blues" shows Dylan's ability to use humor to ridicule contemporary affairs. The great
irony of Dylan being forbidden to perform the song on
television (on "The Ed Sullivan Show" in May 1963) is that
CBS' action amounts to blacklisting, exactly the sort of
attitude that Dylan sends up in the song.[168]

The first disc also reveals Dylan's prowess as a singer,
even at such a young age. He can sing in a Guthriesque drawl
("Hard Times in New York Town," "Rambling, Gambling
Willie"), in a heartfelt, dignified fashion ("He Was a Friend
of Mine," "Kingsport Town"), with infectious good cheer
("Walkin' Down the Line"), or distill all the various inflections into an off the cuff *tour de force* ("Quit Your Low

Down Ways"). The two most breathtaking vocal performances are reserved for the traditional songs "No More Auction Block" and "Moonshiner." Dylan sings "No More Auction Block" as if he were a Negro slave newly liberated from
the shackles of oppression. Dylan's voice floats through the
intimate setting of The Gaslight Cafe as it might have floated
over the American countryside a century earlier. In "Moonshiner," Dylan holds the notes with a skill that belies his
twenty-two years.

The second volume tracks Dylan as his language heads
off into new directions and he turns on the electricity for
outright rock and roll. One of the many treasures of this set
is the inclusion of "Farewell, Angelina," a song that almost
everybody believed had never been recorded by Dylan. The
title would often pop up on bootleg records, and the listener
would discover, infuriatingly enough, that the cut was actually "Farewell."

Even more than the songs on *Another Side of Bob Dylan*,
"Farewell, Angelina" clearly foreshadows where Dylan is
going with his writing. Bauldie mentions Dylan's quotation
about "a chain of flashing images," and this epochal composition certainly personifies that description. Dylan writes
short, direct statements ("The table stands empty / By the
edge of the stream") that seem to spring into the consciousness of the listener as they go by. This is the type of writing
that finds its fullest expression on *Bringing It All Back Home*,
Highway 61 Revisited and *Blonde on Blonde*.

Although "If You Gotta Go, Go Now (or Else You Got
to Stay All Night)" and "Sitting on a Barbed Wire Fence" are
fun, it's clear that the best rock recorded at the sessions for
the above albums made it onto those records, with the
exception of the vituperative "She's Your Lover Now."
"She's Your Lover Now" is a fine Dylan diatribe, as the
narrator manages to trump both his ex-lover and his ex-

lover's new boyfriend ("your friend in the cowboy hat"). But the underlying emotion fueling these attacks is pain, giving the song an entirely new dimension that may be easily overlooked beneath all the surface fuming. This is made clear by the naked piano take recorded at the *Blonde on Blonde* sessions.

From *The Basement Tapes* period, "Santa-Fe" provides an outstanding example of what Dylan alone achieved during this time. John Bauldie dismisses the song as "just for the hell of it," and while there is no particular meaning to the lyrics (the words are largely unintelligible), his assessment fails to do justice to what the track reveals about Dylan's ability as a singer.[169]

There's a passage in Dickens' *David Copperfield* in which the protagonist observes one of the female characters playing the harp and singing a song. Dickens' inimitable description of the scene reads:

> I don't know what it was, in her touch or voice, that made that song the most unearthly I have ever heard in my life, or can imagine. There was something fearful in the reality of it. It was as if it had never been written, or set to music, but sprung out of the passion within her; which found imperfect utterance in the low sounds of her voice, and crouched again when all was still.

Of course, "Santa-Fe" has nothing whatsoever to do with *David Copperfield*, but the quotation may be applied to the experience the listener has while "Santa-Fe" is playing (and, for that matter, "I'm Not There"). It appears that Dylan simply improvised the song on the spot, and the passion within him allows the song to flow forth naturally. When Dylan hums "Dear-dear-dear-dear-dear," the breadth of feeling is remarkable. The unparalleled expressiveness of

Dylan's singing is such that one gets the sense that Dylan could sing "Santa-Fe" with minimal backing and end up with the same results. "Santa-Fe" is a masterpiece of vocalization, evidence that his work in the basement of Big Pink enabled Dylan to experiment successfully with so many different oral techniques.

The later material on disc two showcases Dylan's ability to write love songs and songs of lost love with broad appeal. "Nobody 'Cept You," propelled by Robbie Robertson's guitar work and Dylan's heartfelt singing, concerns the immediate attraction of a woman, and the song leads into the *Blood on the Tracks*' outtakes from the original New York sessions.

Dylan changes the tenses more in the early version of "Tangled Up in Blue"; together with the *Blood on the Tracks* and *Real Live* versions, it indicates how many directions this song can take.

"Call Letter Blues," a song about a man lured into a bordello while thinking about his estranged wife, mixes bitterness with pathos, not unlike the *Blood on the Tracks* version of "Idiot Wind." As Bauldie points out, the anger in that version of "Idiot Wind" is replaced by sorrow in the earlier take.[170] The emotional effect hasn't diminished; Dylan almost chokes when he sings the alternate lyric "Well, I figured I'd lost you anyway, why go on, what's the use?"

"If You See Her, Say Hello" (which belongs on the second disc) has two affecting harmonica solos, some driven guitar playing and a heart-rending vocal performance (Dylan's voice shivers on "used to it"). Unfortunately, one of the original lyrics is problematic: Dylan sings "If you're making love to her, kiss her for the kid," which is crude. It also implies that this person the narrator is confiding in is intimate with this woman, and that doesn't fit with the rest of the song.

The third disc includes some material from Dylan's evangelical phase. "You Changed My Life" and "Need a Woman" are awkwardly performed, but "Ye Shall Be Changed" would have worked quite well as a break from the redundancy of side two of *Slow Train Coming*. The demo version of "Every Grain of Sand" is a touching performance, particularly when the first notes of the tune are heard. The moment with the dog is both funny and strange: the dog barks when Dylan sings about turning around and seeing someone there, then ceases to bark when Dylan says "other times it's only me." Another great performance from the *Shot of Love* sessions is "Angelina," a haunting song.

The *Infidels* outtakes are perhaps the most contentious tracks on *The Bootleg Series* (contentious because many writers believe some of these songs should have made it onto *Infidels*, either in place of other songs or as part of a double album). Two of the songs, "Foot of Pride" and "Blind Willie McTell," are thematically linked with the topical material on *Infidels*. Both songs stress that greed is one of the problems afflicting modern America.

Using as its source the Old Testament proverb about pride going before destruction and a haughty spirit going before the fall, "Foot of Pride" works almost as a sequel to "Desolation Row." Dylan frames the song so that it begins and ends with the narrator attending the funeral of a man whose evil ways catch up with him ("He reached too high and was thrown back to the ground"). At the service, the narrator reflects upon life, bringing in characters ("a retired businessman named Red") who have sold their souls for earthly riches, disturbing situations ("from the stage they'll be trying to get water out of rocks / A whore will pass through here, collect a hundred grand and say 'Thanks'"), and a final warning that judgment for the wicked will be swift. At Dylan's thirtieth anniversary concert, Lou Reed sang the song as if he were trying to decipher its meaning as he performed it.

In "Blind Willie McTell," Dylan travels back in time to the land of slavery, juxtaposing the "big plantations burning" during the Civil War with "the cracking of the whip." Dylan concludes by saying that "power and greed and corruptible seed / Seem to be all that there is."

The blues singer Blind Willie McTell becomes Dylan's muse for the song, and Dylan sings it like a Negro bluesman. In verse four and five, one can hear Dylan's singing and piano playing become more impassioned, as if he suddenly realizes how tremendous the lyrics are that he has written.

"When the Night Comes Falling from the Sky" and "Series of Dreams" conclude *The Bootleg Series*. In the former, Dylan and his musicians (including Steve Van Zandt of the E Street Band) impart a far greater sense of drama to the song than the tedious take on *Empire Burlesque* does. "Series of Dreams," one of Dylan's best songs of the last decade, was used for an impressive promotional video that combined film footage with random lyrics and some artwork.

The Bootleg Series does have a few sub-par tracks. The piano versions of "When the Ship Comes In" and "The Times They Are A-Changin'" are of interest mainly as curiosities, and the tempo has been noticeably slowed, to the songs' detriment. The same holds true for the solo acoustic take of "Subterranean Homesick Blues" and the waltz version of "Like a Rolling Stone." And the rehearsal version of "I'll Keep It with Mine" is a travesty, with Dylan singing in an uninspired manner and the instruments painfully attempting to mesh.

John Bauldie's liner notes are a good read, but the booklet could have used some careful proofreading. "Mama, You Been on My Mind" is from the sessions for *Another Side of Bob Dylan*, not from *Bringing It All Back Home*; "Masters of War," not "A Hard Rain's A-Gonna Fall," replaced "Let Me Die in My Footsteps" on *The Freewheelin' Bob Dylan*; and the line about the fear of bringing children into the world is from "Masters of War," not "A Hard Rain's A-Gonna Fall." And fans can listen in vain, but they will never be able to hear the band playing on "Like a Rolling Stone," or the "spooky organ" in "Idiot Wind."[171]

But these errors are minor; the set has been put together in an attractive package (notice how the lettering in the title is uneven, Columbia's way of poking fun at the tendency of the packaging on bootleg albums to be slapdash), and it is relatively inexpensive. This material should come as a welcome addition to any Dylan library.

CONCLUSION

With the release of *Oh Mercy* (which garnered Dylan his best reviews since *Blood on the Tracks*) and continued touring, Dylan's popularity began to surge once again. The release of *The Traveling Wilburys, Volume Three* and *The Bootleg Series* vitiated the negative press that *Under the Red Sky* had received.

Prior to the release of *The Bootleg Series*, Dylan was given a Lifetime Achievement Award at the 1991 Grammy ceremony. Jack Nicholson, looking like he was reprising his role in *The Shining*, introduced Dylan with a few choice Dylan quotations (all taken out of context), a brief video made up of archival footage was shown, and then Dylan and his new touring band steam-rolled "Masters of War," the only time during the evening that anybody bothered to make reference to the fact that the United States was then bombing

Iraq into submission. Dylan's acceptance speech surpassed the usual routine thanks that artists give for such awards:

> My daddy, he didn't leave me too much, you know. He was a very simple man . . . But what he told me was this . . . he did say, "Son . . ." [pause] He said so many things, you know? But he did say . . . "It's possible to become so defiled in this world that your own mother and father will abandon you. And if that happens, God will always believe in your own ability to mend your own ways.

Detractors found much to parody in Dylan's on-stage demeanor, but his speech reminded listeners that, although he may have lost his way on occasion, in the end, everything turned out okay.

In late 1992, Columbia celebrated thirty years of recordings by Dylan with a much-hyped anniversary concert. Various musical dignitaries of assorted ages, styles and relevance delivered a deluge of bad cover versions of Dylan's songs, including a take of "Like a Rolling Stone" by John Mellencamp that deserved to be censored and a version of "Absolutely Sweet Marie" by George Harrison ("wearing a hideous purple jacket, someone's old mustache, and the world's worst haircut," wrote one British scribe) so out-of-tune that one of the stage hands should have cut the microphone.[172] Dylan was the main offender on a hideous singalong on "My Back Pages"; Dylan later had to re-record his part for the album. Sinead O'Connor provided the evening's low point: having ripped up a picture of the Pope on *Saturday Night Live* a couple of weeks before, O'Connor was booed lustily by the crowd. Instead of just going ahead and performing "I Believe in You" as scheduled, O'Connor began shouting Bob Marley's "War" and then slinked off the stage. Taking on the Pope is always a bad idea; taking on a Madison Square Garden crowd is an even worse one. A stronger artist (i.e.

Dylan circa 1966) would have persevered despite the heckling; O'Connor caved and the stunt effectively destroyed her career.

Dylan himself sang a few songs (aside from "Girl from the North Country," no especial performances). Despite the lousy covers, the concert reinforced the many ways of interpreting Dylan's songs, and the diversity of performers whom Dylan has influenced. Moreso, it called to mind that hoary Columbia records slogan, "Nobody sings Dylan like Dylan."

PART XII

BACK TO THE STARTING POINT

GOOD AS I BEEN TO YOU

RELEASED: NOVEMBER 1992

Thirty years after his debut album, Bob Dylan returned to his folk roots with *Good As I Been to You*. The record consists of thirteen songs, the majority of them plucked from the nether regions of the historical folk songbook, adorned with only guitar and, occasionally, harmonica. Dylan evidently grew leery of working with different producers and the latest studio techniques and decided to make an album quickly and simply, just like in the old days. The result is one of his best records, a stunning collection of tales of adventure, love, adultery, revenge, hardship and triumph.

But the biggest surprise isn't Dylan going acoustic again; it's his singing. In recent concerts, his voice had begun to sound limited, and the material on some of his albums from the past decade tended to be sung in a voice that varied little between songs. On *Good As I Been to You*, Dylan's legendary phrasing is back in place, and although his voice may be showing signs of age, the nuances in his vocals radiate charm. The range of emotion in Dylan's voice on "Jim Jones" is incredible: alternately tender (as on the line, "gone to South

Wales"), poignant (as when he sings, "We toil and toil and when we die / Must fill dishonored graves") and gruff. On Stephen Foster's "Hard Times," he sings the chorus like a man worn out from years of suffering. "Tomorrow Night" is sung with genuine affection. An air of sadness runs through "Arthur McBride," and "Froggie Went A-Courtin'" is sung so delicately that, as a commentator for Q magazine observed, "It's almost as moving as [Dylan's] own classic 'Forever Young.'"[173]

Dylan's guitar work is just as expressive. Throughout, he adopts a fingerpicking style he hadn't used since *Another Side of Bob Dylan*, his last solo outing. On "Sittin' on Top of the World" and "Step It Up and Go," he demonstrates his ability to give folk songs a rock sound. Elsewhere, on songs such as "Froggie Went A-Courtin'" and "Arthur McBride," the glorious strumming perfectly complements his vocals.

These are songs that have had an impact on Dylan's career. "Jim Jones," "Canadee-I-O" and "Arthur McBride" have obvious appeal to Dylan's active imagination. "Frankie and Albert" and "Blackjack Davey" are inspired choices because, like so many of Dylan's songs, they tell tragic stories without slipping into bathos. From "Jim Jones" and "Arthur McBride," Dylan must have picked up a few ideas about how to use the long ballad form.

Some of the songs Dylan covers have more contemporary antecedents, or were learned from other musicians. Dylan tips his hat to Elvis, one of his early influences, on "Tomorrow Night." "Sittin' on Top of the World" is by Howlin' Wolf, and Dylan's biographers report that Howlin' Wolf songs were a regular feature of Dylan's favorite radio program while he was growing up in Hibbing.[174] Dylan also played harmonica on Big Joe Williams' version of the song, for Big Joe's 1962 album *Three Kings and a Queen*. Dylan made an appearance on Ramblin' Jack Elliot's self-titled album in 1964, and one of the songs recorded by Elliot at the sessions was "Diamond Joe" (although Dylan does not play on that particular track).

Good As I Been to You is an album that celebrates the many virtues of folk music. The manner in which Dylan performs these songs reveals how dear they are to him, and, consequently, the songs and performances on *Good As I Been to You* become dear to the listener. Dylan succeeds in showing how the best songs survive through the ages and, in the process, puts together an album that is as timeless as the songs themselves.

WORLD GONE WRONG

RELEASED: NOVEMBER 1993

Dylan's second consecutive solo record of traditional material, the selections on *World Gone Wrong* are just as intriguing as the ones on *Good As I Been to You*. But whereas *Good As I Been to You* is primarily a folk album, *World Gone Wrong* is more of a blues record. This time, the material is even more obscure; "Stack A Lee" is the only readily identifiable lyric.

World Gone Wrong is a much darker album than its predecessor. The title track, "Ragged & Dirty" and "Broke Down Engine" have as their narrator a troubled man who vents his anger at life itself. In "Love Henry," a woman murders her lover and then throws his body down a well. "Delia" ("one sad tale," Dylan says in the liner notes, and it's made even sadder by the heartbreaking refrain, "All the friends I ever had are gone") concerns a cattle rancher who kills a promiscuous woman to get revenge on his competitors. In "Stack A Lee," the title character savagely shoots another man because of a Stetson hat.[175] "Two Soldiers" and "Jack-A-Roe" center around the killing of young men in battle. In "Blood in My Eyes," the narrator pays a hooker, only to have her renege on the deal. The album cover suggest *World Gone Wrong*'s somber content: Dylan poses with hat and cane for a photo that looks like the visual setting for a film adaptation of an Edgar Allan Poe story.

Dylan's voice has the same endearing cragginess that swept through *Good As I Been to You*, but his singing is more bluesy, as he pays tribute to the likes of Blind Willie McTell and Doc Watson. The songs sound a lot like "Sittin' on Top of the World." For the most part, the songs are etched in a broody voice that aptly suits the tales Dylan is telling (as on "World Gone Wrong," "Love Henry," "Jack-A-Roe" and "Blood in My Eyes" [sung in a voice that mixes desire with disgust]). On "Delia," his voice breaks in sorrow when he talks about his love for Delia. And on "Stack A Lee," he lets loose vocally.

Once in a while, his singing does come up a little short. "Two Soldiers" is somewhat too restrained, and "Lone Pilgrim" is sung in a whisper.

Fortunately, his guitar playing is stellar throughout, dashing off guitar runs on "Ragged & Dirty" and "Broke Down Engine," bursting out on "Stack A Lee," fingerpicking through "Two Soldiers," strumming on "Love Henry" and "Delia."

Some of this material has links with a few songs on *Good As I Been to You*. Noted folk musicologist Alan Lomax says that "Frankie and Albert" is a direct descendant of "Love Henry."[176] "Jack-A-Roe" is similar to "Canadee-I-O." And "Delia" and "Diamond Joe" both use the prairies as a backdrop for their stories. By recording songs that follow the same skeletal format, Dylan makes a point of revealing how songs evolve as they are passed down through the ages.

Moreover, it's a particular treat for Dylan fans to see Dylan writing album notes again. The irresistible liner essay gives Dylan a chance to sound off against the problems he sees in the world today, a "New Dark Ages" peopled by "dupes of commerce & politics." Some of the lines are classic Dylan: "no man gains immortality thru public acclaim, truth is shadowy"; "give me a thousand acres of tractable land & all the gang members that exist & you'll see the Authentic alternative lifestyle, the Agrarian one." He even jokes about his touring habits ("there was a Never Ending Tour but it ended in '91 . . . there have been many others since then").

When Dylan asserts in the notes that there aren't any songs like these anymore, he's advocating a return to the roots of modern-day music. As with the songs on *Good As I Been to You,* this material obviously influenced Dylan's songwriting (in writing songs of lust, hardship and love gone sour, in composing ballads, and in writing spirituals with a universal appeal ["Lone Pilgrim"]). One also discovers that "Broke Down Engine" is the source for "the Georgia crawl" that Dylan mentions in "Gonna Change My Way of Thinking" (although people still aren't sure what it is). And, like *Good As I Been to You, World Gone Wrong* may look to the past for its inspiration, but the performances reinforce Dylan's relevance in the present.

BOB DYLAN'S GREATEST HITS, VOLUME III

RELEASED: DECEMBER 1994

Greatest Hits, Volume III is intended to draw attention to Dylan's post-1960s material. All the songs are from 1973 onwards, with one song per album being the general rule.

There are the givens ("Tangled Up in Blue"; "Joker-man"), the radio hits ("Gotta Serve Somebody"; "Knockin' on Heaven's Door"), and a few pleasantly surprising inclusions ("Silvio"; "Ring Them Bells"; "The Groom's Still Waiting at the Altar") on this collection, as well as the token "previously unreleased" song ("Dignity") that no greatest hits album is without nowadays. "Dignity," written for *Oh Mercy* but not used on the record, concludes with words of staid perseverance:

> So many roads, so much at stake
> So many dead ends, I'm at the edge of the lake
> Sometimes I wonder what it's gonna take
> To find dignity.

Despite this new song, *Volume III* seems inconsequential, partly in the wake of *Biograph* and *The Bootleg Series*, partly because *Volume III* attempts to cover twenty-three years of Dylan's career in one package and winds up leaving out innumerable gems. It would have made more sense for Columbia to have released a compilation of live recordings or unreleased tracks instead of another greatest hits collection. It remains a mystery why Columbia continues to hoard so much prime Dylan material.

MTV UNPLUGGED

RELEASED: APRIL 1995

With *MTV Unplugged*, Dylan continued along the acoustic route he had traveled on recent albums, but with his touring band backing him. As was the case with *Good As I Been to You* and *World Gone Wrong*, *Unplugged* is a unified album and, as live offerings go, it is one of Dylan's better ones.

Dylan sounds involved in the proceedings, and his singing is relaxed and confident. Only on occasion (the last verse of "Desolation Row"; the chorus of "Knockin' on Heaven's Door") does his voice slip into an urgent whine that detracts from the performance.

The television special first aired in December 1994; the prospect of Dylan appearing on the show had been rumored since 1992. Dylan seems to be having a good time, shaking hands with audience members at the conclusion of the concert, and cutting short a false start of "Like a Rolling Stone" by saying, "We're gonna start this again. My men are way ahead of me."

The album includes three songs not shown on the program: a rollicking "Tombstone Blues," "Desolation Row," and the little-known "John Brown." "John Brown" is a 1962 composition and was previously released only on 1963's *Broadside Ballads, Volume 1*, with Dylan appearing under the famous pseudonym Blind Boy Grunt.

The moralistic tale regurgitates the theme of "war is hell," but the song's main concern is with the attitudes of parents who envision war as a heroic experience for their sons. John Brown's mother encouragingly sends her reluctant son to battle, only to discover on his return that the boy has been horribly maimed. John Brown directs his anger with war at his mother, and the song ends with the child dropping his medals into his mother's hand. "John Brown" is a disturbing song, done here in an unadorned arrangement.

In "Desolation Row," Dylan's voice flitters along with the notes of the organ, as he substitutes the gloom of the unsurpassable original version with a sorrowful, reflective perspective on the landscape.

Likewise, the tone of "Like a Rolling Stone" differs from the original; here, the song is more a controlled reproach

ANTHONY VARESI

than a venomous broadside. The longer version of the song on *Unplugged* is performed in a bright, casual manner, and it holds up quite well.

In addition to "Desolation Row" and "Like a Rolling Stone," the other classics recorded for *Unplugged* are "All Along the Watchtower," "Rainy Day Women #12 & 35," "The Times They Are A-Changin'" and "Knockin' on Heaven's Door." "All Along the Watchtower," despite a stirring introduction, comes across as a bit stale, and "Rainy Day Women" has a similar drabness about it. But "The Times They Are A-Changin'," in yet another incarnation, sounds better than it has in years, and the musical work on "Heaven's Door" supports Dylan's wayward singing.

The only recent offerings on *Unplugged* are "Shooting Star" and "Dignity." "Shooting Star" is, much like on *Oh Mercy*, sedate; "Dignity" sounds punchier than the version on *Greatest Hits, Volume III*.

Unplugged closes with an excellent version of "With God on Our Side." Dylan leaves out the dated sixth verse concerning the Russians, as well as verse five; the changes notwithstanding, the song does convey a sense of confusion about contemporary America.

Fortunately, Dylan sounds far from confused on this album. Most of the arrangements shine, and the backing allows Dylan to proceed at a comfortable pace. *Unplugged* shows, once again, that Dylan is constantly finding new meaning in his songs, both for himself and for his audience.

CONCLUSION

It seems logical that, with his career into its fourth decade, Dylan would return to making solo albums. In some ways, *Good As I Been to You* and *World Gone Wrong* bring Dylan's art full circle. Among other things, these albums show that Dylan is still respectful of his musical heritage, and still doing what he wants in the way that he wants to do it.

Despite the poor sales of these records and *MTV Unplugged*, Dylan's popularity remained steady during this period, thanks in part to the critical praise these albums received. Among the highlights from his live appearances during this time are a performance with a symphony orchestra at The Great Music Experience in Tokyo, a show that could have been a disaster but instead presented dignified renditions of "Ring Them Bells" and "A Hard Rain's A-Gonna Fall," Dylan's set at Woodstock 1994, at which Dylan won over a much younger audience, and a moving rendition of "Restless Farewell" at Frank Sinatra's eightieth birthday party. Dylan continued to tour during this period, but fans were still waiting anxiously for a new studio album of original material.

PART XIII

SKETCHES FROM MEMORY

TIME OUT OF MIND

RELEASED: SEPTEMBER 1997

Dark and bluesy, *Time Out of Mind* is Dylan's most significant album of the decade, encompassing many of his lifelong themes. There are songs of struggle, survival, heartache and faith. Like many of his finer works, the emotions are laid bare.

Dylan backs up the lyrics with committed vocals, and the help of an assortment of musicians, including members of his touring band (Bucky Baxter, Tony Garnier), and well-known session men (Jim Dickensen, Jim Keltner). And thanks to Daniel Lanois, the production is clean. Having Lanois along as producer inevitably brings forth comparisons to *Oh Mercy,* and both records do have Lanois' trademark echoes and occasionally lush instrumentation. In many ways, however, *Time Out of Mind* is a more complete album than *Oh Mercy.* As fine an album as *Oh Mercy* is, it doesn't quite hang together. At times, the musicians seem distant from the singer, and with Dylan's voice having aged, the lyrics lose some of their impetus. The instrumental breaks in *Oh Mercy* too often sound like empty space. On *Time Out of Mind*, Lanois cloaks the songs in an atmosphere apposite for Dylan's brood.

Time is actually closer in spirit to *Good As I Been to You* and *World Gone Wrong*. It has the same mastery of folk and blues idioms, and Dylan's singing is similar. It's as if Dylan went back to traditional songs to reconnect with his muse, to distance himself from current trends and make records the way he wanted to make them. Some of the lyrics on *Time* show links with the previous records. The line "Gonna walk down that dirt road, until my eyes begin to bleed" in "Dirt Road Blues" is a descendant of "Blood in My Eyes." When Dylan sings, on "Standing in the Doorway," "Don't know if I saw you if I would kiss you or kill you," it recalls the violent misogyny of "I told you, baby, right to your head, / If I don't leave you I would have to kill you dead" in "World Gone Wrong" and "The day you quit me, baby, / That's the day you die, lawd, lawd" in "You're Gonna Quit Me."

Traditional music has a strong place in *Time*, as many folk and blues images appear throughout the album. One of the most famous of these images is the train, which historically can symbolize many things: salvation in "This Train," "Get on Board" and "People Get Ready"; despair in "Broke Down Engine"; loneliness in "900 Miles" and "Mystery Train"; freedom in "The Midnight Special." Many of Dylan's songs utilize a vision of the train. An early composition, "Train A-Travelin'," makes the setting one of desperation ("a firebox of hatred and a furnace full of fears"). "It Takes a Lot to Laugh, It Takes a Train to Cry" is more celebatory – "Don't the brakeman look good, mama, / Flagging down the 'Double E'" – as is "Tonight I'll Be Staying Here with You": "I can hear that whistle blowin', / I see that station-master, too." In the rewritten version of "Tangled Up In Blue" on *Real Live*, Dylan uses the frequently occurring blues phrase "get on that train and ride." And there is the "long-distance train rolling through the rain" of "Where Are You Tonight?," and the "Slow Train."

On *Time*, Dylan speaks of "people on the platforms, waitin' for the trains," generating a picture of time standing still. In the same song, "Tryin' to Get to Heaven," Dylan sings, "Some trains don't pull no gamblers, / No midnight ramblers like they did before," quoting almost verbatim from Guthrie's "This Train": "This train don't pull no gamblers, neither don't pull no midnight ramblers." The narrator of "Tryin' to Get to Heaven" never says if he rides the train, implying he takes his place with the "People on the platforms" in his quest "to get to Heaven before they close the door." In "Standing in the Doorway," the narrator rides "a midnight train / Got ice water in my veins," a stark contrast to the mythical gospel train.

This line reflects the restlessness that infuses *Time*. In "Standing in the Doorway," the search is for an "old love." "Tryin' to Get to Heaven" has the narrator traveling "all around the world" for an inner peace. The opening lines of the album are "I'm walking, / through streets that are dead." "Dirt Road Blues" begins with "Gonna walk down that dirt road' til someone lets me ride." In "Highlands," Dylan sings, "Feel like I'm driftin', driftin' from scene to scene." These lyrics have the same wandering, Guthriesque quality as "Talking New York" and "Song to Woody" on his first album.

Accompanying this restlessness is a profound loneliness and sense of loss. Like a blues singer wishing for his "mama," Dylan gives many of the songs an unmistakable sadness that cuts through any hostility. "Love Sick's" anger over rejection disguises the ironic pathos of the conclusion: "Just don't know what to do / I'd give anything to be with you." Over a caressing melody, the narrator of "Standing in the Doorway" makes a plea for an ex-lover and equates any further relationships with this woman: "Last night I danced with a stranger / But she just reminded me you were the one." The same thing occurs in "Highlands," as the narrator tires of the charade of trading pick-up lines with the waitress and slips out when she isn't looking. "Million Miles," "Can't Wait" and "'Til I Fell in Love with You" continue along similar lines, but the songs are less effective because the tunes are lazy blues arrangements, and some of the lines seem recycled, such as "That's alright, mama" and "Rock me, pretty baby, rock me all at once." Only "Make You Feel My Love" is conciliatory. The lyrics are relatively pedestrian, but the mood created is stirring, as Dylan's voice sails over his piano accompaniment.

Dylan says that the album falls somewhere between despondency and hope, and indeed both emotions are present throughout *Time*.[177] There is a great deal of despair in lines such as "All the laughter is just makin' me sad," "Sometimes my burden is more than I can bear" and "Every nerve in my body is so naked and numb." In the stately "Not Dark Yet," the sense of loss is overwhelming:

Well, my sense of humanity is going down the drain
Behind every beautiful thing, there's been some kind of
  pain.

"Love Sick" seethes with the bitterness of a break-up. "Cold Irons Bound" forecasts troubled times ("Well, the road is rocky and the hillside's mud / Up over my head nothing but clouds of blood"), as does "Can't Wait": "Skies are gray / I'm looking for anything that will bring a happy glow."

The songs that best capture the balance between despondency and hope are "Tryin' to Get to Heaven" and "Highlands," two of Dylan's grandest compositions. "Tryin' to Get to Heaven" is Dylan's masterpiece of the 1990s. The song has the same broad spirituality as "I Shall Be Released," a sense of survival in the face of obstacles. Parts of the song have a Biblical quality to them, as when Dylan sings "I've been walkin' that lonesome valley," and the "land of milk and honey" phrase, "I've been to Sugartown, I shook the sugar down." There are some disheartening lines ("I close my eyes and I wonder if everything is as hollow as it seems"; "When you think that you've lost everything, / You find out you can always lose a little more"), but the mood that prevails is one of ennobling perseverance. The proof is in the performance; as the organ washes over the song, Dylan's voice becomes almost glorious when he sings about "tryin' to get to heaven before they close the door."

"Highlands" will either enthrall or tire the listener; either way, the song is probably too long, due to its slow pace and running time of over sixteen minutes. The narrator muses about being "on anything but a roll" and wishes he could "push back the clock," but he finds harmony in a beatific natural paradise: "the beautiful lake of the Black Swan"; "Honeysuckle blooming in the wildwood air / Blue-bells blazing where the Aberdeen waters flow"; "The wind it whispers to the buckeye trees of rhyme." The conclusion is a vision of contentment:

> There's a way to get there, and I'll figure it out somehow
> Well, I'm already there in my mind and that's good
>   enough for now.

Both "Tryin' to Get to Heaven" and "Highlands" offer plenty of material for fans to ponder. The former's "Miss Mary Jane" from Baltimore – perhaps a nod to Tim Hardin's "The Lady Came from Baltimore" – is only introduced briefly, but she summons a picture of gentility and wealth. One of Dylan's skills is breathing life into characters that appear for a verse or even a couple of lines and then are gone, like Aladdin in "Gates of Eden," the "little neighbor boy" in "The Ballad of Frankie Lee and Judas Priest" and the dealer in "Black Diamond Bay." The same is true of Miss Mary Jane, for the images of her "house in Baltimore" and the narrator "ridin' in a buggy" with her are immediately visualized by the listener.

"Highlands" is filled with gentle humor. "I'm listening to Neil Young, I gotta turn up the sound / Someone's always yellin', 'Turn it down!'" may be making fun of Young's grunge stance of the early 1990s (hence the cry to "'Turn it down!'") or be taken literally, which would link it with the line "At least that's what I think I hear her say" during his conversation with the waitress. Dylan plays on his age when he talks about not knowing "the difference between a real blonde and a fake." And when the waitress says "I know you're an artist, draw a picture of me," Dylan is having some fun at his own expense, self-referencing his book of charcoal paintings, *Drawn Blank*.

"Highlands" is a fine closer for the album, because it puts the narrator at ease ("The sun is beginnin' to shine on me"), heading for the pastoral splendor of the mythical highlands. "My heart's in the Highlands" suggests the narrator is distancing himself from the obsession of "Love Sick" and "Standing in the Doorway," and has purged himself of these feelings and his misgivings about age (in "Not Dark Yet"). The title of the album implies detachment and, musically, a return to the folk and blues melodies that influenced Dylan's development. Like *Blood on the Tracks*, *Time Out of Mind* is the work of an artist confronting his troubles – and walking away the stronger for having done so.

LOVE AND THEFT

RELEASED: SEPTEMBER 2001

Bob Dylan's early albums always struck a good balance between solemnity and amusement. After *Desire*, the records started becoming more one-sided: either they were solemn, moody affairs like *Street Legal* and *Time Out of Mind*, or they threatened to collapse under the weight of their own folly, as with *Down in the Groove* and *Under the Red Sky*. On *Love and Theft*, the jocular meshes perfectly with the profound. This is Dylan's most varied album in a long time, and his most relaxed since *Nashville Skyline*.

The lighter material captures Dylan in fine comedic form. The marvellous Huck Finn tall tale "Po' Boy" works in a knock-knock joke, a groaner about calling room service and requesting a room, and even Shakespearean characters. A dialogue about repeating the past in "Summer Days" crams four lines into a five second span. "Honest with Me" speaks about going into the woods naked and "huntin' bare." "Floater (Too Much To Ask)" has a "Clothes Line Saga"-type charm to it.

On many of the songs, Dylan dips into his past for inspiration. "Honest with Me" is backed by a "Highway 61 Revisited"-style slide guitar. "Highwater" and "Tweedle Dee & Tweedle Dum" include a mixture of characters reminiscent of songs such as "Tombstone Blues" and "Highway 61 Revisited." "Lonesome Day Blues" relies on a back-beat that recalls *Blonde on Blonde*'s musicianship. The early "Only A Hobo" morphs into the sadder, more mature "Po' Boy." And "Cry Awhile" recalls the lasciviousness of *The Basement Tapes*.

But none of the songs can fairly be called copycats of Dylan's prior material. These songs have a vigour all their own. In some cases, they surpass the songs they resemble. For instance, Dylan's evocation of nature is better than on *New Morning* and *Planet Waves*. "Floater" perfectly captures a lazy summer day spent fishing in the backwoods; the sights and sounds wonderfully detailed. "Moonlight" evokes a similar tranquility.

Musically, the songs move seamlessly from one genre to the next. The jazzy swing of "Summer Days" and "Bye and Bye" leads into the rock of "Lonesome Day Blues"; the banjo-tinged "Highwater (For Charley Patton)" precedes the crooning in "Moonlight." Dylan's touring band follows him at just the right pace, allowing Dylan's aged voice to sit comfortably with the backing. Only on "Bye and Bye" is the playing too low in the mix. (Incidentally, some mischievous spirit planted a rumour on the Internet that the album consisted mostly of Dylan alone at the piano. The rumour quickly spread, which only proves that one shouldn't believe everything one reads on the Internet).

Not only does Dylan touch on other musical styles, but he occasionally pays tribute to other musicians and literary figures. Shakespeare is referenced twice on the album, and the penultimate verse in "Lonesome Day Blues" is a Walter Mitty-type fantasy. The opener, "Tweedle Dee & Tweedle Dum," cribs two characters from Lewis Carroll's *Through The Looking-Glass, and What Alice Found There*, and builds on their absurdity and constant quarrelling.

Chuck Berry's influence pops up throughout *Love and Theft*. The lines in "Summer Days" about having eight carburetors and a stalling motor seem straight out of Berry's "Maybelline." Likewise the reference in "Lonesome Day Blues" to "dropping it into overdrive," and the "hopped-up Mustang Ford" of "Highwater." Berry's book *The Autobiog-*

raphy reveals a penchant for the type of laughs that occur throughout *Love and Theft*.

Charley Patton actually gets thanked in a song title, something Dylan has only done before with "Song to Woody" and "Blind Willie McTell" ("See You Later, Allen Ginsberg" doesn't count). Considered the founder of the Delta blues, Patton lived hard and influenced every bluesman who followed, with his ragged voice and poetic guitar picking.

"Highwater (For Charley Patton)" is Dylan's frightening sequel to "Down in the Flood." In Patton's "High Water Everywhere (Part 1)" and "High Water Everywhere (Part 2)," he tells the story of the Mississippi flood of 1927. The song ends with a cry to God that "Oh, Lordy, women and grown men drown." Dylan's song opens with a mention of the great pianist and jazzman Big Joe Turner, and proceeds to document a scene as chaotic as in Patton's song. Dylan's singing on "Down in the Flood" sounds more like a warning; here, his voice is one of menace, as David Kemper's drumrolls at the start of each verse sound like a wave of water. The flooding of the Mississippi Delta comes to symbolize the loss of the great bluesmen like Charley Patton, and the title is Dylan's reminder that their music should never be forgotten.

"Mississippi" is the album's other masterpiece. Originally written for *Time Out of Mind* but then re-recorded, the song has a dignified, moving melody. When Dylan sings that his heart "is not weary," he sounds like a man who will continue to make music until his dying day.

Not all of *Love and Theft* is successful. The chorus to "Sugar Baby" is hectoring, and the song has sounded dull when performed at recent concerts. And while Dylan could play the role of crooner on "Tomorrow Night," on "Moonlight" he just cannot get his voice around the melody.

The most promising aspect of *Love and Theft* is that it shows Dylan's creativity is flourishing. The sheer length of the songs suggests that the writer's block of the early to mid 1990s is long gone. And Dylan seems to be genuinely enjoying himself, as if his brush with death in 1997 has given him a new perspective on writing and performing. A strong follow-up to *Time Out of Mind*, *Love and Theft* sparkles with wit and enthusiasm.

CONCLUSION

Time Out of Mind came in for hefty praise from critics: it made the "top ten" lists of *Q*, *Mojo*, *Spin*, *Rolling Stone* (number one), *People* and *Entertainment Weekly* (among others), and was named second-best album of the year in a panel of Canadian critics. The record received more press than any Dylan album since *Slow Train Coming* and sold over half a million copies, a good showing after the poor sales of his previous records. At the 1998 Grammy Awards, which in recent years have broadened the voting base to reflect somewhat sounder judgment, Dylan received the awards for best male rock vocal performance for "Cold Irons Bound," best contemporary folk album, and album of the year. Dylan even performed "Love Sick," spoiled when someone hopped on the stage and began gyrating foolishly. Dylan responded with a hilarious double-take. The President of the National Academy of Recording Arts and Sciences came on after and, looking furious and embarrassed, apologized to Dylan. In his acceptance speech for album of the year, Dylan mentioned Buddy Holly and Robert Johnson but wasn't quite as cryptic as in his 1991 speech.

Prior to the record's release in late May, Dylan almost died from a rare heart infection and spent several days in

hospital. After his recovery, he played for the Pope in Bolo-
gna in September and became a Kennedy Center honoree in
December. 1997 also saw the release outside the United
States of the otherwise redundant compilation *The Best of
Bob Dylan*, featuring an impressive alternate version of
"Shelter from the Storm," which played over the closing
credits to the film *Jerry Maguire*, and *The Songs of Jimmie
Rodgers: A Tribute*, an album put together by Dylan and
released on Dylan's label Egyptian Records, and featuring
such artists as Bono, Willie Nelson and Jerry Garcia.

In May 1998, Dylan briefly toured with Van Morrison
and Joni Mitchell. In 1999, he paired up for an extensive
North American tour with Paul Simon. Both artists did a full
set of songs, and dueted on four songs, including "The
Sounds of Silence." Dylan seemed to be genuinely enjoying
himself at the shows, and was in good voice. Simon's set
tended to be more conservative and contrasted sharply with
the reworkings Dylan gave his songs. A summer 2000 tour
featured Dylan on a bill with former Grateful Dead bassist
Phil Lesh. Dylan's constant touring suggests that he loves the
road and the opportunity to play his songs in so many
different ways (and it gives the lie to the dialogue between
Martin Scorcese and Robbie Robertson in *The Last Waltz*, in
which touring is described as a "goddamn impossible way of
life").

The one disconcerting aspect of this period was Dylan's
licensing of his songs for use in advertisements, specifically
the *Biograph* version of "Forever Young" for Apple Comput-
ers and "The Times They Are A-Changin'" for the Bank of
Montreal. The first shall be last? Sorry, not for these big
corporations.

After Dylan's appearance at the Golden Globe Awards
(for best original song for "Things Have Changed" from the
film *Wonder Boys*), in early 2001, the award shows and

accolades were starting to become routine, as if Dylan's brush with death in May 1997 made the people responsible for such awards suddenly realize how essential Dylan's music was to popular culture.

At the Academy Awards in April 2001, however, Dylan turned in a performance that brilliantly skewered the ostensible glamour of Hollywood. Appearing via satellite from Australia, where he was on tour at the time (although the eerie, darkened setting made the soundstage look like the centre of the earth), Dylan gnarled his way through "Things Have Changed." The relentless close-ups of Dylan's visage stood in stark contrast to the pearly whites and cosmetically enhanced bodies of the majority of the Hollywood audience. Dylan's appearance was the truest moment of the entire evening.

Following the release of *Love and Theft*, Dylan embarked on a brief United States tour. Many of his older songs retained their relevance in post-September 11 America. When Dylan played "A Hard Rain's A-Gonna Fall" in Seattle, it was heartbreakingly sad, but as the song built to a crescendo in the epic final verse, Dylan's voice resonated with hope in the face of enormous suffering.

Dylan's place in popular culture ranks alongside Elvis and The Beatles amongst twentieth century musicians. No other artists have inspired so much fascination in the public and the press. In their list of the one hundred most influential people of the century, Dylan was named the greatest folk musician and The Beatles the greatest rock musicians of the century by *Time*. One suspects that Dylan was placed in the "folk" category to avoid having to choose between him and The Beatles in the "rock" section. Dylan's greatest gift to folk may have been giving it mainstream acceptance; his greatest gift to rock may have been drawing on his folk influences and his literary influences to give rock a new language. Or his greatest contribution to both may have been his voice, as expressive as any other singer's. Part blues, part country, part pop, part folk: Dylan's voice is unique in popular music.

His influence on both rock and folk is wide-ranging. Where would Peter, Paul and Mary, or Joan Baez, or The Byrds have been without him? Or more modern protest singers like Billy Bragg, Tracy Chapman, or Sinead O'Connor, whose working-class sensibilities gained them recognition? Phil Ochs wrote some fine protest anthems but forever lingered in Dylan's shadow and could never deal with fame as well as his contemporary. "I Ain't a Marchin' Anymore," "Talking Cuban Crisis," "The Ballad of Oxford (Jimmy Meredith)" and "Draft Dodger Rag" are styled after Dylan's songs. Ochs' singing was likewise unconventional, but Dylan's voice made clear that it was perfectly acceptable. Donovan pitched himself as an ultra-hippie Dylan and wrote rip-offs like "Catch the Wind."

Dylan's music spawned innumerable protest songs, including John Lennon's "Give Peace a Chance," "Eve of Destruction" (Barry McGuire), "Street Fighting Man" (The Rolling Stones), "Dawn of Correction" (The Spokesmen), Creedence Clearwater Revival's "Who'll Stop the Rain" and "Fortunate Son," and The Who's "Won't Get Fooled Again."

After Dylan's move to electric music, more and more singer-songwriters emerged in Dylan's wake. Paul Simon mixed pleasant folk songs with Dylanesque excursions like "A Simple Desultory Phillippic" and "Cloudy" ("From Tolstoi to Tinker Bell / Down from Berkeley to Carmel"). The arty "poetry" of Jim Morrison owes much to Dylan; Morrison's lyrics, however, are too often overblown, and his ridiculous behavior during his career was reprehensible, moreso because some cultists actually admire him for it. Patti Smith handled self-loathing much better; like Dylan, she drew inspiration from the Beat poets. Pete Townshend really came into his own as a songwriter after discovering Dylan circa *Another Side*.[178] Elvis Costello's songs bask in the freedom Dylan enabled songwriters to write with.

Of all the "New Dylans," Bruce Springsteen gained the most fame.[179] Part Dylan, part Guthrie, part Chuck Berry, part 1950s rock 'n' roller, plus a great deal of originality, Springsteen enjoyed big success early in his career with *Born to Run* and became an international superstar with the radio-ready *Born in the U.S.A.* But the immense popularity may actually have hurt his career; when 1987's *Tunnel of Love* wasn't more like *Born in the U.S.A.*, all the Springsteen "fans" who had jumped on the bandwagon jumped off; and his subsequent career seems like an attempt to find a comfortable medium between artistic integrity and commercial success. The release of *Human Touch* and *Lucky Town* simultaneously, a cop of Guns 'n' Roses' tactics, struck many as motivated by greed. Ticket sales for his shows dropped, critics snickered at Springsteen doing an electric set on "MTV Unplugged," and the "family man" stance he adopted on *Lucky Town* (à la *New Morning*) alienated many listeners. 1994's *The Ghost of Tom Joad* was a noble but unsuccessful attempt to recapture the greatness of *Nebraska. Nebraska* is Springsteen's finest work, a masterful folk album that heartbreakingly sketches a picture of Americana. "I wouldn't be here without [Dylan]'" Springsteen once said.[180] Dylan's influence appears not only in Springsteen's songwriting (long narratives like "Jungleland," atmospheric songs like "Atlantic City"), but in Springsteen's disdain for music videos, his wariness with the press, and his respect for his musical elders. Dylan retains a perceptible impact on today's musicians, among them Beck and The Wallflowers (fronted by Dylan's son Jakob).

To discuss every musician who is in some way indebted to Dylan is beyond the scope of this work. The examples given above and throughout the book are illustrative of his wide-ranging impact on music.

Dylan's staying power is remarkable. Unlike The Rolling Stones, who have remained immensely popular by constantly reminding people how great they once were, Dylan hasn't trod on his reputation, remaining as withdrawn as ever. Every few years, Dylan comes up with a great album that reinforces his stature. Just when his name seems to have fallen out of fashion for good, he makes it back into the headlines. He did it in the 1970s with the 1974 tour and *Blood on the Tracks*; he did it in the 1980s with *Infidels* and *Oh Mercy*; and he did it in the 1990s with *Time Out of Mind*. Among 1960s musicians still around in the 1990s, only the Stones, Van Morrison, Neil Young and Eric Clapton have managed, like Dylan, to maintain a relatively consistent level of popularity. Others, like Lou Reed, Paul Simon and Pete Townshend, haven't done enough work in the 1990s to sustain critical attention.

Dylan is too fascinating a figure to remain out of the spotlight for too long a period of time. More has been written about him than any popular artist except for Elvis and The Beatles; there are dozens of Internet sites devoted to him; there are fanzines and fan clubs, seminars on his work; every year, dozens of people make a pilgrimage to Hibbing to see where he grew up. It is not just his music that gives him such a following, but the twists and turns of his career, and his determination in the face of opposition. Playing rock and roll at a folk festival; getting booed at every show with The Hawks in 1965-66 and *still* not giving the fans what they wanted; going electric despite being the leader of the folk revival; making *John Wesley Harding* in 1967; going country; becoming a fundamentalist Christian; confounding the Grammy audience in 1991; making the cover of *Newsweek* in 1998: all events that have fueled more controversy, commentary and speculation than some artists experience in their entire career.

Today, popular music encompasses far too many styles for one man to emerge, as Dylan did in the 1960s, and change the direction of pop culture. Popular music owes much of this diversity to Bob Dylan, the man who rewrote the rules for song, liberating rock and roll with his pen and with his voice. As to where Bob Dylan is headed next, who can say? For the only thing predictable about Bob Dylan is that he will always be unpredictable.

NOTES

INTRODUCTION

1   Crowe, Cameron. *Biograph* liner notes, yellow sheets, "Blowin' in the Wind" section.

2   "That difficult task hinged on the authorship and success of "Blowin' in the Wind."" *Ibid.*

3   "Dylan wrote [in "The Lonesome Death of Hattie Carroll"] of the brutal injustice with a masterful touch, never did it approach the heavy-handed." Crowe, p. 10.

4   "Admirers and detractors alike have fallen victim to the 'periodic' fallacy – the notion that the 'folk Dylan' or the 'electric Dylan' or the 'country Dylan' or the 'gospel Dylan' is *the* Dylan, and hence the hero of his own apotheosis or the demon of his own decline." Karlin, Danny. "It Ain't Him, Babe." *London Review of Books*, February 5, 1987, p. 8.

PART I

5   Dave Van Ronk: "We had a terrible falling out about 'House of the Rising Sun.' He was always a sponge, picking up whatever was around him, and he copped my arrangement of the song. Before going into the studio he asked, 'Hey, Dave, mind if I record your version of 'Rising Sun'?' I said, 'Well, Bobby, I'm going into the studio soon and I'd like to record it.' And later he asked me again and I told him I wanted to record it myself, and he said, 'Oops, I already recorded it and can't do anything about it because Columbia wants it.'" Scaduto, Anthony. *Bob Dylan: An Intimate Biography*. New York: Grosset and Dunlap, 1971, p. 105.

6   "He wrote 'Song to Woody' right after that first Sunday visit." Shelton, Robert. *No Direction Home*. New York: William Morrow, 1986, p. 102.

7   "Woody Guthrie was my last idol / he was the last idol / because he was the first idol." "11 Outlined Epitaphs," liner notes to *The Times They Are A-Changin'*.

8   Heylin, Clinton. *Bob Dylan: Behind the Shades*. New York: Summit, 1991, p. 70.

9   Riley, Tim. *Hard Rain: A Dylan Commentary*. New York: Alfred A. Knopf, 1992, p. 61.

10   Karlin, p. 8.

11   Crowe, p. 11.

12   "One of Dylan's prophecies, optimistic and vengeful in heralding the day when evil will be purged." Shelton, p. 214.

13   "There is even a rumor circulating that Dylan did not write 'Blowin' in the Wind,' that it was written by a Millburn (N.J.) High student named Lorre Wyatt, who sold it to the singer. Dylan says he did write the song and Wyatt denies authorship, but several Millburn students claim they heard the song from Wyatt before Dylan ever sang it." Svedburg, Andrea. "I Am My Words." *Newsweek*, November 4, 1963, p. 95.

14   " ['The Times They Are A-Changin'"s] message is *politically* out of date . . . the people who wanted change have rightly lost the optimism of expecting senators and congressmen to heed their political calls." Gray, Michael. *Song and Dance Man: The Art of Bob Dylan*. New York: St. Martin's Press, 1981, p. 131.

15   *Biograph*, p. 5.

16   Spitz, Bob. *Dylan: A Biography*. New York: McGraw-Hill, 1989, p. 78.

17   *Biograph*, p. 26.

18   Humphries, Patrick, and John Bauldie. *Absolutely Dylan*. New York: Viking Studio Books, 1991, p. 44.

19   *Biograph*, yellow sheets, "Masters of War" section.

PART II

20   "Bombarded by visionaries such as Rimbaud, Brecht, Byron, Ginsberg, and the anonymous authors of the Bible, among others, the songs that were beginning to flow from him were growing more transcendent, less concretely objective, increasingly filled with the shapes of vivid fantasy, with the motifs out of the collective unconscious" Scaduto, pp. 177-78. Dave Van Ronk: "On his shelf I discovered a book of translations of French symbolist poets that has obviously been thumbed through over a period of years! I think he probably knew Rimbaud backward and forward . . ." Shelton, p. 99.

21   The incident is recounted, somewhat melodramatically, in Spitz, pp. 263-65.

22   Heylin, *Behind the Shades*, p. 105.

23   Tiring because for every person who insists song lyrics are poetry, somebody else will insist that they are not. Personally, lyrics probably are not poetry *per se* because a songwriter writes differently than a poet, knowing his lyrics will be set to music and necessarily constrained by this fact. Then again, if any songwriter comes closest to being a poet, it's Dylan.

PART III

24   Quoted in Williams, Paul. *Performing Artist: The Music of Bob Dylan, Volume I, 1960-1973*. California: Underwood-Miller, 1990, pp. 137-38.

25   "At the next to last session, Dylan recorded 'Tambourine Man,' 'It's All Right [sic], Ma,' and 'Gates of Eden' one after the other, without hearing a playback . . .This day he announced that these were long numbers and that he didn't want to do them more than once. They were recorded just that way, in one take." Kramer, Daniel. *Bob Dylan*. New York: Citadel Press, 1967, p. 91.

26   Kurt Loder: "Is it true that 'Like a Rolling Stone' was done in one take?" Dylan: "Yeah, one take. It's amazing." *Rolling Stone* editors. *The Rolling Stone Interviews: The 1980's*. New York: St. Martin's Press, 1989, p. 100. The Dylan CD-rom, *Bob Dylan: Highway 61 Interactive*, contains nine takes of the song.

27   "According to Daniel Kramer, Dylan announced that he was going to record 'It's Alright, Ma,' 'Gates of Eden' and 'Mr. Tambourine Man' in one go. If the story is true, Dylan's bravado for once let him down. Though 'It's Alright, Ma' (after one false start) and 'Gates of Eden' came easily enough, 'Mr. Tambourine Man' proved no easier to record than at the previous day's session . . . According to Columbia's files, the *Bringing It All Back Home* version of 'Mr. Tambourine Man' was actually take number six." Heylin, Clinton. *Bob Dylan: The Recording Sessions (1960-1994)*. New York: St. Martin's Press, 1996, p. 36. Heylin doesn't quite succeed in clearing up the issue. Kramer says 'Mr. Tambourine Man' was the first of the three songs recorded, Heylin says it was recorded last. Further, Heylin lists only one take of the song for January 16, 1965, the date Kramer was present in the studio.

28   "I don't know, different things inspired me . . . that Fellini movie? What was it? *La Strada*. It was all sort of like the same thing, you know." *Biograph*, yellow sheets, "Mr. Tambourine Man" section.

29   Riley, p. 107.

30   Spitz, p. 273.

31   "Dylan like Benjamin Franklin can list among his many achievements the authorship of a remarkable number of successful aphorisms." Williams, *Performing Artist, Volume I*, p.123. "... ['It's Alright, Ma' contains] perhaps more memorable aphorisms than in any other popular song ." Heylin, *Behind the Shades*. p.110.

32   "If the other guy hadn't left the damn thing turned on, my career as an organ player would have ended right there. ... After six minutes they'd gotten the first complete take of the day down, and all adjourned to the booth to hear it played back. Thirty seconds into the second verse, Dylan motions towards Tom Wilson. 'Turn the organ up,' he orders. 'Hey, man,' Tom says, 'that cat's not an organ player.' But Dylan isn't buying it. 'Hey, now don't tell me who's an organ player and who's

not. Just turn the organ up.'" Kooper, Al. *Backstage Passes: Rock 'n' Roll Life in the Sixties*. New York: Stein and Day, 1977, p. 55.

33   Speech delivered by Springsteen at the Rock and Roll Hall of Fame induction dinner on January 20, 1988 . Reprinted in Thomson, Elizabeth, and David Gutman, eds. *The Dylan Companion*. London: Macmillan, 1990, p. 286.

34   "You're never sure how many lovers the narrator is addressing: whether his journeys chase the redhead in the first stanza – the slightest verse with the most cliches . . ." Riley, p. 236.

35   *Biograph* yellow sheets, "Abandoned Love" section.

36   ". . . I see Lyndon Johnson as King of the Philistines." Shelton, p. 280. "The word 'Philistines' (easy to think of that word when thinking of Lyndon Johnson, in those days) . . ." Williams, *Performing Artist, Volume I*, p. 161.

37   "The allusion, clinched by that 'castles,' to Kafka's visions . . ." Gray, *Song and Dance Man*, p. 142.

38   Riley, p. 131.

39   ". . . the song as a whole is about persecution . . . it happens to everybody, so don't feel bad . . ." Williams, *Performing Artist Volume I*, p. 192.

40   "You'd think he'd be a little more sensitive to this kind of hate-mongering." Armstrong, John. "Under my thumb . . ." *The Vancouver Sun*, January 9, 1993, p. E-1.

41   "You could stick with the chicaneries of the Schleswig-Holstein affair and end up like Lord Palmerston: 'Only three people ever fully understood it – one is dead, one is mad . . . and I can't remember!' Could almost be Bob Dylan talking about 'Sad-Eyed Lady of the Lowlands.'" Humphries, p. 167.

42   *Biograph*, yellow sheets, "Visions of Johanna" section.

43   Riley, p. 128.

44   "Some nights it sounds like Dylan is about to slump from his stool during the acoustic set." Heylin, Clinton. "Mixed Up Confusion," *Record Collector*, May 1996, p. 23. ". . . Dylan's demeanor onstage during the acoustic sets seemed indicative of someone stoned on marijuana." Heylin, *Behind the Shades*, p. 170. Dylan was certainly stoned during some of the electric sets, specifically the final show at the Royal Albert Hall in London on May 27, at which he prefaced "Like a Rolling Stone" with a long, rambling speech, introducing The Hawks as "all poets," thanking the audience for "sitting in this great, huge place" and dedicating the song to the Taj Mahal.

45   Marcus, Greil *Mystery Train: Images of America in Rock 'n' Roll* (Fourth Revised Edition). New York: Plume, 1997, p. 217

46   "The Hawks considered it the best performance of the tour . . ." Heylin, "Mixed Up Confusion," p. 20.

47   Silber, Irwin. "An Open Letter to Bob Dylan." Reprinted in Benson, Carl. *The Bob Dylan Companion: Four Decades of Commentary*. New York: Schirmer, 1998, p. 28.

48   Heylin, *Behind the Shades*, p. 165.

49   " I wasn't made to be booed . . . I was starting to get real pissed off. It was better for me not to be part of that." Helm, Levon. *This Wheel's On Fire: Levon Helm and the Story of The Band*. New York: William Morrow, 1993, p. 141.

50   "To shout 'Judas' at a Jew was an act of mind-boggling stupidity and senselessness." Lee, C.P., with photos by Paul Kelly. *Like The Night: Bob Dylan and the Road to the Manchester Free Trade Hall*. London: Helter Skelter, 1998, p. 152. Lee argues that the culprit was unaware of the racial implications of his comment, but was merely accusing Dylan of being a sell-out. I would argue that the statement could encompass both sentiments.

51   "The post-concert interviews with fans in *Eat the Document* all come from the Free Trade Hall." Heylin, "Mixed Up Confusion," p. 24.

52   Hoskyns, Barney. *Across the Great Divide: The Band and America*. Toronto: Penguin Books, 1993, p. 105.

53   Queenan, Joe. "The Freefallin' Bob Dylan." *Spy*, August 1991, p. 57.

54   Hoskyns, pp. 100-01.

55   Shelton, p. 366.

PART IV

56   "Rick Danko spoke of 'about 150 songs.'" Gray, Michael and John Bauldie, eds. *All Across the Telegraph*. London: Sidgwick and Jackson, 1987, p. 97. As for the songs that haven't emerged on bootlegs, both Heylin and Marcus suggest that they weren't recorded, or were recorded and deleted. Heylin writes: "The first myth to explode is that there are hours and hours of basement tapes yet to come . . . Hudson only ran the tapes when they felt they wanted to get something down." Heylin, *The Recording Sessions*, pp. 58-9. Marcus says the five-CD bootleg set *The Genuine Basement Tapes*, "with two exceptions, collects Dylan's extant basement pieces." Marcus, Greil. *Invisible Republic: Bob Dylan's Basement Tapes*. New York: Henry Holt, 1997, pp. 236-37.

57   Heylin, *The Recording Sessions*, p. 55.

58   Helm, p. 151. Heylin disputes this, saying that Helm "is surely a few weeks out here." Heylin, *The Recording Sessions*, p. 66.

59   Helm, p. 157.

60   Marcus, *Invisible Republic*, p. 235.

61   *The Basement Tapes* liner notes.

62   *Lyrics* has "I'm standing outside the Taj Mahal / I don't see no one around."

63   Marcus, *The Basement Tapes*.

64   "... Dylan makes slurred noises that only sound like words, like the dummy copy in a rough of an advertisement that only looks like text." Williams, Paul. *Performing Artist, Volume One*, p. 213.

65   "The Vivian in the chorus of 'Too Much of Nothing' has been suggested as T.S. Eliot's first wife Vivienne, who succumbed to the oblivion of madness." Humphries, p. 69.

66   "Indeed, there were suggestions in the press that the album was being released to shore up The Band's depleted funds, which had fallen to a low after two years of relative inactivity and their commercial decline following *Cahoots*." Heylin, *Behind the Shades*, p. 248. "It seems possible that one reason for releasing the basement recordings was to pay for Shangri-La [a ranch purchased by The Band in 1974 and converted into a studio] itself, since the Band had already frittered away so much of the money they'd made." Hoskyns, p. 312.

67   "In fact, the so-called Band basement tapes have nothing to do with the Dylan / Band sessions (of the eight Band cuts on *The Basement Tapes*, two are Richard Manuel Big Pink piano demos from the summer of 1967, with drums and guitars over dubbed in 1975; two are demos cut in New York in September 1967; two are recordings made shortly after Helm rejoined, probably at Big Pink [I'm guessing 'Don't Ya Tell Henry' and 'Long Distance Operator']; and two are actually 1975 recordings made at Shangri-La." Heylin, *The Recording Sessions*, pp. 67-68. (Block parentheses added.)

68   Marcus, *Invisible Republic*, p. 199.

69   To be fair, Columbia has posted "I'm Not There" and "I'm Your Teenage Prayer" on the official Bob Dylan web site (www.bobdylan.com), but fans still have to: a) Get the Internet; b) Have a sound chip in their computer and c) Hear it before Columbia pulls the song.

70   Weisbard, Eric. "The Folk Slingers." Reprinted in Benson, p. 241.

71   For more on the basement tapes, see *Invisible Republic*. For a brave stab at sorting out what was recorded when and where, see Heylin, *The Recording Sessions*, pp. 55-68. For a fascinating study on the history of bootlegs and the bootleg industry, see Heylin, Clinton. *The Great White Wonders: A History of Rock Bootlegs*. New York: Viking, 1994.

72   "... his born-again gospel music ... which became overbearing and grim." Riley, p. 200.

73   Marcus, Greil. "Amazing Chutzpah." Reprinted in Thomson, p. 240.

74   Shelton, p. 389.

75   "One *Melody Maker* reader spoofed: 'If you hold the album cover right-way up, then turn it in a clockwise direction, the record falls out.'" Shelton, p. 391.

76   Williams, *Performing Artist, Volume I*, p. 252.

77   "In The Studio: Charlie McCoy On Dylan." *Record Collector*, September 1992, p. 19.

PART V

78   "I don't know anyone, even vociferous supporters of this album, who plays more than one side at a time." Christgau, Robert. *Rock Albums of the70's: A Critical Guide*. New York: Da Capo, 1981, p. 116.

79   "Down south, Charlie McCoy and Kenny Buttrey were once again recruited to provide instrumentation, but to their surprise the tracks were to be done *without* Bob Dylan. 'It was a real strange session,' Charlie McCoy says of that experience. 'Dylan sent the tapes down [to Nashville] with instructions that we were to just play over what he'd already recorded on it.'" Spitz, pp. 397-98.

80   ". . . [songs] covering the entire range of traditional American music, stopping to pay tribute to bluesmen, cowboys, hillbillies, and a contemporary folksinger or two. Dylan's mellower voice . . . treated the songs well." Gross, Michael. *Bob Dylan: An Illustrated History*. New York: Grossett and Dunlap, 1978, p. 93. "Parts of it seem simply, and quite acceptably, to be the work of a man who is going through a creative drought and has decided to record 'covers' of some of his favorite songs." Heylin, *Behind the Shades*, p. 203.

81   "It is deliberately unoriginal in story, language, structure and overall ethos – and is a terrific parody of the Celtic ballad. I think it still the highlight of the album." Gray, *Song and Dance Man*, p. 167.

82   *The Rolling Stone Interviews: The 1980's*, p. 101.

83   For *Biograph*, Dylan added: *Biograph*, p. 21.

84   A.J. Weberman was a crackpot Dylan follower who gained infamy by rooting through Dylan's garbage. For good discussions of Weberman and his activities, see Spitz, pp. 400-04, and Shelton, pp. 410-12.

85   *The Rolling Stone Interviews*: The 1980's, p. 101.

86   "The roars of dismay along the underground press system made it sound as if Dylan had written a song in support of war, or genocide. One pop newspaper described Princeton as the 'home of Amerika's wealthy, alcoholic post-adolescents' and went on: 'Up on the roster are . . . academic fascists, taking time off from their war contracts to be trustees. Up there with them is Robert Zimmerman . . .'" Scaduto, p. 267.

87   "The songs and performances on *New Morning* are somehow inauthentic." Williams, *Performing Artist, Volume I*, p. 260.

88   Quoted in Williams, *Performing Artist, Volume I*, p. 269.

89   "*Dylan* must stand as his worst, least-representative album, reflecting extreme record-company cynicism . . . Critics described this album as 'corporate dirty pool' . . . In the long run, it probably harmed Columbia more than Dylan." Shelton, p. 428. "All of which is CBS's punishment after Bobby had the bad manners to sign with another label. I wonder how he could imagine that Columbia is less than benevolent." Christgau, p. 117.

90   "Dylan's singing here is as close as anyone has ever gotten to discovering the Lost Chord." Guterman, Jimmy and Owen O'Donnell. *The Worst Rock and Roll Records of All Time: A Fan's Guide to the Stuff You Love to Hate*. New York: Citadel Press, 1991, p. 100.

PART VI

91   Gray, *All Across the Telegraph*, p. 173.

92   Humphries, p. 88.

93   "Songs like 'Just Like a Woman' became stripped of emotion and sounded harsh and unfeeling." Heylin, *Behind the Shades*, p. 235. "Which is more indicative of the 1974 tour with The Band – the riveting 'Ballad of Hollis Brown' at the start, or the mutilated 'Just Like a Woman' at the close?" Lindley, John. "Highway 84 Revisited." Reprinted in Gray, *All Across the Telegraph*, p. 203.

94   *Biograph*, p. 22.

95   Helm, p. 241.

96   Riley, p. 218.

97   *Biograph*, yellow sheets, "You're a Big Girl Now" section.

98   Bauldie, John. *The Bootleg Series, Volumes 1-3* liner notes, p. 48.

99   Quotations and information in this paragraph and the next are from Cartwright, Bert. "The Mysterious Norman Raeben." Reprinted in Bauldie, John, ed. *Wanted Man: In Search of Bob Dylan*. New York: Citadel Underground, 1991, pp. 85-90.

100   *Biograph*, yellow sheets, "Tangled Up in Blue" section.

101   "In 'Simple Twist of Fate' the narrator wakes up after a magical one-night stand, sits in an empty room, and wonders if the woman he paid for the night before is thinking about him at all." Riley, p. 237.

102   " 'If You See Her, Say Hello' was another wistful love song, very much in the tradition of 'Girl from the North Country.'" Gross, p. 118. "A marvelous re-write of 'Girl from the North Country.'" Gray, *Song and Dance Man*, p. 180. "In 'If You See Her, Say Hello,' [Dylan] turns the listener into a reliable distraction from his obsession (as he did in 'Girl from the North Country')." Riley, p. 232

103   Neve, Michael. "Queen Mary." *London Review of Books*, December 20, 1984-January 24, 1985, p. 23. See also Marcus, *Mystery Train*: " 'Studying rain' is symbolism, carried forward into many Bob Dylan songs, echoing back to Shakespeare: it means to contemplate dread, to absorb fear into the soul." p.189. Rain is also used as a metaphor for warfare, as in "A Hard Rain's A-Gonna Fall," or in Creedence Clearwater Revival's masterful anti-Vietnam song "Who'll Stop the Rain?"

104   "The idea of an 'Idiot Wind' brings Shakespeare to mind again, specifically Macbeth's desperate meditation on the meaninglessness of life as 'a tale / Told by an idiot, full of sound and fury, / Signifying nothing.'" Bauldie, *The Bootleg Series*, p. 49.

105   Cartwright, p. 88.

106   Sloman, Larry. *On the Road With Bob Dylan: Rolling With the Thunder.*
      New York: Bantam, 1978, pp. 11-12.

107   "They segued into 'Mozambique,' Stoner says, only Howie hadn't fin-
      ished setting up the drums yet . . . and if you listen to the record you'll
      hear the drums don't come in for a while because Howie hadn't set
      them up.'" Spitz, p. 464.

108   Shepard, Sam. *Rolling Thunder Logbook.* New York: Viking Press,
      1977, p. 53.

109   Jonathan Cott: "But in a song like 'Sara' you seem fairly literal." Dylan:
      "When people say 'Sara' was written . . ." *Rolling Stone* editors. *The
      Rolling Stone Interviews, 1967-1980.* New York: St. Martin's Press,
      1981, p. 358.

110   "I have it on pretty good authority that Dylan wrote 'Sad-Eyed Lady'
      in the studio, just before the songs were recorded." Bangs, Lester. "Bob
      Dylan's Dalliance with Mafia Chic." Reprinted in Thomson, p. 212.
      "Certain lines seem patently untrue — such as his famous one about
      writing 'Sad-Eyed Lady of the Lowlands' in the Chelsea Hotel (it is
      fairly well documented that he wrote it in Nashville), having just taken
      some kind of cure (for what? – it would be another six months before
      he attempted to rid himself of his drug habits)." Heylin, *Behind the
      Shades*, p. 262.

111   Some writers accused Dylan of "using" Carter; "Joey" was lambasted
      by *Rolling Stone*, *The Village Voice*, and in numerous other articles.
      Information on Rubin Carter is from several sources, but primarily
      Shelton, pp. 459-62. Information on Joey Gallo is from Bangs' article,
      pp. 210-22.

112   "Dylan doesn't give a damn about Rubin Carter" (p. 210); " . . . he's
      having trouble coming up with meaningful subject matter closer to
      home . . . " (p. 211); "Dylan merely used Civil Rights and the rest of
      the movement to advance himself in the first place . . ." (pp. 210-11).

113   Ginsberg, Allen. *Desire* liner essay.

114   Heylin, *Behind the Shades*, p. 283.

115   Williams, Paul. *Bob Dylan, Performing Artist, The Middle Years, 1974-
      1986.* California: Underwood-Miller, 1992, p. 85.

116   Bauldie, *The Bootleg Series*, p. 49.

117   "When we open our ears – and it may take a dozen listenings before we
      stop hearing this album in terms of what we expect these songs to sound
      like, or, for the fans, in terms of the performances we think should have
      been included – the rewards and surprises of *Hard Rain* are nearly in-
      exhaustible." Williams, *Performing Artist, The Middle Years*, p. 84.

118   Cott, Jonathan. "Back Inside the Rain." Landau, Jon. "After the
      Flood." *Rolling Stone*, March 13, 1975, pp. 43-51.

PART VII

119 *The Rolling Stone Interviews, 1967-1980*, p. 356.

120 "No wonder this bleak night of the soul was followed by religious conversion." Flanagan, Bill. "Dylan Catalog Revisited." *Entertainment Weekly*, March 29, 1991, p. 32.

121 "Inveterate rock and rollers learn to find charm in boastful, secretly girl-shy adolescents, but boozy-voiced misogynists in their late thirties are a straight drag." Christgau, p. 118.

122 "*Street Legal* comes closest to where my music is going for the rest of time. It has to do with an illusion of time. I mean, what the songs are necessarily about is the illusion of time." Cartwright, p. 90.

123 Bauldie, *The Bootleg Series*, p. 52.

124 Williams, *Performing Artist, The Middle Years*, p. 111.

125 "A few people took against what appeared to be the espousal of a new set of show-business values, but it was really nothing more than Dylan trying something different yet again . . ." Williams, Richard. *Dylan: A Man Called Alias*. London: Bloomsbury, 1992, pp. 146-50.

126 "But the chief problem in performance impact seemed to be that Dylan was ailing." Shelton, p. 482. "'Bob was undoubtedly at the lowest point of his life,' observes a friend who traveled with the *Street Legal* entourage . . . 'His moods were more inconsistent than usual.'" Spitz, p. 526.

PART VIII

127 Information on this period provided by Shelton, pp. 483-87, Spitz, pp. 527-41, Heylin, *Behind the Shades*, pp. 315-23, and Heylin, Clinton. "Saved! Bob Dylan's Conversion To Christianity." Reprinted in Bauldie, *Wanted Man*, pp. 128-34.

128 Rosenbaum, Ron. "Born-Again Bob: Four Theories." Reprinted in Thomson, p. 233.

129 "Nevertheless, Dylan's conversion has some disturbing hints of cult brainwashings . . ." *Ibid.*, p. 237.

130 "Listening to the new Bob Dylan album is something like being accosted in an airport. 'Hello,' a voice seems to say as Dylan twists his voice around the gospel chords of 'When He Returns.' 'Can I talk with you for a moment? Are you new in town? You know, a few months ago I accepted Jesus into my life – 'Uh, sorry, got a plane to catch!' '– and if *you don't* you'll rot in hell!'" Marcus, Greil. "Amazing Chutzpah." Reprinted in Thomson, p. 237.

131 "Much of the writing is insultingly shoddy – some songs are no more than glorified lists." Ibid., p. 238.

132 Humphries, p. 143

133 Gray, *Song and Dance Man*, p. 226.

134 "Though Dylan seems to have seriously considered issuing the songs in the form of a live album, even recording two shows in Toronto in April at his own expense using a twenty-four track mobile studio, CBS dissuaded him . . . " Heylin, Clinton. *Behind the Shades*, p. 342.

135 Riley, p. 270.

136 *Biograph*, yellow sheets, "Every Grain of Sand" section.

137 Shelton, p. 484.

138 Wenner, Jann. "Bob Dylan In Our Times; The Slow Train Is Coming." *Rolling Stone*, September 20, 1979, p. 94.

139 Wolcott, James. "Bob Dylan Beyond Thunderdome." Reprinted in Thomson, p. 277.

140 *Ibid.*

141 "Bob Dylan's Leadbelly Parable." Gray, All Across the*Telegraph*, p. 183.

142 *Biograph*, yellow sheets, "Caribbean Wind" section.

143 Testa, Bart. "The Gospel According to Dylan." *Maclean's*, May 12, 1980, p. 58.

PART IX

144 *The Rolling Stone Interviews: The 1980's*, p. 97.

145 *Ibid.*, pp. 97-98.

146 ". . . an added overlay of what some critics took to be cranky political conservatism . . . " *The Rolling Stone Interviews: The 1980's*, p. 94.

PART X

147 "Dylan sounds as if he were the worse for drink when he recorded the track. When trying to perform his one and only live version of the song, in Sydney in February 1986, he could no longer play the ridiculous, droning melody and wisely abandoned the attempt." Heylin, *Behind the Shades*, p. 376.

148 Information provided by Gray, *All Across the Telegraph*, pp. 266-7; and Williams, *Performing Artist, The Middle Years*, p. 267.

149 Worrell, Denise. "'It's All Right In Front.'" *Time*, November 25, 1985, p. 89.

150 Marcus, Greil. "Bob Dylan: Comeback Time Again." *Village Voice*, August 13, 1985, p. 63.

151 " . . . there aren't any thematic arcs between songs . . ." Riley, p. 273.

152 *Biograph*, yellow sheets, "Every Grain of Sand" section.

153 Worrell, p. 89.

154 *Biograph*, p. 31.

155 *Biograph*, yellow sheets, "Caribbean Wind" section.

156 Gilmore, Mikal. "Positively Dylan." *Rolling Stone*, July 17-31, 1986, p. 135.

157 ". . . I'd always liked . . . 'Lil Junior Parker . . ." *Biograph*, p. 7.

158 Altman, Billy. "Music" section. *The Nation*, September 6, 1986, p. 187.

159 "In The Studio: Al Kooper on Dylan." *Record Collector*, September 1992, p. 18.

160 Gilmore, p. 32.

161 "The pressure of completing the album has reportedly been wearing on Dylan, and his mood is said to have been rather dour and unpredictable these last several days. In fact, somewhere along the line he has decided to put aside most of the rock & roll tracks he had been working on in Topanga, and is apparently now assembling the album from various sessions that have accrued over the last year." Ibid., p. 135.

162 Williams, *A Man Called Alias*, p. 181.

163 "You had to feel sorry for Bob Dylan when he came onstage at Wembley with what looked like a raccoon living in his hair!" Humphries, p. 162. The reference is not exact, but Dylan had the same "hair" in his 1987 shows with Tom Petty (the shows referred to by Humphries) as he did in his 1987 shows with the Dead.

164 ". . . I'd just like to say that I hope that some of the money that's raised for the people in Africa, maybe they could just take a little bit of it – maybe one or two million maybe . . . and use it, say, to pay the . . . mortgages on some of the farms, that the farmers owe to the banks." Dylan comments at Live Aid, July 13, 1985.

PART XI

165 Bauldie, John. "Daniel Lanois and *Oh Mercy*." Reprinted in Bauldie, *Wanted Man*, p. 194.

166 Williams, *A Man Called Alias*, p. 182.

167 "I guess I'd like to do . . . maybe a children's album . . ." *Biograph*, p. 24.

168 For a discussion of the famous "Ed Sullivan" incident, see Spitz, pp. 214-15, and Scaduto, pp. 139-40.

169 Bauldie, *The Bootleg Series*, p. 42.

170 " . . . here the mood is more of sorrow than anger . . ." Ibid., p. 49.

171 "Mama, You Been on My Mind" was recorded on the same night (June 9, 1964) Dylan made *Another Side*. For some reason, the back cover lists it as a *Bringing It All Back Home* outtake. Bauldie says "Let Me Die in My Footsteps" was "excluded at the last moment . . . in favor of 'A Hard Rain's A-Gonna Fall'" (p. 10). Early copies of the album show that "Footsteps" was replaced by "Masters of War." Bauldie notes that "In his great early song, 'A Hard Rain's A-Gonna Fall,' Dylan expressed the thought that the 'worst fear' was 'the fear to bring children into the world'" (p. 57). This phrase is from "Masters of War." The musician

notes to "Like a Rolling Stone" credit Dylan on guitar and harmonica, Mike Bloomfield on guitar, Al Kooper on organ, and Harvey Brooks on bass. Dylan is clearly alone at the piano on this take. There is no "spooky organ" (p. 49) on this take of "Idiot Wind." Bauldie is thinking of another, unreleased version with organ accompaniment that truly is spooky.

172   "I perk up for George Harrison, but that's just out of spite. George is wearing a hideous purple jacket, someone's old mustache and the world's worst haircut. It looks like he's rented it for a bet." Jones, Allan. "Million Dollar Bash." *Melody Maker*, October 31, 1992, p. 43.

PART XII

173   Snow, Mat. "Unlikely." *Q*, December 1992, p. 116.

174   " . . . another deejay took over, jazzing up the show's final segment with records by Lightnin' Hopkins, Howlin' Wolf . . ." Spitz, p 46. "Bob would spend hours listening to Gatemouth Page, a disk jockey . . . who played Muddy Waters and Howlin' Wolf." Scaduto, p. 6.

175   For an excellent study of the history behind "Stack A Lee," see Marcus, *Mystery Train*, pp. 65-68, 227-40.

176   "The ballad of little Frankie is the modern counterpart of the same old story." Lomax, John A. and Alan Lomax. *Folk Song U.S.A.* New York: Duell, Sloan & Pearce, 1947, p. 367.

PART XIII

177   "I try to live within that line between despondency and hope. I'm suited to walk that line, right between the fire . . . I see [the album] right straight down the middle of the line, really." Associated Press, December 16, 1997.

178   "Dylan liberated him from the need to write self-consciously 'teen' songs, and allowed him to write even more self-conscious songs about adolescents struggling toward maturity: coded versions of his own dilemma." Marsh, Dave. *Before I Get Old: The Story of the Who*. New York: St. Martin's Press, 1988, p. 118.

179   For an amusing list, see "Greil Marcus Lists 100 New Dylans." Marsh, Dave and James Bernard. *The New Book of Rock Lists*. New York: Fireside, 1994, p. 334.

180   Thomson, p. 287.

SELECTED BIBLIOGRAPHY

Bauldie, John. *The Bootleg Series, Volumes 1-3* liner notes.

_____ ed. *Wanted Man: In Search of Bob Dylan*. New York: Citadel Underground, 1991.

Benson, Carl. *The Bob Dylan Companion: Four Decades of Commentary*. New York: Scribner, 1998.

Christgau, Robert. *Rock Albums of the '70's: A Critical Guide*. New York: Da Capo, 1981.

Crowe, Cameron. *Biograph* liner notes.

DeCurtis, Anthony and James Henke, and Holly George-Warren, eds. *The Rolling Stone Album Guide*. New York: Random House, 1992.

Dylan, Bob. *Drawn Blank*. New York: Random House, 1994.

_____. *Lyrics, 1962-1985*. New York: Alfred A. Knopf, 1985.

_____. *Tarantula*. New York: Macmillan, 1971.

_____. *Writings and Drawings*. New York: Alfred A. Knopf, 1973.

Flanagan, Bill. *Written in My Soul*. Chicago: Contemporary, 1985.

Ginsberg, Allen. *Desire* liner essay.

Glover, Tony. *The Bootleg Series, Volume 4* liner notes.

Gray, Michael. *Song and Dance Man: The Art of Bob Dylan*. New York: E.P. Dutton, 1973. Updated, New York: St. Martin's Press, 1981.

_____ and John Bauldie, eds. *All Across the Telegraph*. London: Sidgwick and Jackson, 1987.

Gross, Michael. *Bob Dylan: An Illustrated History*. New York: Grossett & Dunlap, 1978.

Guterman, Jimmy and Owen O'Donnell. *The Worst Rock-and-Roll Records of All Time: A Fan's Guide to the Stuff You Love to Hate*. New York: Citadel Press, 1991.

Guthrie, Woody. *Bound for Glory*. New York: E.P. Dutton, 1943.

Hamill, Pete. *Blood on the Tracks* liner notes.

Helm, Levon with Stephen Davis. *This Wheel's On Fire: Levon Helm and the Story of The Band*. New York: William Morrow, 1993.

Heylin, Clinton. *Bob Dylan: Behind the Shades*. New York: Summit, 1991.

_____. *Bob Dylan: A Life in Stolen Moments: Day By Day 1941-1995*. New York: Schirmer, 1996.

_____. *Bob Dylan: The Recording Sessions, 1960-1994*. New York: St. Martin's Press, 1996.

_____. *The Great White Wonders: A History of Rock Bootlegs*. New York: Viking, 1994.

Hoskyns, Barney. *Across the Great Divide: The Band and America*. Toronto: Penguin Books, 1993.

Humphries, Patrick, and John Bauldie. *Absolutely Dylan*. New York: Viking Studio Books, 1991.

Kooper, Al. *Backstage Passes: Rock 'n' Roll Life in the Sixties*. New York: Stein and Day, 1977.

Kramer, Daniel. *Bob Dylan*. New York: Citadel Press, 1967.

Lee, C.P., with photos by Paul Kelly. *Like The Night: Bob Dylan and the Road to the Manchester Free Trade Hall*. London: Helter Skelter, 1998.

Lomax, John A., and Alan Lomax. *Folk Song U.S.A*. New York: Duell, Sloan & Pearce,1947.

Marcus, Greil. *The Basement Tapes* liner notes.

_____. *Invisible Republic: Bob Dylan's Basement Tapes*. New York: Henry Holt, 1997.

_____. *Mystery Train: Images of America in Rock 'n' Roll Music*. (Fourth Revised Edition). New York: Plume, 1997.

Marsh, Dave. *The Heart of Rock and Soul: The 1001 Greatest Singles Ever Made*. New York: Plume, 1989.

_____ and James Bernard. *The New Book of Rock Lists*. New York: Fireside, 1994

_____ and John Swenson, eds. *The New Rolling Stone Record Guide*. New York: Rolling Stone Press / Random House, 1983.

McGregor, Craig, ed. *Bob Dylan: A Retrospective*. New York: William Morrow, 1972.

Pascall, Jeremy. *The Illustrated History of Rock Music*. New York: Hamlyn, 1978.

Pickering, Stephen. *Bob Dylan Approximately: A Portrait of the Jewish Poet in Search of God: A Midrash*. New York: David McKay, 1975.

Riley, Tim. *Hard Rain: A Dylan Commentary*. New York: Alfred A. Knopf, 1992.

Rodnitzky, Jerome L. *Minstrels of the Dawn: The Folk-Protest Singer as a Cultural Hero*. Chicago: Nelson-Hall, 1976.

Rolling Stone editors. *Knockin' on Dylan's Door: On the Road in '74*. New York: Pocket Books, 1974.

_____. *The Rolling Stone Interviews, 1967-1980*. New York: St. Martin's Press, 1981.

_____. *The Rolling Stone Interviews: The 1980's*. New York: St. Martin's Press, 1989.

Scaduto, Anthony. *Bob Dylan: An Intimate Biography*. New York: Grosset and Dunlap, 1971.

Scobie, Stephen. *Alias Bob Dylan*. Alberta: Red Deer, 1991.

Shelton, Robert. *No Direction Home*. New York: William Morrow, 1986.

Shepard, Sam. *Rolling Thunder Logbook*. New York: Viking Press, 1977.

Sloman, Larry. *On the Road with Bob Dylan: Rolling with the Thunder*. New York: Bantam, 1978.

Spitz, Bob. *Dylan: A Biography*. New York: McGraw-Hill, 1989.

Thomson, Elizabeth, and David Gutman, eds, *The Dylan Companion*. London: Macmillan, 1990.

Thompson, Toby. *Positively Main Street: An Unorthodox View of Bob Dylan*. New York: Coward-McCann, 1971.

Williams, Paul. *Bob Dylan: Performing Artist, The Middle Years, 1974-1986*. California: Underwood-Miller, 1992.

_____. *Performing Artist: The Music of Bob Dylan, Volume II, 1960-1973*. California: Underwood-Miller, 1990.

Williams, Richard. *Dylan: A Man Called Alias*. London: Bloomsbury, 1992.

DISCOGRAPHY

PART A

OFFICIALLY RELEASED RECORDINGS BY BOB DYLAN

This section lists all Bob Dylan albums to have been released in the United States. *Planet Waves* and *Before the Flood* were originally released by Asylum Records but are now available on Columbia Records. All of the following are available at present on Columbia, with the exception of *Dylan*, which is available as a Japanese import. Most are available in cassette and compact disc formats, but as cassettes become obsolete, most retailers only stock compact discs.

BOB DYLAN
(RELEASED MARCH 1962)

Side One: You're No Good / Talkin' New York / In My Time of Dyin' / Man of Constant Sorrow / Fixin' to Die / Pretty Peggy-O / Highway 51

Side Two: Gospel Plow / Baby, Let Me Follow You Down / House of the Risin' Sun / Freight Train Blues / Song to Woody / See That My Grave is Kept Clean

THE FREEWHEELIN' BOB DYLAN
(RELEASED MAY 1963)

Side One: Blowin' in the Wind / Girl from the North Country / Masters of War / Down the Highway / Bob Dylan's Blues / A Hard Rain's A-Gonna Fall

Side Two: Don't Think Twice, It's All Right / Bob Dylan's Dream / Oxford Town / Talking World War III Blues / Corrina, Corrina / Honey, Just Allow Me One More Chance / I Shall Be Free

THE TIMES THEY ARE A-CHANGIN'
(RELEASED JANUARY 1964)

Side One: The Times They Are A-Changin' / Ballad of Hollis Brown / With God on Our Side / One Too Many Mornings / North Country Blues

Side Two: Only a Pawn in Their Game / Boots of Spanish Leather / When the Ship Comes In / The Lonesome Death of Hattie Carroll / Restless Farewell

ANOTHER SIDE OF BOB DYLAN
(RELEASED AUGUST 1964)

Side One: All I Really Want to Do / Black Crow Blues / Spanish Harlem Incident / Chimes of Freedom / I Shall Be Free No. 10 / To Ramona

Side Two: Motorpsycho Nightmare / My Back Pages / I Don't Believe You / Ballad in Plain D / It Ain't Me, Babe

BRINGING IT ALL BACK HOME
(RELEASED MARCH 1965)

Side One: Subterranean Homesick Blues / She Belongs to Me / Maggie's Farm / Love Minus Zero No Limit / Outlaw Blues / On the Road Again / Bob Dylan's 115th Dream

Side Two: Mr. Tambourine Man / Gates of Eden / It's Alright, Ma (I'm Only Bleeding) / It's All Over Now, Baby Blue

HIGHWAY 61 REVISITED
(RELEASED AUGUST 1965)

Side One: Like a Rolling Stone / Tombstone Blues / It Takes a Lot to Laugh, It Takes a Train to Cry / From a Buick 6 / Ballad of a Thin Man

Side Two: Queen Jane Approximately / Highway 61 Revisited / Just Like Tom Thumb's Blues / Desolation Row

BLONDE ON BLONDE
(RELEASED JUNE 1966)

Side One: Rainy Day Women #12 & 35 / Pledging My Time / Visions of Johanna / One of Us Must Know (Sooner or Later)

Side Two: I Want You / Stuck Inside of Mobile with the Memphis Blues Again / Leopard-Skin Pill-Box Hat / Just Like a Woman

Side Three: Most Likely You Go Your Way (and I'll Go Mine) / Temporary Like Achilles / Absolutely Sweet Marie / 4th Time Around / Obviously 5 Believers

Side Four: Sad-Eyed Lady of the Lowlands

BOB DYLAN'S GREATEST HITS
(RELEASED MARCH 1967)

Side One: Rainy Day Women #12 & 35 / Blowin' in the Wind / The Times They Are A-Changin' / It Ain't Me, Babe / Like a Rolling Stone

Side Two: Mr. Tambourine Man / Subterranean Homesick Blues / I Want You / Positively 4th Street / Just Like a Woman

JOHN WESLEY HARDING
(RELEASED DECEMBER 1967)

Side One: John Wesley Harding / As I Went Out One Morning / I Dreamed I Saw St. Augustine / All Along the Watchtower / The Ballad of Frankie Lee and Judas Priest / Drifter's Escape

Side Two: Dear Landlord / I Am a Lonesome Hobo / I Pity the Poor Immigrant / The Wicked Messenger / Down Along the Cove / I'll Be Your Baby Tonight

NASHVILLE SKYLINE
(RELEASED APRIL 1969)

Side One: Girl from the North Country (with Johnny Cash) / Nashville Skyline Rag / To Be Alone with You / I Threw It All Away / Peggy Day

Side Two: Lay, Lady, Lay / One More Night / Tell Me That It Isn't True / Country Pie / Tonight I'll Be Staying Here with You

SELF PORTRAIT
(RELEASED JUNE 1970)

Side One: All the Tired Horses / Alberta #1 / I Forgot More Than You'll Ever Know / Days of 49 / Early Mornin' Rain / In Search of Little Sadie

Side Two: Let It Be Me / Little Sadie / Woogie Boogie / Belle Isle / Living the Blues / Like a Rolling Stone

Side Three: Copper Kettle / Gotta Travel On / Blue Moon / The Boxer / Quinn the Eskimo (The Mighty Quinn) / Take Me as I Am (or Let Me Go)

Side Four: Take a Message to Mary / It Hurts Me Too / Minstrel Boy / She Belongs to Me / Wigwam / Alberta #2

NEW MORNING
(RELEASED OCTOBER 1970)

Side One: If Not for You / Day of the Locusts / Time Passes Slowly / Went to See the Gypsy / Winterlude / If Dogs Run Free

Side Two: New Morning / Sign on the Window / One More Weekend / The Man in Me / Three Angles / Father of Night

BOB DYLAN'S GREATEST HITS, VOLUME II

(RELEASED NOVEMBER 1971)

Side One: Watching the River Flow / Don't Think Twice, It's All Right / Lay, Lady, Lay / Stuck Inside of Mobile with the Memphis Blues Again /

Side Two: I'll Be Your Baby Tonight / All I Really Want to Do / My Back Pages / Maggie's Farm / Tonight I'll Be Staying Here with You

Side Three: She Belongs to Me / All Along the Watchtower / Quinn the Eskimo (The Mighty Quinn) / Just Like Tom Thumb's Blues /A Hard Rain's A-Gonna Fall

Side Four: If Not for You / It's All Over Now, Baby Blue / Tomorrow Is a Long Time /When I Paint My Masterpiece / I Shall Be Released / You Ain't Goin' Nowhere / Down in the Flood

PAT GARRETT & BILLY THE KID

(RELEASED JULY 1973)

Side One: Main Title Theme (Billy) / Cantina Theme (Workin' for the Law) / Billy Bunkhouse Theme / River Theme

Side Two: Turkey Chase / Knockin' on Heaven's Door / Final Theme / Billy 4 / Billy 7

DYLAN

(RELEASED NOVEMBER 1973)

Side One: Lily of the West / Can't Help Falling in Love / Sarah Jane / The Ballad of Ira Hayes

Side Two: Mr. Bojangles / Mary Ann / Big Yellow Taxi / A Fool Such as I / Spanish is the Loving Tongue

PLANET WAVES
(RELEASED JANUARY 1974)

Side One: On a Night Like This / Going, Going, Gone / Tough Mama / Hazel / Something There Is About You / Forever Young

Side Two: Forever Young / Dirge / You Angel You / Never Say Goodbye / Wedding Song

BEFORE THE FLOOD
(RELEASED JUNE 1974)

Side One: Most Likely You Go Your Way (and I'll Go Mine) / Lay, Lady, Lay / Rainy Day Women #12 & 35 / Knockin' on Heaven's Door / It Ain't Me, Babe / Ballad of a Thin Man

Side Two: Up on Cripple Creek* / I Shall Be Released* / Endless Highway* / The Night They Drove Old Dixie Down* / Stage Fright*

Side Three: Don't Think Twice, It's All Right / Just Like a Woman / It's Alright, Ma (I'm Only Bleeding) / The Shape I'm In* / When You Awake* / The Weight*

Side Four: All Along the Watchtower / Highway 61 Revisited / Like a Rolling Stone / Blowin' in the Wind

(*performed by The Band)

BLOOD ON THE TRACKS
(RELEASED JANUARY 1975)

Side One: Tangled Up in Blue / Simple Twist of Fate / You're a Big Girl Now / Idiot Wind / You're Gonna Make Me Lonesome When You Go

Side Two: Meet Me in the Morning / Lily, Rosemary and the Jack of Hearts / If You See Her, Say Hello / Shelter from the Storm / Buckets of Rain

THE BASEMENT TAPES
(RELEASED JUNE 1975)

Side One: Odds and Ends / Orange Juice Blues (Blues for Breakfast)* / Million Dollar Bash / Yazoo Street Scandal* / Goin' to Acapulco / Katie's Been Gone*

Side Two: Lo and Behold! / Bessie Smith* / Clothes Line Saga / Apple Suckling Tree / Please, Mrs. Henry / Tears of Rage

Side Three: Too Much of Nothing / Yea! Heavy and a Bottle of Bread / Ain't No More Cane* / Down in the Flood / Ruben Remus* / Tiny Montgomery

Side Four: You Ain't Goin' Nowhere / Don't Ya Tell Henry* / Nothing Was Delivered / Open the Door, Homer / Long Distance Operator* / This Wheel's on Fire

(*performed by The Band)

DESIRE
(RELEASED JANUARY 1976)

Side One: Hurricane / Isis / Mozambique / One More Cup of Coffee (Valley Below) / Oh, Sister

Side Two: Joey / Romance in Durango / Black Diamond Bay / Sara

HARD RAIN
(RELEASED SEPTEMBER 1976)

Side One: Maggie's Farm / One Too Many Mornings / Stuck Inside of Mobile with the Memphis Blues Again / Oh, Sister / Lay, Lady, Lay

Side Two: Shelter from the Storm / You're a Big Girl Now / I Threw It All Away / Idiot Wind

STREET LEGAL
(RELEASED JUNE 1978;
REMIXED AND RELEASED JULY 1999)

Side One: Changing of the Guards / New Pony / No Time to Think / Baby Stop Crying

Side Two: Is Your Love in Vain? / Señor (Tales of Yankee Power) / True Love Tends to Forget / We Better Talk This Over / Where Are You Tonight? (Journey Through Dark Heat)

BOB DYLAN AT BUDOKAN
(RELEASED APRIL 1979)

Side One: Mr. Tambourine Man / Shelter from the Storm / Love Minus Zero-No Limit / Ballad of a Thin Man / Don't Think Twice, It's All Right

Side Two: Maggie's Farm / One More Cup of Coffee (Valley Below) / Like a Rolling Stone / I Shall Be Released / Is Your Love in Vain? / Going, Going, Gone

Side Three: Blowin' in the Wind / Just Like a Woman / Oh, Sister / Simple Twist of Fate / All Along the Watchtower / I Want You

Side Four: All I Really Want to Do / Knockin' on Heaven's Door / It's Alright, Ma (I'm Only Bleeding) / Forever Young / The Times They Are A-Changin'

SLOW TRAIN COMING
(RELEASED AUGUST 1979)

Side One: Gotta Serve Somebody / Precious Angel / I Believe in You / Slow Train

Side Two: Gonna Change My Way of Thinking / Do Right to Me, Baby (Do Unto Others) / When You Gonna Wake Up? / Man Gave Names to All the Animals / When He Returns

SAVED
(RELEASED JUNE 1980)

Side One: A Satisfied Mind / Saved / Covenant Woman / What Can I Do for You? / Solid Rock

Side Two: Pressing On / In the Garden / Saving Grace / Are You Ready?

SHOT OF LOVE
(RELEASED AUGUST 1981)

Side One: Shot of Love / Heart of Mine / Property of Jesus / Lenny Bruce / Watered-Down Love

Side Two: Dead Man, Dead Man / In the Summertime / Trouble / Every Grain of Sand (note: "The Groom's Still Waiting at the Altar" was later added to the album)

INFIDELS
(RELEASED NOVEMBER 1983)

Side One: Jokerman / Sweetheart Like You / Neighbourhood Bully / License to Kill

Side Two: Man of Peace / Union Sundown / I and I / Don't Fall Apart on Me Tonight

REAL LIVE
(RELEASED NOVEMBER 1984)

Side One: Highway 61 Revisited / Maggie's Farm / I and I / License to Kill / It Ain't Me, Babe

Side Two: Tangled Up in Blue / Masters of War / Ballad of a Thin Man / Girl from the North Country / Tombstone Blues

EMPIRE BURLESQUE
(RELEASED MAY 1985)

Side One: Tight Connection to My Heart (Has Anybody Seen My Love) / Seeing the Real You at Last / I'll Remember You / Clean-Cut Kid / Never Gonna Be the Same Again

Side Two: Trust Yourself / Emotionally Yours / When the Night Comes Falling from the Sky / Something's Burning, Baby / Dark Eyes

BIOGRAPH
(RELEASED NOVEMBER 1985)

Side One: Lay, Lady, Lay / Baby, Let Me Follow You Down / If Not for You / I'll Be Your Baby Tonight / I'll Keep It with Mine

Side Two: The Times They Are A-Changin' / Blowin' in the Wind / Masters of War / Lonesome Death of Hattie Carroll / Percy's Song

Side Three: Mixed-Up Confusion / Tombstone Blues / The Groom's Still Waiting at the Altar / Most Likely You Go Your Way (and I'll Go Mine) / Like a Rolling Stone / Jet Pilot

Side Four: Lay Down Your Weary Tune / Subterranean Homesick Blues / I Don't Believe You / Visions of Johanna / Every Grain of Sand

Side Five: Quinn the Eskimo (The Mighty Quinn) / Mr. Tambourine Man / Dear Landlord / It Ain't Me, Babe / You Angel You / Million Dollar Bash

Side Six: To Ramona / You're a Big Girl Now / Abandoned Love / Tangled Up in Blue / It's All Over Now, Baby Blue

Side Seven: Can You Please Crawl Out Your Window? / Positively 4th Street / Isis / Caribbean Wind / Up to Me

Side Eight: Baby, I'm in the Mood for You / I Wanna Be Your Lover / I Want You / Heart of Mine / On a Night Like This / Just Like a Woman

Side Nine: Romance in Durango / Señor (Tales of Yankee Power) / Gotta Serve Somebody / I Believe in You /Time Passes Slowly

Side Ten: I Shall Be Released / Knockin' on Heaven's Door / All Along the Watchtower / Solid Rock / Forever Young

KNOCKED OUT LOADED
(RELEASED JULY 1986)

Side One: You Wanna Ramble / They Killed Him / Driftin' Too Far from Shore / Precious Memories / Maybe Someday

Side Two: Brownsville Girl / Got My Mind Made Up / Under Your Spell

DOWN IN THE GROOVE
(RELEASED JUNE 1988)

Side One: Let's Stick Together / When Did You Leave Heaven? / Sally Sue Brown / Death Is Not the End / Had a Dream About You, Baby

Side Two: Ugliest Girl in the World / Silvio / Ninety Miles an Hour (Down a Dead End Street) / Shenandoah / Rank Strangers to Me

DYLAN & THE DEAD
(RELEASED FEBRUARY 1989)

Side One: Slow Train / I Want You / Gotta Serve Somebody / Queen Jane Approximately

Side Two: Joey / All Along the Watchtower / Knockin' on Heaven's Door

OH MERCY
(RELEASED SEPTEMBER 1989)

Side One: Political World / Where Teardrops Fall / Everything Is Broken / Ring Them Bells / Man in the Long Black Coat

Side Two: Most of the Time / What Good Am I? / Disease of Conceit / What Was It You Wanted? / Shooting Star

UNDER THE RED SKY
(RELEASED SEPTEMBER 1990)

Side One: Wiggle Wiggle / Under the Red Sky / Unbelievable / Born in Time / T.V. Talkin' Song

Side Two: 10,000 Men / 2*2 / God Knows / Handy Dandy / Cat's in the Well

THE BOOTLEG SERIES, VOLUMES 1-3
[RARE AND UNRELEASED], 1961-1991
(RELEASED MARCH 1991)

Volume One: Hard Times in New York Town / He Was a Friend of Mine / Man on the Street / No More Auction Block / House Carpenter / Talkin' Bear Mountain Picnic Massacre Blues / Let Me Die in My Footsteps / Rambling, Gambling Willie / Talkin' Hava Negeilah Blues / Quit Your Low Down Ways / Worried Blues / Kingsport Town / Walkin' Down the Line / Walls of Red Wing / Paths of Victory / Talkin' John Birch Paranoid Blues / Who Killed Davey Moore? / Only a Hobo / Moonshiner / When the Ship Comes In / The Times They Are A-Changin' / Last Thoughts on Woody Guthrie

Volume Two: Seven Curses / Eternal Circle / Suze (the Cough Song) / Mama, You Been on My Mind / Farewell, Angelina / Subterranean Homesick Blues / If You Gotta Go, Go Now (or Else You Got to Stay All Night) / Sitting on a Barbed Wire Fence / Like a Rolling Stone / It Takes a Lot to Laugh, It Takes a Train to Cry / I'll Keep It with Mine / She's Your Lover Now / I Shall Be Released / Santa Fe / If Not for You / Wallflower / Nobody 'Cept You / Tangled Up in Blue / Call Letter Blues / Idiot Wind

Volume Three: If You See Her, Say Hello / Golden Loon / Catfish / Seven Days / Ye Shall Be Changed / Every Grain of Sand / You Changed My Life / Need a Woman / Angelina / Someone's Got a Hold of My Heart / Tell Me / Lord, Protect My Child / Foot of Pride / Blind Willie McTell / When the Night Comes Falling from the Sky / Series of Dreams

GOOD AS I BEEN TO YOU
(RELEASED NOVEMBER 1992)

Side One: Frankie & Albert / Jim Jones / Blackjack Davey / Canadee-I-O / Sittin' on Top of the World / Little Maggie / Hard Times

Side Two: Step It Up and Go / Tomorrow Night / Arthur Me Bride / You're Gonna Quit Me / Diamond Joe / Froggie Went A-Courtin'

WORLD GONE WRONG
(RELEASED NOVEMBER 1993)

Side One: World Gone Wrong / Love Henry / Ragged & Dirty / Blood in My Eyes / Broke Down Engine

Side Two: Delia / Stack A Lee / Two Soldiers / Jack-A-Roe / Lone Pilgrim

BOB DYLAN'S GREATEST HITS, VOLUME III
(RELEASED DECEMBER 1994)

Side One: Tangled Up in Blue / Changing of the Guards / The Groom's Still Waiting at the Altar / Hurricane / Forever Young / Jokerman / Dignity

Side Two: Silvio / Ring Them Bells / Gotta Serve Somebody / Series of Dreams / Brownsville Girl / Under the Red Sky / Knockin' on Heaven's Door

MTV UNPLUGGED
(RELEASED APRIL 1995)

Side One: Tombstone Blues / Shooting Star / All Along the Watchtower / The Times They Are A-Changin' / John Brown / Rainy Day Women #12 & 35 / Desolation Row

Side Two: Dignity / Knockin' on Heaven's Door / Like a Rolling Stone / With God on Our Side (note: "Love Minus Zero-No Limit" was later added to the album)

TIME OUT OF MIND
(RELEASED SEPTEMBER 1997)

Side One: Love Sick / Dirt Road Blues / Standing in the Doorway / Million Miles / Tryin' to Get to Heaven / 'Til I Fell In Love With You

Side Two: Cold Irons Bound / Make You Feel My Love / Can't Wait / Highlands

THE BOOTLEG SERIES, VOLUME 4: LIVE 1966, "THE "ROYAL ALBERT HALL" CONCERT
(RELEASED OCTOBER 1998)

Disc One: She Belongs to Me / Fourth Time Around / Visions of Johanna / It's All Over Now, Baby Blue / Desolation Row / Just Like a Woman / Mr. Tambourine Man

Disc Two: Tell Me, Momma / I Don't Believe You / Baby, Let Me Follow You Down / Just Like Tom Thumb's Blues / Leopard-Skin Pill-Box Hat / One Too Many Mornings / Ballad of a Thin Man / Like a Rolling Stone

THE ESSENTIAL BOB DYLAN
(RELEASED OCTOBER 2000)

Disc One: Blowin' in the Wind / Don't Think Twice, It's All Right / The Times They Are A-Changin' / It Ain't Me, Babe / Maggie's Farm / It's All Over Now, Baby Blue / Mr. Tambourine Man / Subterranean Homesick Blues / Like a Rolling Stone / Positively 4th Street / Just Like a Woman / Rainy Day Women # 12 & 35 / All Along the Watchtower / Quinn the Eskimo (The Mighty Quinn) / I'll Be Your Baby Tonight

Disc Two: Lay, Lady, Lay / If Not for You / I Shall Be Released / You Ain't Goin' Nowhere / Knockin' On Heaven's Door / Forever Young / Tangled Up in Blue / Shelter from the Storm / Hurricane / Gotta Serve Somebody / Jokerman / Silvio / Everything Is Broken / Not Dark Yet / Things Have Changed

LOVE AND THEFT
(Released September 2001)

Tweedle Dee & Tweedle Dum / Mississippi / Summer Days / Bye and Bye / Lonesome Day Blues / Floater (Too Much To Ask) / High Water (For Charley Patton) / Moonlight / Honest with Me / Po' Boy / Cry A While / Sugar Baby

PART B

This section lists other albums referred to in the text. Dylan contributes to these albums. With the exception of the two Travelling Wilburys records, only Dylan's contribution is cited.

BROADSIDE BALLADS, VOLUME I
(released September 1963)

Dylan, appearing under the pseudonym Blind Boy Grunt, performs "John Brown," "Only a Hobo" and "Talkin' Devil."

JACK ELLIOTT, JACK ELLIOTT
(released 1964)

Dylan plays harmonica on "Will the Circle be Unbroken."

BIG JOE WILLIAMS, BIG JOE WILLIAMS
(RELEASED 1964)

Dylan plays harmonica and adds vocals on "Sittin' on Top of the World," and plays harmonica on "Wichita."

BROADSIDE REUNION
(DYLAN'S PERFORMANCES RECORDED 1962; RELEASED NOVEMBER 1971)

Dylan, appearing under the pseudonym Blind Boy Grunt, performs "Train A-Travelin'," "I'd Hate to Be You on That Dreadful Day," "The Death of Emmett Till" and "The Ballad of Donald White."

THE CONCERT FOR BANGLADESH
(RELEASED DECEMBER 1971)

A Hard Rain's A-Gonna Fall / It Takes a Lot to Laugh, It Takes a Train to Cry / Blowin' in the Wind / Mr. Tambourine Man / Just Like a Woman

THE BAND, THE LAST WALTZ
(RECORDED NOVEMBER 1976; RELEASED APRIL 1978)

Baby, Let Me Follow You Down / I Don't Believe You / Forever Young / Baby, Let Me Follow You Down / I Shall Be Released

BOB DYLAN, MASTERPIECES
(RELEASED MARCH 1978 IN JAPAN, AUSTRALIA
AND NEW ZEALAND; AVAILABLE AS AN IMPORT)

Side One: Knockin' on Heaven's Door / Mr. Tambourine Man / Just Like a Woman / I Shall Be Released / Tears of Rage / All Along the Watchtower / One More Cup of Coffee (Valley Below)

Side Two: Like a Rolling Stone / Quinn the Eskimo (The Mighty Quinn) / Tomorrow Is a Long Time / Lay, Lady, Lay / Idiot Wind

Side Three: Mixed-Up Confusion / Positively 4th Street / Can You Please Crawl Out Your Window? / Just Like Tom Thumb's Blues / Spanish Is the Loving Tongue / George Jackson (Big Band Version) / Rita May

Side Four: Blowin' in the Wind / A Hard Rain's A-Gonna Fall / The Times They Are A-Changin' / Masters of War / Hurricane

Side Five: Maggie's Farm / Subterranean Homesick Blues / Ballad of a Thin Man / Mozambique / This Wheel's on Fire / I Want You / Rainy Day Women #12 & 35

Side Six: Don't Think Twice, It's All Right / Song to Woody / It Ain't Me, Babe / Love Minus Zero-No Limit / I'll Be Your Baby Tonight / If Not for You / If You See Her, Say Hello / Sara

HEARTS OF FIRE
(SOUNDTRACK, RELEASED OCTOBER 1987)

The Usual / Had a Dream About You, Baby / Night after Night

FOLKWAYS, A VISION SHARED: A TRIBUTE TO WOODY GUTHRIE AND LEADBELLY
(RELEASED AUGUST 1988)

Pretty Boy Floyd

TRAVELING WILBURYS, VOLUME ONE
(RELEASED OCTOBER 1988)

Side One: Handle with Care / Dirty World / Rattled / Last Night / Not Alone Any More

Side Two: Congratulations / Heading for the Light / Margarita / Tweeter and the Monkey Man / End of the Line

TRAVELING WILBURYS, VOLUME THREE
(RELEASED OCTOBER 1990)

Side One: She's My Baby / Inside Out / If You Belonged to Me / The Devil's Been Busy / 7 Deadly Sins / Poor House

Side Two: Where Were You Last Night? / Cool Dry Place / New Blue Moon / You Took My Breath Away / Wilbury Twist

BOB DYLAN: THE 30TH ANNIVERSARY CONCERT CELEBRATION
(RELEASED AUGUST 1993)

It's Alright, Ma (I'm Only Bleeding) / My Back Pages / Knockin' on Heaven's Door / Girl from the North Country

WOODSTOCK '94
(RELEASED DECEMBER 1994)

Highway 61 Revisited

THE BEST OF BOB DYLAN

(RELEASED AUGUST 1997 IN EUROPE AND CANADA)

Side One: Blowin' in the Wind / The Times They Are A-Changin' / Don't Think Twice, It's All Right / Mr. Tambourine Man / Like a Rolling Stone / Just Like a Woman / All Along the Watchtower / Lay, Lady, Lay / I Shall Be Released / If Not For You

Side Two: Knockin' on Heaven's Door / Forever Young / Tangled Up in Blue / Oh, Sister / Gotta Serve Somebody / Jokerman / Everything Is Broken / Shelter from the Storm

THE SONGS OF JIMMIE RODGERS: A TRIBUTE

(RELEASED SEPTEMBER 1997)

Sweet Liza Jane